Faded Glory

A&M travel guides

FADED GLORY

A CENTURY OF FORGOTTEN TEXAS MILITARY SITES, THEN AND NOW

Thomas E. Alexander and Dan K. Utley

TEXAS A&M UNIVERSITY PRESS

College Station

This paper meets the requirements of ANSI/NISO Z39.48-1992 (Permanence of Paper).
Binding materials have been chosen for durability.

Library of Congress Cataloging-in-Publication Data

Alexander, Thomas E., 1931–
Faded glory : a century of forgotten Texas military sites, then and now /
Thomas E. Alexander and Dan K. Utley. — 1st ed.
p. cm. — (Tarleton State University southwestern studies in the humanities ; no. 25)
"A Texas A&M travel guide."
Includes bibliographical references and index.
ISBN-13: 978-1-60344-699-0 (flex : alk. paper)
ISBN-10: 1-60344-699-0 (flex : alk. paper)
ISBN-13: 978-1-60344-753-9 (e-book)
ISBN-10: 1-60344-753-9 (e-book)
1. Military bases—Texas. 2. Fortification—Texas. 3. Battlefields—Texas.
4. Historic sites—Texas. 5. Texas—History, Millitary. 6. Texas—Antiquities.
I. Utley, Dan K. II. Title. III. Series: Tarleton State University
southwestern studies in the humanities ; no. 25.
F387.A526 2012
355.009764—dc23
2011050695

DEDICATED TO

Capy Alexander for taking excellent photos,
trekking tirelessly through countless deserted sites,
editing the manuscripts of six books, and just putting up with Tom in general;

Debby Davis Utley for her boundless encouragement, unwavering
support of Dan's myriad projects, and willingness, even in the wee small hours
of the morning, to offer honest insights on a finished chapter.

We are additionally indebted to Debby and Capy
for encouraging the friendship that is an integral part of the
collaborative effort represented by this book.

CONTENTS

MAPS

ACKNOWLEDGMENTS

Any attempt to recognize all the individuals who assisted us with this project must begin with three distinct understandings. First, this book was first and foremost a team effort by two authors, and each member of that team relied on the other countless times for input, guidance, friendship, encouragement, and perhaps most important, good humor under pressure. That team effort extends to our spouses as well, so this book is duly dedicated to them.

Second, any such list of acknowledgments is, by its very nature, incomplete. Many individuals provided noteworthy assistance related to research, writing, or editing, and many more simply kept us going by showing genuine interest in the work, enthusiastically supporting its core idea, or sharing personal reminiscences of kindred stories. To those unnamed individuals, we offer our sincerest thanks. And finally, to all those whose names are included here, we must acknowledge that we can never fully repay you for your kindness, patience, and direction. This work is the sum of many parts from many contributors, and we are fortunate indeed to live and work among such extraordinary individuals.

Our heartfelt thanks go to the Texas A&M University Press staff, especially editor Mary Lenn Dixon. With her boundless enthusiasm, engaging smile, positive encouragement, and quiet grace, she made us feel, even from our first presentation of the book proposal, that we had a good idea and that we had the right editorial and marketing teams backing us up. This book represents the culmination of a lengthy process, one made incredibly smooth by the good folks at the press. As a result, the authors—a Colorado Buffalo and a Texas Longhorn—step outside the bounds of tradition to offer a hearty "Gig 'em" to our Aggie friends.

We offer special thanks to a number of dedicated staff members at the Texas Historical Commission's Austin headquarters: to Lillie Thompson for locating research materials; to Pat Mercado-Allinger for tracking down a recent photo of Brazos Santiago; to Lyman Labry for fighting his way through the Ruidosa village dump to photograph what remains of Camp Ruidosa; to Charles Sadnick, Bob Brinkman, Bratten Thomason, and Kimberly Gamble for providing historical file materials; and to the indefatigable William McWhorter, military site historian extraordinaire, for his assistance with research materials and photographs. We also thank Michael "Buddy" Garza, site manager at Fort McKavett State Historic Site, for searching through files for just the right photograph, and Chris Elliott, site manager at Fort Lancaster State

Historic Site, for taking time to help determine where an artist must have stood in 1861 to sketch the fort.

Any mention of the help we received from the Texas Historical Commission would be incomplete without naming two key volunteers from the preservation partners at the county level: J. Travis Roberts in Brewster County for taking time to journey to remote Glenn Spring, saving the authors an extended return trip; and Bernie Sargent in El Paso County, for a personal tour of many historic locations in the area and for reviewing the manuscript for accuracy on Old Fort Bliss and the Mexican Revolution.

At Sul Ross State University in Alpine, one of our favorite places in Texas, special thanks go to archivist Melleta R. Bell and her assistant, Jerry Garza, for help in using the vast collections on the Big Bend, and to archeologist Robert J. Mallouf, retired director of the Center for Big Bend Studies, for opening the doors to the remarkable Camp Holland site. Others in West Texas whom we specially acknowledge are retired Lt. Col. William F. Haenn, president of the Fort Clark Historical Society, for generosity with his time and collection access, and Clay Riley, Brownwood, for leading the way to the vast photographic resources of the Brown County Historical Museum. And we also extend heartfelt thanks, in memorial, to the late Fritz Kahl, former instructor pilot and mayor at Marfa, for telling the real story of Marfa Army Airfield.

With regard to military sites in Central Texas, there were a number of people who provided vital leads and assistance in maneuvering overgrown research trails. At Baylor University in Waco, special thanks go to the great staff at the Texas Collection, particularly director John Wilson and archivist Geoff Hunt, who combed their files to find maps, oral histories, photographs, papers, and clippings related to Camp MacArthur and Rich Field. With regard to those topics, too, the authors recognize Internet friend and aviation historian Ben Guttery, of Fort Worth, who helped tie up loose research ends, and also Georgetown residents Milton and Anne Jordan, who provided map-reading skills and driving assistance for photos.

At Austin's Camp Mabry, a remarkable team of volunteers and museum staff maintain one of the state's most extensive military collections, but particular thanks go to Museum Registrar Lisa Sharik, who assisted with both research and photographs. With regard to sites in San Antonio, the authors are indebted to Maria Watson Pfeiffer, their colleague on the Antiquities Advisory Board, and a respected historian and preservationist. On the topic of Camp Ford, thanks go to Alston Thoms of Texas A&M University, whose ground-truth work on the site of the Confederate prisoner-of-war camp at Tyler set high standards for archeological investigations, and to Stephen L. Black of Texas State University–San Marcos for providing photos of the work. For research related to Sabine Pass and Galveston, special thanks go to Edward Cotham Jr. of Houston, an attorney and military historian who has helped preserve

those stories and others through his personal research and his advocacy for site preservation and interpretation. His passion for good history is admirable and infectious,
and his commitment to this project went far beyond what was expected.

One of the true highlights of the research for this book happened at the Palo Alto
Battlefield National Historical Park, administered by the National Park Service. There,
two individuals—Superintendent Mark E. Spier and Archeologist/Chief of Resource
Management Rolando L. Garza—generously allowed us vital access to sites and information and provided us with copies of historic and satellite maps that helped us
interpret the often confusing nature of early installations and battlefields from the
opening days of the Mexican War. Both men work tirelessly to tell an important but
lesser-known story of American history that played out on the South Texas Plains.
Particular thanks go to archeologist Garza, who took time from his busy schedule to
not only personally lead a tour of various sites but also answer our myriad questions.
Clearly knowledgeable about military history in the area and enthusiastically devoted
to the National Park Service mission at the park, he is the consummate public history
ambassador to the heritage tourists who seek out the site.

As with any "then and now" treatment of history, good photographs are essential
to the effort. In addition to the folks previously noted, several others equally deserve
recognition for assisting us in the search for the best available images, both past and
present. They are Patrick Lemelle and Tom Shelton at the Institute of Texan Cultures, part of the University of Texas at San Antonio; Cathy Spitzenberger at Special
Collections, University of Texas at Arlington Library; Cynthia Brandimarte and Nola
Davis, Texas Parks and Wildlife Department; John Anderson, Texas State Library and
Archives Commission; Howard C. Williams, Orange County Historical Commission;
and Michael Grauer, Curator of Art, Panhandle-Plains Historical Society Museum,
Canyon, Texas. Others who unselfishly provided assistance with photograph leads,
helped set up the shots, or traveled along on photo excursions were T. Lindsay Baker,
Susan Oglesbee, Clara Ruddell, and Chuck Blanks. For the maps in this book, we
would not have considered anyone else but Austin artist and cartographer Molly
O'Halloran, who is not only exceptionally talented but also one of the nicest people
with whom we worked. She was an integral part of the team.

It has been both an extreme pleasure and a humbling experience for us to work
with people of such high caliber and genuine dedication. If we succeed in meeting this
book's original objective, causing travelers, history enthusiasts, preservation planners,
and young people to take special notice of significant sites that might disappear without some measure of collective interest, education, and planning, it is due in large part
to those who helped and encouraged us along the way. We are in your debt.

INTRODUCTION

The first full century of Texas statehood, from 1845 through 1945, can be clearly defined by specific military confrontations. These confrontations, viewed by some as glorious and as odious by others, came to mold virtually all social, economic, and political characteristics of the state. Indeed, the unique and universally recognized cartographical shape of Texas is itself the result of armed conflict.

This book features the brief story of 34 historic military sites that played a significant role in those conflicts and illustrates how each appeared at the zenith of its usefulness compared with how it looks today. Although the sites were chosen using various criteria, each site represents a key facet in the overall broad sweep of Texas military history. Some are military only in the general sense that shots were fired there in anger, although not necessarily by soldiers in uniform. Other sites directly contributed to the winning of major wars that raged far from the borders of Texas.

Unfortunately, there is little physical evidence of these volatile early years in the Lone Star State. Many of the sites we describe have been totally obliterated by the relentless waves of time. Some have surrendered to urban development while others, doomed by climate and public apathy, have simply melted back into the earth, their location unmarked and all but forgotten.

Likewise, sprawling military installations once home to tens of thousands of soldiers have disappeared completely, having been transformed in some cases into teeming subdivisions whose inhabitants have little if any knowledge of or interest in the fascinating history that now lies buried beneath their feet. Other sites, once vital to a specific military purpose, now seem too remote to encourage casual visitation. Still others are secured with locked gates and are not accessible by the public.

Fortunately, the Texas state government has, over the years, taken exemplary steps through the Texas Historical Commission and the Texas Parks and Wildlife Department to identify, record, interpret, and preserve the still-visible evidence of the state's historic military heritage. It is at the local level, however, that the challenge of identification and preservation must first be fully met.

Famous soldiers served at many of these sites, and numerous history books make note of their presence in Texas. Ulysses S. Grant passed through on his way to future fame, as did the likes of Zachary Taylor, Phil Sheridan, William Sherman, George Pickett, James Longstreet, George Custer, Douglas MacArthur, Teddy Roosevelt, John Pershing, George Patton, and of course, Robert E. Lee. If tradition is to be accepted as truth, the iconic Virginian appears to have been at many Texas posts in the years prior to the War between the States. Other far less celebrated soldiers from foreign lands spent involuntary time in Texas as well. Veterans of German Gen. Erwin Rommel's Afrika Korps, along with countless Italian prisoners of war, found themselves in Texas camps located all across the state during World War II.

As the decades have passed, the true significance of the early military history of Texas has become all but obscured by more urgent issues, both domestic and international. It is the intent of this book to restore, at least in the mind's eye, something of the vitality of these now largely forgotten sites. Further, we hope the stories and illustrations of these sites will encourage visitors to seek them out, and perhaps to preserve similar locales for future generations.

While the drama and excitement created long ago by the thunder of cannon, the rattle of sabers, the bugles' blare, and the ruffle of drums are now but distant echoes, the enduring heritage of each site remains. Viewed as a whole, that heritage forms a tapestry that is too rich in color and too vibrant in reflected glory to ever be allowed to fade completely into darkness.

Faded Glory

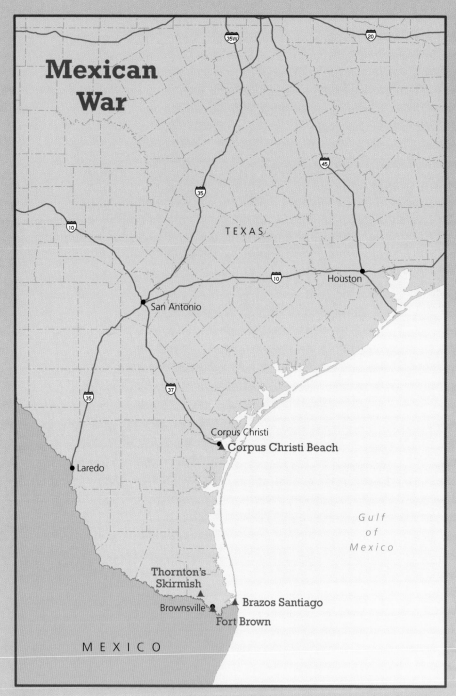

Map by Molly O'Halloran

1

THE MEXICAN WAR
1846–1848

*Wars as such may
best be forgotten, but
the period of the Mexican
War was an important
era, one of upheaval,
of passion, of heroism,
of bitterness, and of
triumph.*

—John S. D. Eisenhower

While all wars are controversial by nature, few have proved to be quite as lastingly contentious as the relatively brief but hugely significant war between the United States and Mexico. Beginning on the banks of the Rio Grande at the southern tip of Texas in May 1846, the often fierce conflict came to its close less than 18 months later when the victorious American army marched into Mexico City.

The magnitude of the spoils of the war is beyond dispute. In defeat, Mexico forfeited more than 1 million square miles of its territory to the United States. In time, those vast lands became the states of California, Arizona, and New Mexico, with sizeable portions of Colorado, Utah, and Nevada included in the war-wrought transaction. Texas, then only recently annexed into the Union, was by treaty finally made free of the long-standing claim of ownership by Mexico. In addition, the defeated nation was forced to recognize the Rio Grande as the formal boundary separating it from the United States.

For many politicians at the time, as well as for numerous historians since who have made the Mexican War their favorite subject, the controversy that still swirls around it has provided ample fodder for argument. For example, Abraham Lincoln, as a 38-year-old freshman congressman from Illinois, railed against the rationale for going to

3

war with Mexico so vehemently that his colleagues and supporters called into question his personal loyalty to the Union.

As is always the case, the writing of the war's history fell largely to the victor's own historians. In this instance, however, some of these scholars have depicted the winning side as the villainous perpetrator of the whole affair. No less a military authority than Ulysses S. Grant, a participant in and a chronicler of the Mexican War, decried it as being "the most unjust war ever waged by a stronger nation against a weaker nation." His analysis, offered years after the Union general Grant himself had led the forces of a stronger nation in a war against a weaker one, puts his quote in clear perspective.

With the passage of time, however, the American invasion of Mexico now seems to have taken refuge in the handy observation that the ends justify the means. In the case of the Mexican War, the ends were a weakened Mexico and an enlarged United States suddenly without any strong strategic challenger on the North American continent. It is not only the end, however, that has stirred the controversy over the years but the means as well. Just how and why this pivotal war came about remain the key questions. While it is not within the scope of this chapter to review in any depth the war's causes and effects, we offer a short abstract of the more salient issues. Those seeking a comprehensive study of the conflict are urged to read John S. D. Eisenhower's excellent book, *So Far from God,* as well as Robert Selph Henry's equally compelling treatment, *The Story of the Mexican War.*

In this short version of that story, the overarching reason for the Mexican War was American expansionism. The United States apparently had no desire to expand deeply into Mexico proper, but rather, slice across its northern territory in pursuit of what US president James Knox Polk saw as his nation's manifest destiny. Like other presidents before him, he envisioned a United States that stretched the full 3,000 miles from the Atlantic Coast on the east to California's Pacific shores on the west. A cursory glance at an 1840s-era map of North America reveals that the most expedient way to accomplish this bold ambition would be to persuade Mexico to relinquish its claim to much of its northern territory, which ran from Texas westward to the Pacific.

At first, the Polk administration attempted to purchase the thousands of square miles of desired Mexican territory. It quickly became clear, however, that Mexico had no interest in selling its valuable lands at any price. When pressed on the issue, the Mexican government countered with a bellicose note to the effect that if the Republic of Texas, still viewed by Mexico as being its legal possession, were to become an American state, a condition of war would immediately exist between the two neighboring nations.

Likely recognizing that a war with Mexico might well be the only viable key to his aspirations, Polk promptly cleared the path for Congress to annex Texas. In a rather transparent move, the United States next sent more than half its entire army into the newly annexed state to protect it from any overt military manifestations of Mexico's threatened declaration of hostilities.

The American army under the command of Gen. Zachary Taylor encamped on the shoreline of Corpus Christi Bay in Texas from July 31, 1845, until March 8, 1846. From the Mexican viewpoint, this camp was actually inside Mexico. A long-standing dispute between Mexico and the now defunct Republic of Texas about the boundary line separating the two had become an issue with the United States. While the Mexican government had always maintained that boundary line was the Nueces River, the United States chose to accept the old Republic's claim that the Rio Grande, located many miles farther south, was the true international boundary.

Clearly intending to prove that his national domain did now indeed extend to the Rio Grande by virtue of the annexation of Texas, President Polk ordered Taylor to march some 160 miles south to the river. When the army reached the site of present-day Brownsville, Taylor ordered that a fort be constructed directly across the Rio Grande from the Mexican village of Matamoros. An apparently temporary American army camp on the beach of Corpus Christi Bay was one thing, but a small but permanent fort built on what the Mexicans believed to be their indisputable terrain was something else altogether. The gauntlet had been thrown down by the invading United States forces.

The challenge was quickly answered when on April 25, 1846, a Mexican force of some 1,600 men ambushed a US cavalry patrol, resulting in over 60 American casualties. When word of the first clash of arms in Texas reached Washington, it triggered a swift reaction. Claiming that "American blood had been shed on American soil," Polk quickly orchestrated a congressional declaration of war against Mexico. That the newly declared enemy had every reason to believe the blood of American invaders had actually been spilled on Mexican soil did not alter the course of events that followed.

The war was often hotly contested, with the Mexican forces proving to be much better trained than the Americans had assumed. Eventually, however, the Americans' better leadership, superior firepower, and efficient logistical support won battle after battle across Mexico and, in short order, the war itself. It was a costly conflict. Over 13,000 Americans died in battle, as did countless thousands of Mexican soldiers. Among the survivors were some 300 junior American officers who would in just 13 years serve as generals on both sides in their divided nation's tragic Civil War. Among them were Robert E. Lee, James Longstreet, George McClelland, George Pickett, Thomas "Stonewall" Jackson, Joseph E. Johnston, and, of course, Ulysses S. Grant.

The war over, America's wide path to the Pacific seemed clear. Serious concerns about slavery issues in the newly acquired territory were eventually resolved, and Polk's dream of manifest destiny became a reality. History holds, generally, that what is often referred to as "Mr. Polk's War" made that dream come true. However, whether that highly desired end justified his allegedly provocative means continues to be debated on both sides of the Rio Grande.

CORPUS CHRISTI BEACH
(1845)

The congress of the Republic of Texas voted on July 4, 1845, to approve annexation to the United States, and three weeks later American forces were in position at Corpus Christi to quell any possible Mexican attempt to invade what would become the nation's newest state upon formal approval by the US Congress. The aptly named "Army of Occupation" established its massive encampment on the beach of Corpus Christi Bay on July 31, 1845. Its very name and immense size demonstrated that the American army had immediate plans to invade and then occupy something far more significant than a desolate bay front in a tiny village in the newly annexed state of Texas. A lithograph made at the time shows impeccable rows of canvas tents stretching eight deep along the edge of the bay for miles, only to disappear beyond the horizon. According to army records, there were exactly 8,509 American men in uniform in the year of the lithograph's creation, and by most accounts just slightly less than half the entire regular American army lived in that tent city by the bay.

Many of the soldiers arrived in Corpus Christi by sea. They had marched from Fort Jessup, Louisiana, to New Orleans to board the steamboat *Alabama* and other smaller vessels for the three-week, 90-mile passage across the Gulf of Mexico to land on St. Joseph Island, a barrier island off the Texas coast. Because the waters between the barrier island and the mainland were too shallow to accommodate oceangoing vessels such as the *Alabama,* the troops relied on shallow-draft vessels to transport them from the steamboat to the little village of Corpus Christi. In the first of many poorly planned logistical episodes in this campaign, the men were compelled to stay on the desolate island for five days until the transport vessels finally arrived to shuttle them to the mainland and their bay front campsite.

There was also great confusion about which river Mexican forces would have to cross to invade American territory. Having never officially recognized the Republic of Texas after the battle at San Jacinto in 1836, Mexico at first continued to claim the

Sabine River as its border with the United States. When it became clear the Sabine premise could not be defended, the Mexican government concluded that the Nueces River was a more practical choice as its international boundary with Texas. But Texas during its 10-year existence as a republic claimed the Rio Grande as the legal boundary, and the United States, upon annexing Texas, eagerly endorsed the Rio Grande border.

For almost seven months some 4,000 American troops awaited a resolution of the border issue on the hot and humid shore of Corpus Christi Bay. Nearly half the soldiers were foreign born, and having no particular interest in the strategic plans of their adopted country, many often slipped away from camp to escape the heat and the constant drilling imposed upon them in an effort both to maintain discipline as well as to occupy the long, hot hours between sunrise and sunset.

The leader of this large contingent of bored and restless soldiers, and the man who demanded the endless hours of drill, was Bvt. Brig. Gen. Zachary Taylor. Today, Taylor would be called a "soldiers' general." Like other commanders in history who have been admired and respected by their troops, Taylor had a nickname, "Old Rough and Ready," in common use throughout the tent city and later in combat. It was a particularly apt title for a man who, at age 61, was definitely old at a time when reaching one's 50th birthday represented a remarkable feat. Taylor was also rough, both in the sense of his disdain for accepted military practices and procedures as well as his disregard for social niceties. Capt. Franklin Smith of the 1st Mississippi Rifle Regiment commented that Taylor "swore worse than even Andy Jackson," who it was said could burn the bark off a tree by hurling crude epithets at it. Smith also found Taylor to be outrageous and a man who "pummels with his fists anyone who comes in his way."

Descriptions of the general in letters written by some of his soldiers portrayed him as being short, bowlegged, and fat. His disregard for military uniforms led him to wear whatever sort of clothing seemed comfortable for the occasion. He sometimes wore trousers made of a purple-colored cloth and a shabby and tattered greenish leather overshirt, as well as all manner of headgear, including a soiled oil cloth cap and a well-worn Mexican straw sombrero. Apparently, he only once wore the official army uniform to which his high rank entitled him, on the occasion of a meeting with an equally high-ranked naval officer. In an ironic twist worthy of the author O. Henry, the navy commodore came to the meeting wearing his most informal uniform in deference to Taylor's widely known dislike of pretentious military frills.

A young lieutenant who had just arrived at camp once saw what he perceived to be a fat old man sitting outside a tent, polishing a sword. He offered his own sword to the old fellow with a promise to pay him a dollar if he were to shine it, as well as direct him to the commanding general. To his dismay, the "old fatty," as the lieutenant had addressed him, barked, "Lieutenant, I *am* the commanding general and I will take that dollar."

Being old and rough, Taylor was also ready. He had been the first American army officer to earn a brevet promotion for bravery in battle. He served in the War of 1812 and received another promotion for bravery during the Seminole War in Florida. Just as soon as he had arrived at Corpus Christi, the general seemed more than ready to move on to the next stage in the border river disputes with Mexico, but political intrigues in Washington, DC, and Mexico City thwarted him. Taylor's army remained on the beach for over half a year, much to his dismay and to his men's discomfort. Under the direct supervision of such West Point–trained junior officers as Ulysses S. Grant, Braxton Bragg, and George Meade, the troops drilled by the hour and then refreshed themselves with frequent frolics in the calm waters of Corpus Christi Bay.

The village of Corpus Christi, virtually adjacent to a portion of the sprawling but orderly city of tents, could boast of no more than 200 residents when General Taylor and his troops arrived to make camp. It had been founded as a trading post in 1839 by Col. Henry L. Kinney, a somewhat shady early Texas entrepreneur. The longer the troops stayed on its bay front, the larger Corpus Christi became. By the time the army broke camp and moved south to the Rio Grande, the population had increased more than tenfold. The reason for the explosive growth in population was the golden opportunity to cater to the more basic needs of the thousands of soldiers virtually stranded on the beach with at least some money in their uniform pockets and no-where else to spend it. Saloons and gambling houses sprang up almost overnight. The combination of high-priced but barely drinkable liquor and crushing boredom fre-quently generated a predictable flurry of drunken brawls involving the enlisted men.

When they were not busy disciplining errant soldiers or drilling the troops for hours each day, officers found numerous ways to amuse themselves. Horseracing along the water's edge was a popular pastime, as were card games and checker tour-naments. Those officers seeking more intellectual pursuits formed a book club. Other off-duty diversions included attending one of the many circuses that somehow fre-quently found their way to the Gulf Coast. A drama club formed to help quell the malaise that stemmed from having few official duties to perform. Soldiers created a theater by arranging canvas tent panels in a large circular pattern. Enlisted men constructed the floor of the stage and the scenery, and received front-row seating in exchange for their labors. Although the primitive theater-in-the-round had no roof, most of the 800 seats it contained reportedly remained filled during every perfor-mance. Many younger officers who in 15 years would become generals on both sides of America's Civil War took part in the productions. Longstreet, Grant, and other junior officers often accepted challenging roles in Shakespearian plays, and due to the absence of any genuine actresses, men commonly served as female leads. In one production of *Othello,* Grant took on the role of Desdemona but in such a slovenly manner as to cause the male actor in the leading role to stalk off the stage in disgust midway through the first act.

Despite General Taylor's badgering of the War Department to issue orders to move on to the Rio Grande, the army remained on the beach. Even though the food and entertainment made available to his troops were in most respects superior to those found in other military camps at the time, the men grew as impatient as their general to move on. When diplomatic efforts to resolve the international boundary and other issues with Mexico abruptly came to an end, orders to vacate the camp and move south finally came from Washington. As a result, Taylor had his columns marching toward the Rio Grande by March 8, 1846. Some large equipment, supplies, and a number of troops made their way back across the bay to St. Joseph's Island to then be transported by sea to the new American supply port at Brazos Santiago while the general joined most of his men in the 160-mile march to the Rio Grande. Three weeks later, the Army of Occupation took up its position on the river directly across from the important Mexican trade hub city of Matamoros.

With the forces of both the United States and Mexico thus poised for long-anticipated battle, the inevitable military clash that led to a full-blown war soon occurred. On April 25, a small cavalry patrol under the command of Capt. Seth Thornton rode blindly into an ambush by a much larger Mexican force. Zachary Taylor quickly proceeded to claim victory in a number of battles in Mexico that would eventually propel him into the White House as the 12th president of the United States, and a very long way from the beach on Corpus Christi Bay.

Over a century and a half later, the bay is still there, of course, but virtually everything else has changed from its days of military importance. A beautiful bay front featuring towering skyscrapers has replaced the 1845 city of cotton canvas tents. The original natural beach is covered by a seawall and a manicured sweep of handsome boulevard. No vestige of Taylor's camp managed to survive the decades of necessary improvements that have elevated the terrain where the many tents of his army once swayed in the Gulf's sea breeze. A cemetery several city blocks inland from the shore contains the graves of sailors killed in a ship's boiler explosion that occurred on the bay during the time of the encampment on the beach. A marker in nearby Artesian Park indicates a possible site of Taylor's personal tent, while other accounts suggest the general actually spent his spare time by the bay at a location one and a half mile to the north.

It is possible to stand atop the seawall that spans the bay front and look to the

Gen. Zachary Taylor's Army of Occupation arrived at Corpus Christi's bay front on July 31, 1845. Nearly half the entire US Army encamped there for more than seven months before the Mexican War began. *Lithograph by Daniel Whiting. Library of Congress, USZ 62–126, October 1845.*

south along the curve of the shoreline to get at least a fleeting sense of the magnitude and sweep of Taylor's encampment. On the far horizon, some five miles distant, a thin peninsula juts out into the bay. That same landmark is clearly visible in the lithograph made in 1845 when the army's tents filled nearly every square foot of the beach that has now disappeared beneath a seawall.

Location: On Corpus Christi bay front, extending from five blocks north of the Ship Channel Bridge (Highway 181) south along Shoreline Boulevard to Taylor Street.

Access: Open to the public.

The actual Corpus Christi beach location of Zachary Taylor's 1845 Army of Occupation has been obliterated by 165 years of seawall and landfill construction. The encampment stretched from north of today's Ship Channel on the right to roughly midway on the shoreline in this photograph. *Thomas E. Alexander Collection.*

THORNTON'S SKIRMISH
(1846)

As US forces under Gen. Zachary Taylor made their way to the Rio Grande in March 1846, hopes for a diplomatic détente with Mexico ended with President Polk's recall of Commissioner John Slidell. Both sides readied themselves for war. Mexico viewed Taylor's *entrada* below the Nueces River and his establishment of a fortification along the Rio Grande as acts of aggression, and quickly moved troops into Matamoros to prepare for what appeared to them to be a certain attack. With the opposing forces clearly in view of each other across the disputed border, there were occasional checks on the positions, with sporadic reports of isolated sniper fire and even sightings of small scouting parties back and forth across the river.

Despite such tension, the tenuous and uneasy military line nevertheless remained largely uncontested for weeks. That began to change by mid-April, when Mexican Gen. Pedro de Ampudia sent a communiqué to Taylor demanding withdrawal of US forces back north of the Nueces River. The US general responded by ordering naval forces to move forward to blockade the mouth of the Rio Grande. Within days, Gen. Mariano Arista replaced Ampudia as the frontline commander, and with that change the inevitability of war greatly increased as the Mexican forces prepared for a punitive drive across the river. Known as a brash and aggressive field leader, Arista quickly assessed Taylor's vulnerable position and exposed supply line extending back to Port Isabel, and assumed the time was right to move forward.

On April 24, word reached Taylor that Mexican troops had crossed the river above and below the Fort Texas position, and he responded by sending scouting parties in both directions. As rumors of several thousand soldiers crossing upriver were particularly disturbing, Taylor directed Capt. Seth B. Thornton, with assistance from Capt. William J. Hardee, to lead two companies of the Second Dragoons to reconnoiter. Thornton seemed the logical choice for the assignment. A native of Virginia and a member of the Second Dragoons since their inception in 1836, the year Texas gained its independence from Mexico, he had extensive field experience in the Second Seminole War, 1835–42. Described in *The Mexican War and Its Heroes* (1854) as "being of a small stature and delicate constitution," he nevertheless had a reputation as a formidable fighter and seasoned cavalry officer, albeit impetuous. Georgia-born Hardee, his second in command, who would later gain prominence as a Confederate general during the Civil War in such battles as Shiloh, Perryville, and Stones River, seemed equally prepared.

Utilizing a local guide, who proved both reluctant and unreliable, Thornton's unit left camp that evening, halting for rest only after it had covered 15 miles. The march resumed at daybreak, and at a point some eight miles farther west, after the guide had turned back, the dragoons approached a site known as Rancho de Carricitos along the river. There, Thornton made a fateful tactical decision based on his presumption that either the Mexican forces had not crossed in large numbers or that they would not engage the US forces if encountered. Electing not to post sentries or to reconnoiter the surrounding area beforehand, Thornton instead proceeded directly toward several houses by means of a large corral. In effect, the corral was a vast open field surrounded by fencing and nearly impenetrable thickets of native chaparral. Thornton's men followed him into the corral, with Hardee bringing up the rear, but there was little order to the operation, and the troops quickly fanned out in search of someone associated with the property. They soon found an old man, and as Thornton engaged him in conversation, Mexican forces surrounded the corral, sealing off any hope of escape. As the dragoons sensed their precarious situation, a general panic ensued, and the Mexican infantry opened fire while Thornton vainly tried to regroup his men. As Hardee wrote the following day in his report of the incident: "Our gallant commander immediately gave the command to charge, and himself led the advance; but it was too late; the enemy had secured the entrance, and it was impossible to force it. The officers and men did every thing that fearless intrepidity could accomplish; but the infantry had stationed themselves in the field on the right of the passage way, and the cavalry lined the exterior fence, and our retreat was hopelessly cut off."

While desperately seeking a weakness in the enemy line by circling the interior line, Thornton called for the charge and spurred his horse against the perimeter, somehow managing to break through, although presumably meeting instant death on the other side. No one followed. In the meantime, Hardee did his best to rally the troops in another direction. Recalling the pandemonium of the moment, he noted:

> I made for the river, intending either to swim it or place myself in a position for defense. I found the bank too boggy to accomplish the former, and I therefore rallied the men, forming them in order of battle in the open field, and without the range of the infantry behind the fence. . . . In five minutes from the time the first shot was fired, the field was surrounded by a numerous body of men. However, I determined to sell our lives as dearly as possible if I could not secure good treatment, and accordingly I went forward and arranged with an officer that I should deliver myself and men as prisoners of war, to be treated with all the consideration to which such unfortunates are entitled by the rules of civilized warfare.

Hardee's report, which mentioned seven fatalities, went immediately to Taylor, who relayed the information to Washington along with his one-line assessment: "Hostilities may now be considered as commenced." A few days later, Taylor received an additional report, this time from Captain Thornton, who wrote that he had survived his break through the fence and managed to elude pursuing troops for two days, making it within six miles of Fort Texas before capture by an advance guard that escorted him to Matamoros, where he joined Hardee and the other survivors.

Taylor's message to President Polk would take weeks to reach Washington, and in the meantime the general prepared for the inevitable battles to come. His immediate plan was simply to secure and hold his positions until the arrival of reinforcements. Sensing Fort Texas was duly prepared for an assault from the forces then massed in Matamoros, he opted to return to Port Isabel, 25 miles to the northeast, to strengthen his supply base. Soon after his arrival there, though, he received the first reports about the siege of Fort Texas. Delaying his response long enough to ensure the security of the port fortifications, he then organized his forces and was back on the road to the Rio Grande by May 7. The following day he encountered the Mexican army under the command of General Arista at a place called Palo Alto along the Matamoros Road. Not wishing to engage the enemy at that point due to its superior numbers and to the vulnerability of his supply train, Taylor cautiously chose to hold his ground. Arista then took the offensive, ordering Gen. Anastasio Torrejón to strike at the supply line, but Taylor's tactical use of light artillery—the so-called flying artillery that proved to be an integral part of military maneuvers later in the Mexican War—thwarted two major attacks.

As the battle extended into the evening hours, amid the cries of the wounded and the eerie glow of brush fires burning across the landscape, Arista realized his losses were significant and that his primary objective had failed. Opting to withdraw back along the Matamoros Road rather than prepare for another day on the battlefield, he gambled that Taylor would not pursue. Despite such advice from his key aides, though, Taylor ordered the troops to press forward and the following day engaged the Mexicans at their position along the Resaca de la Palma. Buoyed by their successes the day before, the US troops maintained the pressure, although it was the infantry and not the flying artillery that won the day. With the enemy forces in disarray, the lines collapsed, and what followed was a running battle that extended back to the Rio Grande, with the enemy moving across to Matamoros. Taylor's forces thus triumphantly reentered Fort Texas—soon to be renamed Fort Brown for its commander who had fallen in battle only a few days before—breaking the siege.

On May 8, as fighting commenced at Palo Alto, President Polk met with Commissioner Slidell in Washington. With details of the failed diplomatic effort in hand, but yet without knowledge of either Thornton's skirmish or the fighting then underway along the Rio Grande, Polk met with his cabinet the following day and ascertained their strong commitment to war. At the time, though, Polk's position was tenuous at best, based largely on private commercial claims against Mexico and a failure of deliberations that would have pursued other options for redress, namely an agreement on the international border and the purchase of land. Early that evening, though, the president received Taylor's note about the Thornton incident along with the general's assessment that war, in reality, was already underway. This was the missing element Polk felt he needed to petition Congress for a declaration of war, and he did so on Monday, May 11. In his call for military action, he carefully outlined the complex deterioration of US-Mexico relations following the annexation of Texas, including the report on the Thornton incident, and provided a detailed justification of his administration's actions to that point. Referencing directly the spark that touched off the war, though, Polk wrote, "But now, after reiterated menaces, Mexico has passed the boundary of the United States, has invaded our territory and shed American blood upon the American soil." As a result, he added, "the two nations are at war."

Two days later, on March 13, the president received formal notice Congress had approved the war declaration. Coincidentally, while political leaders in Washington deliberated on the war issue, an exchange of prisoners along the Rio Grande following the fighting at Resaca de la Palma resulted in the return of several soldiers, including captains Thornton and Hardee, to Taylor's command. Thornton was immediately placed under arrest, however, pending a formal review of his battlefield actions at Rancho de Carricitos. At the hearing, Hardee testified on Thornton's behalf, and his persuasive argument figured prominently in the court's decision for acquittal. Seth Thornton subsequently returned to military duty with the dragoons, but on August 18, 1847, near the settlement of San Antonio outside Mexico City, while providing escort for a party of engineers, he died when an 18-pound cannon shot tore through his body. Just over five months later, officials of the United States and Mexico met in the town of Guadalupe Hidalgo to sign the treaty that ended the Mexican War.

Today, the National Park Service provides extensive interpretation for the opening battles of the Mexican War at both Palo Alto and Resaca de la Palma. Visitors can also view the site of Fort Brown along the Rio Grande in downtown Brownsville. Few, however, make the drive west from town along the Military Highway to seek out the site of Thornton's Skirmish, where the international war began. Two miles west of the little settlement of Las Rusias (Rucias), against the backdrop of vast agricultural fields, is a small roadside commemorative exhibit that features a 1936 Texas Centennial gray granite monument—now heavily damaged and missing its metal wreath. Without mentioning the Mexican War, the monument's brief, historically understated inscription simply notes, "The spot where 'American blood was shed on American soil' April 25, 1846; here Capt. Seth B. Thornton and 62 dragoons were attacked by Mexican troops." Nearby is a cannon—not of Mexican War vintage—on concrete supports, with a small stone marker attributing placement of the artillery piece to a local chapter of the Daughters of the American Revolution. Complicating the interpretation at the site is an Official Texas Historical Marker honoring the 17th-century expeditions of explorer Alonso de León through the area. Nowhere at the site is there information on the outcome of the 1846 skirmish, and likewise there is no list of those who died or were wounded in battle that fateful day. More important for those who seek history where it occurred, there is also no indication that the commemorative site is only in the general vicinity of the battlefield, for the exact location of the historic ranch and the skirmish remains unknown. As the National Park Service notes through its online interpretation of the Mexican War, "somewhere

This scene, published in *The Pictorial History of the Mexican War and Mexico,* depicts the close-quarter fighting and general chaos involved in the attack on the US Second Dragoons at Rancho de Carricitos. *Digital reimaging of the lithograph found on page 202 of* The Pictorial History of the Mexican War and Mexico, *by John Frost (Philadelphia: Published by Thomas, Cowperthwait and Co. for J. A. Bill, 1849).*

amidst the lush cane fields, rich soil, and dense chaparral of the modern Rio Grande Valley the spot where the war began in 1846 remains hidden." Although lost for now, presumably it is still extant as archeological artifacts. Vestiges of Thornton's skirmish may someday surface through professional field investigations, providing important analytical analysis that will promote a greater understanding of and appreciation for the pivotal military encounter and the significant role it played in the history of two nations.

Location: Commemorative area is 24 miles west of Brownsville (two miles west of the Las Rusias community) on the north side of US Highway 281 in a roadside park. Actual site of the skirmish remains unknown.
Access: Open.

The exact location of Thornton's Skirmish is undetermined, but a small roadside park along the heavily traveled Military Road (US 281) near the small community of Las Rusias commemorates the 1846 incident with a state centennial marker. The cannon at the site is from the 1850s and therefore not contemporaneous with the Mexican War era. *Photo by Dan K. Utley, 2010.*

BRAZOS SANTIAGO
(1845)

Although not all current general-purpose maps of the lower Texas Gulf Coast indicate the location of Brazos Santiago Pass, it was a prominent feature on Spanish maps of the region as early as 1519. In the summer of that year, the explorer Alonso Álvarez de Pineda charted the pass at the southern tip of what would later become known as Padre Island. He gave it the name that in English would translate into "Arms of Saint James." A map drawn in 1788 showed a small village identified as Brazos Santiago existed on the south shore of this narrow pass at the tip of Brazos Island. One historian claims that the tiny assortment of crude thatched huts comprised essentially a summer resort presumably for those seeking the relative coolness of breezes coming ashore off the Gulf of Mexico.

By 1823, the onetime seaside resort had been reconfigured into a deepwater port at which the cargoes of oceangoing ships could be off-loaded to be transported down Brazos Island to the town of Matamoros located a short distance inland on the Rio Grande. From Matamoros, which the Mexican government soon designated an official port of entry, foreign goods reached all of Mexico, which at the time included Texas. Products to be exported from Mexico went to Matamoros and then by mule trains or wagons back over the same island roadway to Brazos Santiago. There, workers loaded the goods onto ocean-worthy ships and sent them on to the markets of the world. By the early 1830s, Matamoros had become a major international commercial hub, and Brazos Santiago, its gulfside gateway to worldwide trade, had emerged as an important port second only to Veracruz on the Gulf Coast of Mexico. One author even suggests that Mexico's concerns over losing the port to the United States in the event Texas became annexed was a major factor leading to the Mexican War in 1846.

For several years before that war, a number of American tradesmen and shippers had come to Matamoros eager to participate in the lucrative import and export businesses that flourished there and at other points up the Rio Grande. Although the dangerous bar and constantly shifting sands at its mouth at the Gulf often made entrance to it impossible, the river was more than deep enough a few miles upstream from its mouth to permit safe and profitable navigation. Well over a century prior to the flood control and water diversion projects along its lengthy course deprived it of its powerful thrust, the Rio Grande was a vital waterway of international trade. Relatively shallow-draft riverboats with flat-bottom hulls plied its twisting course to and from Matamoros carrying goods that had initially been unloaded at Brazos Santiago.

The village that had changed from summer resort to international port in less than 40 years became a Mexican military installation during the ultimately successful Texas struggle for independence. In 1836, the army constructed a gun battery to guard against possible attack by the Texas Navy. According to a visitor to the site at the time, the cannon mounted on the solidly constructed gun platform had a "commanding view of the entrance of the harbor" as well as of the village. The Mexican government also maintained a revenue station to levy tariffs on incoming goods.

In 1837 a hurricane, the first recorded storm in a long string of frequent Gulf hurricanes to devastate the port, destroyed the revenue outpost. The military encampment with its multiple gun emplacements survived the 1837 tempest only to be washed away by another storm some seven years later.

Although the destruction of its gun platform by the 1844 hurricane ended the Mexican army's presence at Brazos Santiago, a much larger American force would soon make use of the pass to build a key installation on the northern tip of Brazos Island itself. The annexation of the Republic of Texas by the Union in 1845 in effect lit the short fuse that led to the beginning of the war with the United States.

By late March 1846, Gen. Zachary Taylor's army left its encampment at Corpus Christi to establish a far more invasive installation on the left bank of the Rio Grande directly opposite Matamoros. Recognizing the absolute necessity of adequately supplying his large army in such hostile territory, Taylor ordered the immediate construction of two key logistical centers near the mouth of the Rio Grande that separated Matamoros and the newly established American position on the Texas side. He had his principal supply depot built on the mainland on the shore of the Laguna Madre at a village known as El Fronton and later as Point (Port) Isabel. The second link in Taylor's chain of supply was on the northern tip of Brazos Island at the site of the old Mexican gun battery.

The port that developed at Brazos Santiago provided a harbor where oceangoing vessels could unload their cargoes of men and supplies from the island installation. Those cargoes could then be either trans-shipped to Point Isabel on shallow draft boats or hauled on wagon trains down the short length of the island to arrive at Taylor's new camp on the Rio Grande. Ships sailing from Galveston, New Orleans, and beyond soon docked at the wharves of Brazos Santiago. As the treeless island could provide no lumber for the construction of the wharves, timbers salvaged from the many wrecked ships that ran aground on the island over the years provided the building materials. The army built the seaport rapidly but substantially. It constructed a warehouse, several dwellings, and stables to accommodate the flood of military supplies required of an invading army not yet officially at war.

The army's quartermasters clearly knew of the historic logistical significance of Brazos Santiago. Being aware that the bar at the mouth of the Rio Grande could not be reliably crossed by ships, the army simply copied the long-established practices of generations of Mexican tradesmen and used the pass at Brazos Island to gain access to the Texas mainland and the key strategic waterway of the Rio Grande. The overland route from the Gulf port to the supply depot on the mainland was just over 16 miles. The journey sometimes required fording the shallow and narrow Boca Chica inlet that during storms and unusually high tides cleaved the island into two parts. Most of the time silt covered the inlet, allowing easy passage of the wagon trains, but under adverse conditions the angry waters of the Gulf washed away the silt to create a treacherous strip of water that made the wagon road impassable. To ensure reliable passage over this unpredictable stretch of the road, Taylor's engineers constructed a short trestle bridge. The pylons for the bridge reached deep into the surprisingly firm clay that underlies the sand of the barrier island.

According to army records, the flow of supplies from Brazos Santiago to Point Isabel proved to be extensive. One quartermaster report for an 18-month period, from April 1847 to the end of October 1848, mentions that fewer than 1,200 vessels had docked at the harbor. In their collective holds were 5 million pounds of hay, 560,000 bushels of oats, and 115,940 bushels of corn. Feeding of the army's invaluable horses and mules was clearly a high priority. As the invader in a hostile land whose huge population by no means favored feeding either their horses or their soldiers, the American army's own self-sufficient logistical network was vital. As the war progressed, the lines of supply grew longer and increasingly susceptible to enemy action by military troops, hungry civilians, and larcenous bandits.

As a consequence of the mounting demand for supplies to support thousands of troops marching and fighting across Mexico, the army continually expanded the depot at Brazos Santiago. By the war's end in 1848, it had built additional large warehouses, along with better housing for officers, men, and their horses. The site included ship repair facilities, as well as a complete foundry capable of manufacturing reliable parts for steam engines in need of repair.

Troops arriving in Mexico fresh from American ports of embarkation passed through the busy port harbor installation before marching down the island and onto the mainland to go into battle. Although the men were likely relieved to have enjoyed safe passage across the often treacherous waters of the Gulf, few seemed much impressed by what they found on Brazos Island. Apart from the bustling harbor, there was little to behold. The island was just over three miles long and about two miles wide. It lacked trees of any description and, far more important, it had no freshwater source. Potable water reached the harbor installation in barrels on the wagons returning to the Brazos from the mainland.

Capt. William P. Rogers, who served in Col. Jefferson Davis's 1st Mississippi Rifle Regiment, seemed appalled at his first view of the island. He had arrived during the summer to what he described as a "lone and desolate sand beach." Other Mississippians who sailed through the pass along with Captain Rogers noted "the merciless sun," a complaint that raises doubts about the viability of the 18th-century summer resort that once reportedly occupied the island. During the short war, some 8,000 American soldiers touched Mexican soil for the first time at Brazos Santiago. Each spent an average of five days there awaiting transportation for the overland trip to Fort Polk or beyond.

Capt. Luther Giddings of the 1st Ohio Volunteers arrived at Brazos Island to find it "alive with busy men, soldiers, sailors, and others who were running to and fro like ants." He also noted that the only real work being done was by Mexican laborers unloading the ocean ships and loading the wagons. The captain also commented on the many civilian merchants who had set up shop to sell their wares at inflated prices.

While Zachary Taylor and his men engaged in heavy fighting in northern Mexico, his superior officer planned for a more aggressive use of the US Army's burgeoning supply depot on Brazos Island. Gen. Winfield Scott, the army's top commander, called for what would become the first amphibious landing in history of American troops on enemy soil. To provide the logistical support for his unique campaign, Scott needed a final gathering point for his supplies. Because of its strategic location and well-developed harbor facilities, Brazos Santiago was his clear choice. Scott's siege and invasion of Veracruz, Mexico, had been in the planning stages for at least eight months prior to its successful execution in mid-March 1847. At the core of the planning was Scott's confidence in the capability of the facilities at the island. That confidence proved well placed. It was from the soon-vanquished city of Veracruz that the well-supplied Scott was next able to march westward over the mountains to capture Mexico City, yet only after a series of challenging and costly battles.

The occupation of Mexico City eventually ended the war, although the army apparently intended to maintain indefinitely its facility on Brazos Island. However, a severe hurricane on September 19, 1848, destroyed most of the buildings that remained after the war. Another storm in May 1849 inflicted further damage, even though about 90 carpenters, blacksmiths, and other craftsmen reportedly still lived and worked at what remained of the facility after the storms had passed.

With the Mexican War over, the entire lower Rio Grande region entered a period of rapid commercial development. Boat traffic up and down the river put the importance of the Brazos Santiago Pass into a new perspective. Enterprising captains such as Mifflin Kenedy and Richard King perfected the means to reach the Gulf port by sailing directly to it across the Laguna Madre from the mainland. Using shallow-draft vessels, Kenedy, King, and others forever eliminated the time-consuming overland trek down Brazos Island in order to reach the navigable stream of the Rio Grande. In 1850, increased traffic through the Brazos Pass caused the US Congress to approve funds for a lighthouse on the site of Zachary Taylor's old Fort Polk. The purpose of the facility was to guide mariners as they approached the mainland. Completed in 1852, the lighthouse still stands today.

Brazos Santiago's history following the Mexican War and the economic boom the war made possible along the Rio Grande is beyond the scope of this brief narrative. While it played roles of varying significance during America's Civil War, it also suffered as the target of frequent, powerful hurricanes. On rare occasions, however, hurricanes can afford a valuable glimpse of historic human activity at sites totally destroyed by previous storms. In 1980, for example, when Hurricane Allen swept across Brazos Island, there were no longer any structures to level on the barrier island, but the high winds and the surging tides laid bare evidence of both the Mexican War port and the Civil War fortification that had replaced it in 1861. A previous storm in 1933 temporarily exposed artifacts of both eras, unfortunately long enough to permit looters to cart them away. They reportedly found belt buckles, rifle balls, and some insignia.

The deadly storm known as Beulah also roared across the barren island in 1967 to reveal what some claimed to be the remains of a bridge built by General Taylor's soldiers in 1846. The pilings that reappeared were thought to be part of the trestle

In the spring of 1846, the US Army established a bustling port of entry on the northern tip of Brazos Island on the Gulf of Mexico. From there, men and materiel were either transported across the Laguna Madre to Port Isabel on the Texas mainland or on down the island proper to reach the mainland by wagon road. *Courtesy of Institute of Texan Cultures, University of Texas at San Antonio, #076–0424. Source: Thomas B. Thorpe, "Our Army" on the Rio Grande (Philadelphia: Carey & Hart, 1846).*

that permitted the transporting of army troops and supplies across the usually silted over Boca Chica inlet. In his study of the Mexican War, John S. D. Eisenhower says in a footnote on the subject that he saw the pilings in 1984 and had archeologists confirm that they were remains of Taylor's structure. In 1994, the remnants of the bridge remained clearly visible at low tide. Some historians offer a counterclaim that the pilings are part of a railroad bridge built over the always unreliable Boca Chica inlet during the Civil War. There are others who contend that the Civil War rail bridge used the very same pilings originally put in place by Taylor's engineers 16 years earlier during the Mexican War. At any rate, the stark sun- and salt-bleached timbers stand on the Texas Gulf beach as an enduring reminder of the tempestuous past of Brazos Santiago and its historic island military outpost.

The entire island is still as barren and treeless as it was when Jefferson Davis brought his Mississippians ashore there in 1847. From time to time, military artifacts are surrendered by the waters of the Gulf in mute testimony of a time when the small island was the key to successful military campaigns on the mainland.

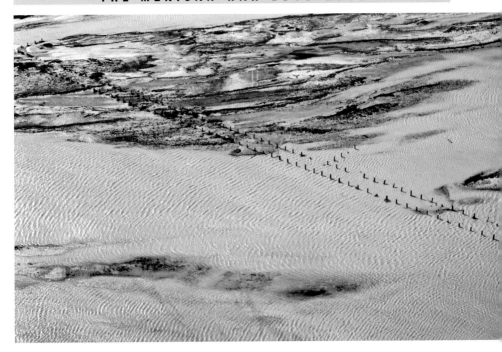

No longer a haven for tall ships and an invading American army, Brazos Island is today a sand-covered wilderness. The vertical posts are said by some to be vestiges of the causeway built by General Taylor's engineers in 1846. Historian John S. D. Eisenhower supports this assumption. *Courtesy of Texas Historical Commission, Austin, Texas.*

Location of Brazos Santiago Depot: At the tip of Brazos Island, four miles north of the end of Texas Highway 4 at the Gulf of Mexico. Access: Difficult; requires driving on the beach at low tide.

FORT BROWN
(1846–1946)

After enduring seven months of mind-numbing inactivity at Corpus Christi, Zachary Taylor's Army of Occupation decamped with few if any regrets on March 8, 1846. The command apparently made no attempt to keep secret the destination to be reached at the end of the march. Exactly where on the disputed Rio Grande they were bound was not widely known to the men, but they knew they were marching south toward the river and moving closer to Mexico. Some of the officers and men in Taylor's force left Corpus

Christi on foot or on horseback while others traveled by sea from St. Joseph's Island to Brazos Santiago. The marchers departed their bay-front encampment and briefly hiked west along the banks of the Nueces River for about 10 miles before swinging south on a route known locally as either the Matamoros Road or the Arroyo Colorado Trail. More a rough pathway for smugglers and bandits than a suitable roadway for an army on the march, the route cut through treeless prairie mostly devoid of potable water. Although the troops appeared well rested after their lengthy sojourn on the bay at Corpus Christi, the long treks between reliable sources of water tested their endurance. On several occasions, the distance between waterholes made it necessary to be without fresh drinking water for more than two days.

Late springtime in South Texas is often much like deep summer elsewhere. An intensely burning sun combined with the constant high humidity steaming off the nearby Gulf of Mexico made the average eight miles the men marched each day tiring and difficult, particularly when drinking water became scarce. As the columns of soldiers moved closer to the Rio Grande, the landscape became more verdant. When rare rainfall came, small clusters of wildflowers bloomed amid the ever-present cacti. Pvt. Enos W. Murfin, who made the 150-mile march to the Rio Grande in 1846, kept a journal in which he noted each day's happenings along with his observations about the terrain he passed through. On March 23 he wrote, "All the land I have seen around here is so flat that when it commences to rain, the water's got no place to run off to, so the flowers grew wild and pretty." After this colorful entry, Murfin next expressed a thought not uncommon among foot soldiers throughout history. "If old Cap would only let us slow down a tad," he complained, "I would surely like to rest here for a spell."

Private Murfin's unidentified "Old Cap" was in all likelihood being pushed hard by his own superior officer, Zachary Taylor. The general stayed with his troops throughout the three-week march to the river. Being among the last to leave the Corpus Christi campsite, Taylor had ridden 30 miles to catch up with the lead unit in the marching columns. Along the route, he suffered as much as his men. His recently acquired straw sombrero already showed signs of frequent wear and had proven to be only partially successful in blocking the blistering rays of the South Texas sun. One of his lieutenants caught a glimpse of him eating breakfast while sitting on a camp stool that seemed likely to give way at any moment under the old general's sturdy frame. Despite his misplaced reliance on his once-new sombrero, the lieutenant noticed that Taylor's nose was white as a result of post-sunburn peeling skin and his lips raw from long hours on the trail.

Although Taylor's army had camped for months at Corpus Christi, the Mexican military had made no effort to drive the Americans back across the Nueces River. At Arroyo Colorado, however, Taylor's men encountered a Mexican military force for the first time. Nothing came from the encounter when Taylor simply ignored a demand that he halt his advance. As the American army continued marching south, the officer in charge of the Mexican unit withdrew his challenge and the old general rode blithely past him. Before his army reached the Rio Grande, Taylor briefly left the column to inspect Point Isabel, the location of his soon-to-be-built supply depot on the Laguna Madre, immediately inland from the port at Brazos Santiago. Satisfied that he would have the necessary logistical network to supply his troops, he rode back to his army, which then arrived at long last on the banks of the Rio Grande. Although it is difficult today to imagine the river as being a wide and navigable waterway, it was over 100 feet across when General Taylor first saw it on March 28, 1846. Directly opposite Fort Texas, the hastily constructed American position on the river's left bank, stood the Mexican city of Matamoros. As Taylor and his men gazed at the bustling town, they could clearly make out uniformed soldiers placing artillery pieces along the waterfront.

While the Americans went about improving their own fortifications on the Texas side of the river, they also saw fit to taunt onlookers on the Mexican side. The soldiers hoisted the US flag to the top of a hurriedly erected pole as bugles loudly blared and drums beat a hearty cadence. This show of patriotic fervor soon had the desired effect. Gen. Francisco Mejia, commandant of the detachment in Matamoros, sent formal messages at all hours to his noisy taunters across the river demanding that the Army of Occupation leave at once and go back to beyond the Nueces. When his demands were ignored, General Mejia ordered even larger caliber artillery brought to the riverfront, aimed directly at the American position on the opposite shore. Taylor, as might be expected, countered by bringing his own big guns to bear on what at any moment could become the active guns of his nation's new enemy. It was now only a matter of time until the shooting would begin.

In further preparation for the inevitable war, Taylor ordered a defensive fortification built a few short yards from what the US government had repeatedly insisted was its side of the Rio Grande. When completed, the earthen fortress was some 800 yards in circumference with walls nine feet tall. The ditches from which the earth for the walls had been removed provided a moatlike trench that surrounded the entire structure. The trench was 20 feet wide and 10 feet deep on average. The Americans constructed the six-sided fortification in the shape of a star with each of its points capable of mounting either artillery pieces or small squads of riflemen. The so-called star fort initially bore the name Fort Texas, in all likelihood to further antagonize the Mexican soldiers who watched it being built within a stone's throw of their drill field in Matamoros. Fort Texas was nearly complete when General Taylor's scouts reported that a sizeable Mexican force had crossed the river and headed toward the new US supply depot at Fort Polk. Leaving behind a small detachment commanded by Maj. Jacob Brown, Taylor hurriedly marched the bulk of his army to his vital supply depot located on the Laguna Madre nearly 20 miles to the east.

No sooner had Taylor's large force reached Fort Polk, which they found well defended and secure, when they heard faintly the sound of artillery fire coming from back at Fort Texas. According to most accounts, Taylor at first ordered his men to return quickly to the sounds of the cannon. Then, apparently believing Major Brown's small contingent of soldiers augmented by the field battery of Lt. Braxton Bragg fully capable of defending the star fort, Taylor decided to stay at Fort Polk. After putting his men to work on further strengthening the defenses of the supply depot, Taylor ordered a scouting party to return to Fort Texas to determine its status. The scouts soon returned with a report from Major Brown that all was well even though Mexican forces surrounded his little fort and shells from their batteries landed inside the works, albeit with little effect.

When he believed Fort Polk had been satisfactorily reinforced, Taylor ordered his men to march back to the besieged Fort Texas. Mexican Gen. Mariano Arista had anticipated Taylor's intentions, and his army's efforts to halt the return of the American soldiers resulted in the first two full-scale clashes between the new enemies, one at the battle of Palo Alto on May 8, 1846, and then at Resaca de la Palma the next day. Taylor's forces easily prevailed in both battles. Upon his return to Fort Texas, the victorious Taylor was saddened to learn that Major Brown had been struck by a Mexican shell fragment during the siege and died a few days later. In honor of his friend and subordinate, the general changed the name of the little fortification to Fort Brown. It was a name to be borne proudly by the army installation that flourished at the site for 100 years.

A week after his twin defeats at Palo Alto and at the Resaca, General Arista withdrew all his troops from Texas. In just over a week, he had evacuated the city of Matamoros in advance of what proved to be an uncontested occupation by American forces. During the remaining months of the war, Fort Brown played a highly significant role. As Taylor's army continued up the Rio Grande from Matamoros, vital supplies moved by steamboat to ports located on the Mexican side of the river. From there, the supplies went to support Taylor's advance deep into northern Mexico.

Immediately following the end of the war in February 1848, construction began on a new Fort Brown at a site less than a half mile from the original star-shaped earthen structure. Workers built the new buildings utilizing lumber salvaged from the many warehouses that had been located at Fort Polk during the war. A tall wall separated the fort from the town of Brownsville that began to develop during the war. The soldiers set aside a parade ground at the center of the new installation, which soon boasted more than 10 sturdy buildings. At the base of the flagpole on the parade ground they laid to rest the fallen heroes of the first battles of the Mexican War, including Maj. Jacob Brown.

The fort continued to be an important military installation through the Civil War, the Mexican Revolution, World War I, and World War II. It underwent modifications many times over, with brick and stone eventually replacing the old timbers from the Mexican War–era supply depots. In 1945, the army deactivated the fort, and a portion of the land was transferred to the city of Brownsville to be used as a college. At the beginning of the 21st century, much of the latter-day Fort Brown is still in remarkably good condition, although many new buildings have been constructed since 1945. The fort's hospital building remains intact, as do the morgue, the commissary, and several barracks. There is very little to be found that reflects the fort's earliest years. Yet, on one corner of the golf course that covers the area closest to the river, one fascinating remnant can be discerned. Barely visible above the well-tended grass, a fading image of the outline of the original six-sided star-shaped fort remains. Surrounding the mounds that were its earthen walls is a shallow indentation, which is all that is left of the once-deep trench from which came the earth used to form the fort's walls in 1846. A large cannon barrel is imbedded in the ground near the outline of the fort. It is said to be implanted at the exact spot where Jacob Brown fell from a Mexican shell in the first days of the war. As the weapon is from a later war, the historic authenticity of the cannon site's importance cannot be determined.

There is a distinctly modern irony in the Fort Brown story. The old fort was placed on the Rio Grande to be within shooting distance of Matamoros during the Mexican War, but it now suffers from that once desirable proximity. In September 2009, the university that now occupies much of the land that was once the fort had to close its campus for several days because of bullets flying across the river out of Mexico. Local citizens on the Texas side reported hearing several hours of rifle and pistol fire coming from what was later identified as a battle in Mexico's ongoing war between drug cartels. Some of the projectiles fired from Matamoros struck buildings and vehicles located on the fort's historic grounds. Over a century and a half after the Mexican War, bullets are still crossing the Rio Grande to strike the very spot where "Old Rough and Ready" built his fort.

Location of the original Fort Brown: Within the boundaries of the golf
     course on Southmost College at the east end of Elizabeth Street in
     Brownsville.
Access: Limited to golf course patrons.

This dramatic if somewhat fanciful vista of Fort Brown in 1846 shows clearly the star-shaped earthwork that was built virtually on the banks of the Rio Grande, a short cannon shot away from the Mexican port city of Matamoros. The grave is that of Col. Trueman Cross, the US Army's chief quartermaster, who was likely the first American casualty of the Mexican War. *Courtesy of Institute of Texan Cultures, University of Texas at San Antonio, #076–0423. Source: Thomas B. Thorpe, "Our Army" on the Rio Grande (Philadelphia: Carey & Hart, 1846).*

Despite 16 decades of hurricanes, erosion, and aggressive golf course construction, enough remains of the old star fort to offer a good idea of Fort Brown's original layout. The vertical cannon barrel on the right was cast at West Point Foundry in 1837. *Thomas E. Alexander Collection.*

SOURCES

Bauer, K. Jack. *The Mexican War, 1846–1848.* New York: Macmillan, 1974.

Borneman, Walter R. *Polk: The Man Who Transformed the Presidency and America.* New York: Random House, 2008.

Chance, Joseph E., ed. *Jefferson Davis's Mexican War Regiment.* Jackson: University of Mississippi Press, 1991.

———, ed. *The Mexican War Journal of Captain Franklin Smith.* Jackson: University of Mississippi Press, 1991.

Dana, Napolean Jackson Tecumseh. *Monterey Is Ours! The Mexican War Letters of Lieutenant Dana, 1845–1847,* edited by Robert H. Ferrell. Lexington: University Press of Kentucky, 1990.

Davis, William C. *Jefferson Davis: The Man and His Hour.* New York: Harper Collins, 1991.

Descendants of Mexican War Veterans, www.dmwv.org (accessed March 24, 2010).

DuFour, Charles L. *The Mexican War: A Compact History, 1846–1848.* New York: Hawthorn Books, 1968.

Eisenhower, John S. D. *So Far from God: The US War with Mexico, 1846–1848.* New York: Doubleday, 1989.

Grant, Ulysses Simpson. *Personal Memoirs of U. S. Grant.* New York: DaCapo Press, 1982.

Henry, Robert Selph. *The Story of the Mexican War.* New York: Frederick Ungar, 1950.

Horgan, Paul. *Great River: The Rio Grande in North American History,* 2 vols. New York: Holt, Rinehart & Winston, 1968.

Hughes, Nathaniel Cheairs Jr. *General William J. Hardee: Old Reliable.* Baton Rouge: Louisiana State University Press, 1965.

McCaslin, Richard B. *Fighting Stock: John S. "Rip" Ford of Texas.* Fort Worth: Texas Christian University Press, 2011.

The Mexican War and Its Heroes: Being a Complete History of the Mexican War, Embracing All the Operations under Generals Taylor and Scott, with a Biography of the Officers. Philadelphia: Lippincott, Grambo & Co., 1854.

Nevin, David. *The Mexican War.* Alexandria, VA: Time-Life Books, 1978.

Nichols, Edward J. *Zach Taylor's Little Army.* Garden City, NY: Doubleday & Co., 1963.

Singletary, Otis A. *The Mexican War.* Chicago: University of Chicago Press, 1960.

Strode, Hudson, ed. *Jefferson Davis: Private Papers, 1823–1889.* New York: DaCapo Press, 1995.

Texas Historical Commission. Marker files, Cameron County.

Thompson, Jerry. *Sabers on the Rio Grande.* Austin, TX: Presidial Press, 1975.

Tyler, Ron, ed. *The New Handbook of Texas,* 6 vols. Austin: Texas State Historical Association, 1996.

Warner, Ezra J. *Generals in Blue: Lives of the Union Commanders.* Baton Rouge: Louisiana State University Press, 1964.

———, *Generals in Gray: Lives of the Confederate Commanders.* Baton Rouge: Louisiana State University Press, 1959.

Weigley, Russell F. *History of the United States Army.* New York: MacMillan Publishing Co., 1967.

Winders, Bruce Richard. *Mr. Polk's Army: The Military Experience in the Mexican War.* College Station: Texas A&M University Press, 1997

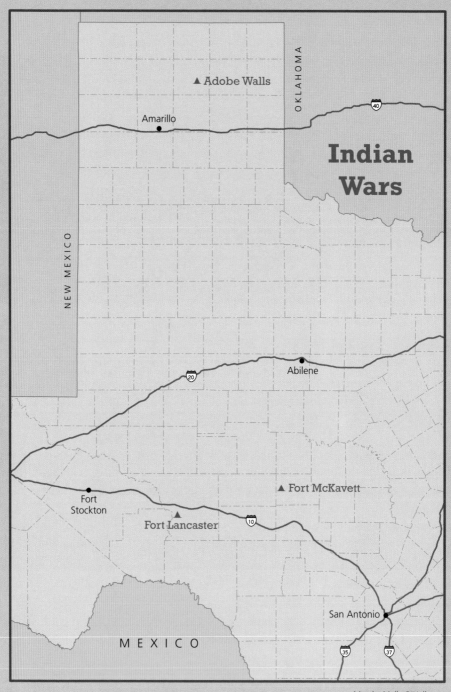

Indian
Wars

OKLAHOMA

NEW MEXICO

▲ Adobe Walls

Amarillo

Abilene

Fort
Stockton

▲ Fort Lancaster

▲ Fort McKavett

San Antonio

MEXICO

Map by Molly O'Halloran

2

THE INDIAN WARS
1848-1875

We took away their country and their means of support, broke up their mode of living, their habits of life, introduced disease and decay among them, and it was for this they made war. Could anyone expect less?

—Lt. Gen. Philip H. Sheridan

Philip Henry Sheridan is considered to have been one of the three most famous Union Army generals in America's Civil War. Short in stature but long on ruthlessness, the blunt-spoken cavalryman had a reputation for his fiery temperament, as well as his tenacious determination to overcome any obstacles that blocked the accomplishment of his mission. He was not known, however, to possess the keen sense of heavy irony that is reflected in his quoted words above. It was, after all, General Sheridan and the soldiers in his post–Civil War army who inflicted upon the Indians of Texas the evils he so accurately identified. After outlining all that he had directly caused to befall the tribes during his tenure as commander of all army forces in Texas in the latter part of the 19th century, Sheridan seemingly asked himself if anyone could possibly expect the maltreated Indians to do anything but make war in retaliation. The general had made clear his intentions about the Indians early on in his new position as commanding general. "Indians," he declared, "were the enemies of our race and our civilization." He then vowed to rid Texas of these enemies even "if it ends in the utter annihilation" of the tribes.

Sheridan's harsh words essentially parroted those spoken by Mirabeau B. Lamar, president of the Republic of Texas in 1839. "The white man and the red man cannot dwell in harmony together," said the president. "Nature forbids it." When asked how the Republic intended to deal with its then large population of Native Americans, Lamar responded, "The proper policy to be pursued toward the barbarian race is absolute expulsion from the country." Through the uncompromising efforts of Philip Sheridan, the Indian policy of President Lamar became a national reality just 36 years later. Sheridan's successful war with the Indians of Texas sputtered to its conclusion when the final band of Quahadi Comanches moved onto a federal reservation in 1875. It was the final moment in a bitter cultural confrontation that raged for more than 300 years in every corner of the vast expanse of land that would in time be known as Texas.

While most Native American tribes had been engaged in intramural battles for countless years, it was the invasion of their ancestral hunting grounds by Europeans that triggered what came to be termed "The Indian Wars." The unwelcome arrival of Spanish and other European adventurers early in the 16th century began the lengthy Texas chapter of those wars. Seeking to impose Christianity upon the native people while at the same time hoping to garner vast mineral wealth, the explorers surged across Texas. Though the natives had no concept of the legal ownership of land, they soon realized that the newcomers believed all the territory they had invaded was indisputably theirs, claimed in the name of some far-off crown. Threatened with the loss of their traditional hunting grounds and nomadic folkways, the Indians forcibly resisted the advance of the white man's civilization. The result was the heated clash of cultures destined to rage for more than three centuries. In retrospect, it is easy to view the Indian wars as having been inevitable. However, as historian Frederick Rathjen aptly put it, "The surprise is not that the red man eventually lost, but that Stone Age people held out so well for so long against the forces of an industrial society." At the beginning of the wars, however, the white man's society was not really all that industrialized, though it was further advanced than that of the Stone Age people it sought to conquer. The tightly woven mail armor of the conquistadors, for example, offered more protection from Indian spears and arrows than did a mere deerskin breechclout against the swords and flintlock muskets of the Spanish soldiers.

To put the Indian Wars in Texas into perspective, the time period involved can be roughly divided into four phases. First, the Europeans came in the early 1500s bent on conquering, subjugating, converting, and exploiting the native population. The next phase covered the westward surge of the white man's culture across Texas, which immediately followed the American victory in the Mexican War and slowed only at the outbreak of the Civil War in 1861. To protect travelers bound for the goldfields of California, as well as settlers seeking cheap land in the newly annexed Lone Star State, the US Army marched west in large numbers to build forts along the principal routes of travel. In the process, the troopers prepared to do battle with any Indian bands that dared block the progress of white civilization. The third phase of the Indian War saga saw the rapid withdrawal of the federal army at the beginning of the Civil

War and the abandonment of its line of protective forts. From 1861 until late 1865, the western frontier actually receded back to the east, providing the long-embattled natives a too-good-to-be-true period of renewed raiding opportunities and the reclaiming of their traditional domain. In the fourth phase, however, the US Army returned in even greater numbers after the Civil War to build new forts farther west than before. Very soon, a tidal wave of white emigrants flooded the wagon roads to seek their fortunes far from the states recently ravaged by war. Greatly outnumbered and relentlessly hounded by the men of Sheridan's army, the Indians retreated and eventually submitted to the unceasing white expansion. As a result, organized Indian resistance ended throughout the state in the early 1870s.

Even the most intensely dramatic of the armed clashes between the Native Americans and their white antagonists seldom resembled the Hollywood-style film depictions of such battles. Rather than blindly hurling themselves against the well-defended army outposts, the Indians usually employed stealth as a tactic rather than the hard-charging and war-whooping frontal assaults made famous by the likes of movie director John Ford. Most times, small bands of marauding warriors would strike the less-fortified settlements and ranches to steal horses and cattle, set buildings afire, kill any hapless residents, and generally let the whites know that their way west was not to go unimpeded. There were, of course, direct, open clashes between troopers and braves. At other times, skirmishes involved nonmilitary, vigilante-type groups of outraged citizens seeking to attack Indian encampments in retaliation for particular recent native transgressions.

In some ways, it was this thirst for retaliation that helped fuel the forward motion of the Texas frontier, incident by incident. Warriors seeking food, plunder, and blood sport would, for example, strike an isolated ranch. Then, survivors of the raid or friends of its victims would stage a counterraid to seek out and punish the guilty native raiders. If the Indians caught up in the killing frenzy eventually proved to have been innocent, and if their women and children perished in the crossfire, no one on the opposing side, including the US Army, seemed to mind. Other Indians in the vicinity, enraged by the white man's response to the initial raid, would then strike another ranch in revenge. The vicious cycle of retaliation would then start anew. The deciding factor in this violent exchange was that after 1865, greater numbers of ranchers, settlers, and soldiers opposed a diminishing population of Native Americans willing or able to keep the cycle in motion. As a result, what had long been a fluctuating frontier began to move steadily westward until it finally reached the shores of the Pacific. During the time when the frontier ebbed and flowed, General Sheridan set about ridding Texas of its vexing "Indian problem" once and for all. The general was a master of the dark art of total war, which features no rules of engagement, no mercy shown, and no quarter given. During the Civil War, as a cavalry general, he had laid waste to Virginia's beautiful Shenandoah Valley to such a degree that, as he boasted, "A crow could not fly from Winchester to Staunton without taking its rations along." A brilliant tactician, Sheridan correctly assumed that what had worked so well in Virginia in 1864 was certain to work on the Texas plains in 1871 and beyond. Under his orders, his men burned Indian villages and either killed all their occupants or, if possible, moved them to government reservations. Further, the general orchestrated the mass slaughter of the bison herds that were the very stuff of life to the Plains Indians. The nomadic tribes freely roaming the plains in pursuit of vital game gave way involuntarily to an ill-fitting existence as hardscrabble farmers under the watchful eyes of Indian agents and Phil Sheridan's soldiers.

Today, few physical remains mark the long course of the Indian Wars in Texas. Only Fort Clark has retained much of its original 19th-century appearance. Other forts, such as Davis and Concho, have been reconstructed to provide a clear impression of army installations during the peak years of the conflict. Forts Lancaster, McKavett, and Griffin have remained largely untouched. As a result, each exudes an almost eerie sense of the dangerous isolation encountered at such installations in the mid-19th century. The sites of such memorable Indian fights as Adobe Walls and the Buffalo Wallow have simply melted back into the patch of Texas earth once so hotly contested.

General Sheridan unquestionably accomplished his mission by ridding Texas of its perceived hostile Indian population entirely. Never a great fan of the state in which he served as commander, he once famously observed, "If I owned both Hell and Texas, I'd rent out Texas and live in Hell." While survivors of his sweep down the Shenandoah Valley or his wrathful taming of the Texas plains might have gleefully speculated on the general's final destination, that information can only remain speculative. There can be no question, however, that despite his heavy-handed methods, Phil Sheridan, the self-described but wholly imaginary landlord of all Texas, quickly and efficiently made the state much safer for all tenants eager to take up residence.

FORT McKAVETT
(1852–1883)

The discovery of immense gold deposits in the newly acquired state of California in 1849 triggered an immediate westward flow of immigration unmatched before or since in American history. The vast western territories claimed by the United States as the spoils of its highly beneficial victory in the Mexican War of 1846–48 opened the way for the seemingly endless throngs of treasure seekers and restless pioneers bound for the Pacific coast.

It soon became apparent, however, that the Native American tribes, the traditional stewards of all the massive hunting grounds that lay west of the Nueces River, had no intention of recognizing any claims of legal ownership of their lands, whether the claimants were Spanish, Mexican, or later, American. The savage vehemence with which such warlike tribes as the Kickapoo, Kiowa, Apache, and Comanche bitterly resisted the surge of white civilization swiftly prompted the US government to employ its military might to protect its citizens as they sought their fortunes either in California or perhaps at more convenient stops along the wagon routes.

By 1851, Gen. Persifor F. Smith, commander of the Military Department of Texas, completed an inspection of the frontier as it then existed in the state. As a result, he decreed that a line of frontier forts be established as quickly as possible. These installations would serve as fortified anchors along the frontier from which troops could be deployed to protect westbound travelers as well as homesteading settlers from Indian attack. The eventual line of fortifications extended from Fort Belknap on the Brazos River in the north to Fort Duncan on the Rio Grande in the south. In early 1852, the army built one of these forts on the banks of the San Saba River some 50 miles west of an existing military installation at Fort Mason. Temporarily known appropriately enough as the "Camp near Fort Mason," the fledgling fort sat near the so-called Upper Road that stretched from San Antonio some 550 miles across West Texas to the well-established Fort Bliss at El Paso. Travelers along this relatively well-protected route then proceeded on to California. The initial name of the installation changed briefly to Camp San Saba before it attained its permanent title of Fort McKavett in 1853. The new name honored Capt. Henry McKavett, an officer of the 8th Infantry who fell at the Battle of Monterrey during the Mexican War some six years earlier.

The new fort encompassed more than 2,000 acres. Its location near the ever-flowing spring that was the source of the San Saba River ensured a permanent supply of water. The site also contained an abundant quantity of building stone that could readily be quarried to construct long-standing structures. As there were few civilians living in the area, enlisted men built the entire fort, with each company charged with the construction of its own quarters. All the men working in concert built the headquarters, commissary, and other such general use structures. By 1856, the fort boasted 21 stone buildings, including a hospital, officers quarters, enlisted barracks, and other necessary administration and headquarters facilities. Some wooden structures were made of oak and pecan found near the site. Although its frontier location near the increasingly well-traveled Upper Road was vital, the fort's remoteness and distance from regular supply sources presented serious challenges. Heavily armed contract supply trains carried provisions to the fort from the army's established logistical depot in San Antonio. While the costs associated with such freighting were considered quite high, the importance of the fort and its mission made the issue of supply expense secondary.

As important as the protection against Indian harassment was at the time of constantly increasing travel to the west, Fort McKavett proved to be only nominally successful in accomplishing its mission. Most of the troops posted to the fort from its inception in 1852 until it temporarily closed in 1859 were infantrymen. Using foot soldiers to guard the Upper Road and its general vicinity was largely a futile undertaking. The fort's mere existence probably did more to discourage Indian horsemen from attacking wagon trains than did any fear of unmounted troopers.

By the late 1850s, the sheer force and mass of the westward immigration pushed the frontier well beyond the reach of Fort McKavett. Many of those who had intended to be prospectors for gold in California had wearied of the trail and decided to become Texas ranchers or farmers instead. Small communities developed throughout the region in support of new agricultural activity. As the ranches and settlements began to take permanent root on the eastern side of what had been the wild frontier only seven years earlier, the threat from the typically wide-ranging Indian marauders slowly diminished. In March 1859, when the army no longer deemed Fort McKavett necessary, it abandoned the post. Local citizens promptly took advantage of the soundly built stone buildings and converted them into residences and barns.

The coming of the American Civil War in 1861, though fought primarily in the east, had a profound effect on what had become the western frontier. US Army leaders simply surrendered forts and outposts to troops of Confederate Texas. Eventually, when the pressing military needs of the Confederacy on the battlefields of Virginia, Mississippi, and Tennessee required the presence of virtually every one of its soldiers, the prewar frontier forts closed. The Indians, once the unchallenged occupants of the territory, soon proved to have been only briefly displaced. With no soldiers to effectively block their return to the land, the tribesmen raided ranches and settlements with neither mercy nor fear of retaliation by either Union or Confederate troops.

As a result of this Civil War–caused vacuum along the western frontier, the surge of white civilization toward the Pacific all but halted, at least for a time. From 1861 until the end of the war in 1865, the Texas frontier receded. It proved to be a brief recession; when the war ended, the pent-up thirst for western expansion again gripped the reunited nation. With the peace came new waves of emigrants eagerly seeking both land and opportunity. As might be expected, this renewed surge of white expansion resulted in vigorous Indian opposition. The tribesmen, having lost much of their domain to the white man prior to the Civil War, now seemed particularly intent on not losing it again.

As had been the case before the Civil War, it became the mission of the American army to provide protection for settlers who now arrived by the thousands by pushing the Indian frontier back to the west. To facilitate that mission, some of the antebellum forts that had been optimistically closed in the 1850s in the belief the "Indian problem" had been solved reopened under War Department orders. Fort McKavett, sitting vacant atop its West Texas hill, was among the old outposts restored to active status. On April 1, 1868, two companies of cavalry and three infantry companies took possession of what little was left of the site. During its nine-year period of abandonment, the fort had deteriorated greatly. The walls of all but one of the buildings had fallen and all the roofs had collapsed. The enlisted men who were detailed to build an essentially new Fort McKavett lived in tents as their work progressed.

Nearly a year later before the new fort began to emerge from the rubble. The man responsible for the Fort McKavett that is still visible to this day rode through its gate in March 1869 with two companies of cavalry and another two of infantry. Not only would Ranald Slidell Mackenzie change forever the look of Fort McKavett, he would also do the same to the whole Indian frontier of Texas. Curiously, many historians give Mackenzie a permanent colonel's rank even though he was in fact a brevet major general and, in time, a full-fledged regular army brigadier. George Armstrong Custer, on the other hand, is almost always referred to as "General Custer" when his actual rank on the Little Bighorn was that of lieutenant colonel. The two Indian fighters, regardless of relative military rank, have often been compared, or perhaps more accurately, contrasted. Colonel Custer, flamboyant and blessed with an adoring wife who made of him a posthumous legend, is widely regarded as the most famous, if fatally flawed, of the heroes of the so-called Indian Wars. General Mackenzie, on the other hand, is little known today, although he was by far the most successful of all the army's Indian campaign leaders. Of the two officers, it is Mackenzie who accomplished more in terms of the total subjugation of the large American tribes in the West. Custer, of course, died in a botched battle with the Sioux, while Mackenzie, long after outgeneraling all the war chiefs of the Kickapoo and the Comanche, had the great misfortune of dying without a wife to sing his praises to all who would listen.

And it was Ranald Mackenzie who brought a new life to Fort McKavett beginning in 1869. From there, with his "buffalo soldiers" as important contributors, the general began the relentless and merciless pursuit of his Native American quarry until such time as they could no longer resist. To provide a suitable base for his cavalrymen and foot soldiers, Mackenzie oversaw the final reconstruction of the fort from 1869 until 1871. During that time his men raised officers quarters, enlisted barracks, a large hospital, a morgue, and a fine headquarters building, along with a bakery, a post office, and, of course, a guardhouse. So sturdy were Mackenzie's buildings that more than 10 are still virtually intact almost 140 years later. The last large building to be added to the fort was a schoolhouse erected in 1878. That building became the center of a civilian community that developed on the fort site a few years later. It, too, is still standing.

In hindsight, the renovation and reconstruction of Fort McKavett were perhaps not really necessary. Forts Clark and Concho, among others, were the primary posts used by General Mackenzie during the course of his successful two decades of fighting with Indians in the American West and even across the Rio Grande in Mexico. By 1880, just 11 years after its final renovation, the army marked Fort McKavett for closure for the second time in its history. By June 1883, the fort permanently closed. An inspection report taken on the installation's last day of official activity indicated 40 buildings still in use.

The history of the fort revolves largely around two principal factors, with the first being the often valorous exploits of the buffalo soldiers who comprised the 9th and 10th Cavalries under the command of Mackenzie. The other factor was the importance of the fort as a logistical supply depot for a more remote military installation located farther west and closer to the expanding frontier. One superintendent at the State Historic Site that the old fort has now become likens its logistical function to that of a modern-day Walmart Distribution Center. All manner of supplies shipped from the main depot at San Antonio were warehoused at McKavett before being sent on to Fort Concho at San Angelo and other outposts.

When not escorting the supply trains and riding patrols along the emigrant trails, the African American buffalo soldiers of Fort McKavett often engaged in running battles with marauding Indians in retaliation for raiding and kidnapping. As the leader of one such foray, one soldier became a highly decorated if unsung hero. His name was Emanuel Stance, a diminutive trooper who became a sergeant just 10 months following his enlistment in Company F of the 9th Cavalry garrisoned at McKavett. For his heroic actions against the Kickapoo and the daring rescue of two kidnapped children on July 24, 1870, Sergeant Stance became the first African American soldier to earn the nation's Medal of Honor in the post–Civil War era. The tiny quarters once occupied by Stance in the enlisted men's barracks at the old fort still exists.

After the US Army abandoned Fort McKavett for the second time in June 1883, the Robinson family, which owned the property following the first abandonment in 1859, moved into the buildings on the site. Although the family had legally purchased the original site and subsequently rented it to the US government when the army returned in 1868, this fact was apparently unknown to General Mackenzie. When his landlord presented him with an invoice for past due rent in 1870, Mackenzie was said to be both shocked and angered. Only after he received a direct order by the War Department to pay did the general comply with his landlord's demands.

The Robinson family soon had many neighbors living close by in the deserted army buildings or, in some instances, in tents left behind by the army. A large number of civilians had moved onto the old fort from Scabtown, a cluster of saloons, gambling dens, and bordellos that flourished a mile from McKavett. When soldiers were still garrisoned at the post, many of them often sought escape from the traditional bore-dom of army life on the frontier by visiting Scabtown. With the closing of the fort, all of Scabtown's uniformed customers had marched away to Fort Concho, which had an even more colorful version of Scabtown just outside its main gate in San Angelo. The denizens of Fort McKavett's sinful satellite settlement, realizing their customers as well as their protectors were gone forever, sought security in the village that devel-oped on the site of the then abandoned fort.

Within a year after the closing of Fort McKavett, the settlement that assumed the name of the army fort boasted several reputable businesses. There were two general stores and, perhaps not surprisingly, two saloons. In addition, there was a hotel, two doctors' offices, a blacksmith's forge, two feed yards, and a school held in the same school building constructed by the army a few years earlier. The little community also had its own newspaper, appropriately called *The Breeze*. Advertisements in the paper carried the schedule for the San Angelo & McKavett stage that left the settlement early every morning except Sunday in order to arrive in San Angelo the same day.

With the Indian threat no longer a factor, the village of Fort McKavett, Texas, be-came a prosperous supply and recreational center for the growing number of cattle ranches and goat stock farms. By the mid-1890s, the little town had a population of nearly 80. Although *The New Handbook of Texas* credits the settlement with having a population of 45 as recently as 1990, the handful of former residents who still come back to the townsite to participate in reunions believe that no more than 10 inhabit-ants actually resided on the fort site in the 1920s and beyond.

Those former residents who still attend the annual homecoming event on the site meet in the old schoolhouse where many of them studied years before. Some of the military buildings built under the watchful eye of General Mackenzie are also still standing. A handful of the buildings have been fully restored and another 10 remain just as they appeared when the State of Texas acquired the site a half century ago. The unrestored buildings have been stabilized to prevent further deterioration. The blending of restored and unrestored buildings lends an atmosphere of authenticity to the site, now operated by the Texas Historical Commission. Unlike some former mili-tary sites that have been so completely restored as to resemble Hollywood sets, Fort McKavett provides its visitors with a genuine sense of the past without the artificially recreated appearance of certain tourist attractions.

Location: At the intersection of Ranch Road 1674 and Ranch Road 864, 26 miles north of Interstate 10.

Access: A Texas Historical Commission property, the site is open daily from 8:00 A.M. to 5:00 P.M.

Shown here some 50 years after it was abandoned, the commander's quarters at Fort McKavett were occupied for a time by Col. Ranald S. Mackenzie. Guests over the years were said to be future generals Albert Sidney Johnston and Robert E. Lee, the latter of whom purportedly stayed in the northwest room on the first floor. *Courtesy of Fort McKavett State Historic Site, Texas Historical Commission.*

FORT LANCASTER
(1855–1873)

In 1851, Col. (later Maj. Gen.) Joseph King Fenno Mansfield received orders to commence what proved to be a 10-year-long inspection tour of every army installation along the western frontier. Mansfield was apparently a demanding inspector, and his written evaluations of most of the posts he visited bristle with harsh criticism. His 1856 report on Fort Lancaster, however, was mostly complimentary and included the rare observation that

The former commanding officers quarters at Fort McKavett was all but totally destroyed by a fire on December 7, 1941, the day of the Japanese attack on Pearl Harbor. The window opening for the room possibly used by Robert E. Lee is on the lower level, extreme right of the photo. *Thomas E. Alexander Collection.*

the post "cannot be dispensed with." The men who had served at the fort from its opening in 1855 until its abandonment in 1873 might have found good reason to wish that it could have been "dispensed with" the very day they first saw the post. Located some 200 miles west of San Antonio in a valley that proved unbearably hot most of the time and bone-chillingly cold otherwise, the fortification offered its garrison little but boredom interrupted by mindless drilling. The remote location of the site made it eligible to be a "double ration post," one of only three to be so designated in Texas in the years prior to the Civil War. Although the army rarely rewarded its soldiers stationed at such remote posts in this way, the men at Fort Lancaster received twice the standard daily pay in recognition of their unfortunate luck in duty assignments. Even at double pay, a private at Fort Lancaster received less than eight dollars per month.

There were several reasons for placing the post at its location in a broad desert valley flanked on the east by a towering limestone lip of the Edwards Plateau. A short distance to the south, the always treacherous Pecos River snaked its way down toward the Rio Grande on the Mexican border. A frequently crossed ford on the nearby Pecos was part of a route traditionally used by Mescalero Apache and Comanche raiding parties. The surveillance of and perhaps the ultimate destruction of these warlike tribesmen were among the initial missions of the post. The fact that the Indian ford on the Pecos was so close to the army's Lower Road made placing a military installation in the immediate vicinity a necessity, despite the obvious drawbacks of climate and remoteness. The Lower Road connected San Antonio and El Paso, two of the most important commercial and military cities in Texas at the time. The site selected for the location of Fort Lancaster was more or less halfway along the Lower Road between Fort Clark and Fort Davis to the west. Protecting the civilians headed to the Pacific Coast from attacks at first by the Apache and later the Comanche was another prime mission for the Fort Lancaster troopers. "It [the fort] undoubtedly has and will save many valuable lives," reported Colonel Mansfield, who went on to say that the tribes in the vicinity were "highwaymen and murderers." Despite the colonel's rare words of support for the fort that opened just one year before he came to inspect it, Fort Lancaster was never a large post garrisoned by a substantial detachment. When finally and fully completed in 1860, the post could boast of no more than 25 buildings. Records indicate there were never more than 175 officers and men stationed at the facility at any one time. The same records, however, indicate the relatively few troops stationed at Fort Lancaster managed to accomplish their various missions admirably.

Just a year following Mansfield's inspection, a historic event occurred that gave the fort a distinction it would share with only a few other installations along the Lower Road. On July 9, 1857, the army's experimental Camel Corps crossed the tall escarpment overlooking Fort Lancaster and made its way carefully down the steep road into the valley. The men of the camel caravan camped on a creek near the fort to rest before being invited to share whatever hospitality could be offered at the installation itself. The arrival of Capt. Edward Beale and his 40-man entourage with 25 camels, over 100 sheep, and a large herd of horses and mules without doubt shattered for the moment the leaden boredom at the post. Capt. Stephen D. Carpenter, commanding officer of the small detachment at Lancaster, reluctantly agreed to ride one of the strange-looking animals, and he found it to be a pleasurable experience, noting that he preferred riding the camel to bouncing about on the back of an "ornery mule."

Tragedy soon darkened the circuslike atmosphere that briefly prevailed at the fort with the arrival of the camels. The infant son of one of the caravan's escorting officers, Capt. Arthur Lee, had taken mortally ill on the trail. His death just after he arrived at the fort cast a long shadow over the remainder of the caravan's stay. Young

Arthur Lee Jr. was buried in the post cemetery. His tiny grave is still there, marked by a simple stone put in place by soldiers after his mother and father had departed with the westbound caravan the day after his death.

Although what came to be called the "Great Camel Experiment" proved that the imported animals were exceptionally well suited for carrying heavy loads across the arid terrain of the western frontier, the army permanently discontinued the entire undertaking during the Civil War. The officially given reason was that the softness of the pads on the animals' hooves made travel over rocky terrain painful and therefore unreliable. Many observers of the camel experiment, however, believe there were other significant reasons behind its cancellation. Some say it was the animals' notoriously foul temperament coupled with their propensity to terrify, and thus make unmanageable, horses and mules. Others contend that if Jefferson Davis, the originator of the camel scheme, had not gone on to become president of the Confederate States of America during the Civil War, the experiment would have continued and eventually might well have been pronounced a success. Although the overall camel plan ultimately failed for whatever reason, the caravan's brief visit to Fort Lancaster did much to boost morale at the desolate site. Aside from the arrival of Butterfield Overland stagecoaches three times a month, little occurred to break the monotony of army life on the bleak frontier.

When Texas seceded from the Union to join the Confederate cause on February 23, 1861, the federal troops stationed at the fort knew, likely with considerable relief, that they would soon be leaving the fort, as well as Texas itself. Indeed, a small detachment of Confederate soldiers would take over the abandoned post and remain there for the first full year of the Civil War. On November 28, 1861, the Lancaster soldiers witnessed part of a significant if ultimately unsuccessful adventure in the short history of the Confederate States of America. Sibley's Brigade, under the command of Brig. Gen. Henry Hopkins Sibley, marched into the fort on its trek west from San Antonio to El Paso. A West Point graduate and veteran of both the Mexican War and the earlier Indian Wars, Sibley was a personal friend of newly elected Confederate president Jefferson Davis. Taking full advantage of that friendship, Sibley convinced Davis that the Confederacy should move at once to take control of the New Mexico Territory, as well as Colorado and California. As Sibley saw it, the benefits derived from a successful military occupation in those territories could be significant. Thus Sibley assumed command of his own brigade with orders to move westward at once along the Lower Road across Texas before turning north from El Paso's Fort Bliss to march up the Rio Grande to capture the New Mexican Territory. The initial portion of his campaign brought the general and thousands of his soldiers into Fort Lancaster, where they were met by the hundred or so men of the remote garrison. To show the proper respect for a visiting general widely known to be a friend of President Davis, the post's commander ordered his soldiers to don their otherwise seldom-worn dress uniforms. One account notes Sibley felt obliged to recognize the welcoming ardor of the smartly dressed Lancaster garrison by personally taking charge of a morning drill assembly.

If there was anything at which the bored men of Fort Lancaster were proficient it was drilling, as they had done little else since their arrival following the departure of the Union troops. With Sibley barking orders from his saddle, the colorfully turned-out soldiers wheeled and marched and countermarched perfectly in response to each of the general's commands. It was not until Sibley ordered the drilling men to "file left" that the good impression being created by the Lancaster troops instantly faded. Perhaps a sudden gust of capricious West Texas wind muted the second but most important word in the barked command. At any rate, the men proceeded to march to the right in perfect order, through the gate of the fort, and well up the slope of a nearby hill. Sibley watched in dismay as the participants in his honorary parade left the drill ground. He made no effort to order them to halt or march to the rear but merely looked on in bemusement. Finally, turning to his aide, the general muttered, "Gone to Hell," before riding out the main gate to move onward to Fort Bliss.

By April 1862, all regular soldiers of the Confederacy left Fort Lancaster. A company of Texas Rangers then occupied the installation, but with little in the way of official duties to perform. During the several periods when the fort was without a garrison of any description, it fell victim to vandals and even partial destruction by fire.

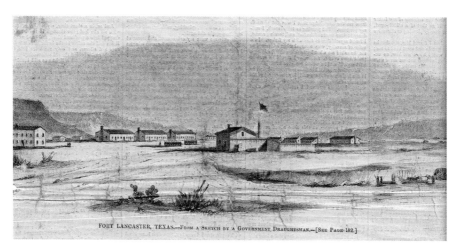

FORT LANCASTER, TEXAS.—From a Sketch by a Government Draughtsman.—[See Page 182.]

Surviving plats of Fort Lancaster showing its layout in 1861 strongly suggest that the "Government Draughtsman" who sketched this view used a good deal of imagination in creating his work. *From* Harper's Weekly, *March 23, 1861. Courtesy of Fort Lancaster State Historic Site, Texas Historical Commission.*

Although Fort Lancaster was never more than a subpost in the years immediately following the Civil War, it did experience a rare frontal attack by a large force of well-armed and tactically proficient warriors of the Lipan Apache and Kickapoo tribes, augmented perhaps by a few renegade Mexican soldiers. On December 26, 1867, the attackers, said to number from 900 to 1,200, surrounded the buffalo soldiers of Company K, 9th Cavalry, stationed within the fort. Unlike most Indian attacks, the raiders moved along four well-defined lines of advance. The battle reportedly lasted three hours, with at least 20 of the attackers being killed and "many others wounded." The only army casualties were three men captured and carried away by Indians during the attack. Their remains were discovered three months later and brought back to the fort for burial. Their crudely marked graves have been located on what is now private land north of the state-owned Fort Lancaster State Historic Site.

When the army permanently abandoned the installation in 1873, the local citizenry quickly dismantled most of the buildings to cart away the rocks to build their ranch houses. By 1912, only a few extant walls and a single chimney remained. Fortunately,

A modern vista of Fort Lancaster taken from the identical vantage point used in the 1861 sketch shows the mountains on the horizon to match perfectly. The ruins in the center of the photo are of the fort's blacksmith shop. *Photograph by Daphne Elliott, Fort Lancaster, Texas, 2010.*

more recent years have been kinder to this historic frontier fort. Preservation efforts have resulted in the stabilization of walls left standing, the excavation of long-gone buildings, and some limited reconstruction, although not in an effort to "recreate" the old post. Probably because of the absence of overbearing but well-intentioned commercial reconstruction efforts, today's Fort Lancaster site still generates the genuine sense of desolation that confronted army men in mid-19th-century Texas. No modern-day buildings are visible in any direction. Few vehicles pass by today on what was the Lower Road, but the trace of that once well-traveled roadway can easily be discerned descending from the hilltop on the eastern edge of the valley.

A rare 1857 lithograph of Fort Lancaster shows neat rows of barracks and other buildings situated close to a mountain that looms over the rooftops. Standing at the exact point of perspective used by the artist so long ago, it quickly becomes obvious that he employed a great deal of creative license in picturing the fort. An actual diagram of the facility clearly indicates that the artist placed buildings in his work where no buildings ever existed. He also saw fit to enlarge the eastern ridge to well beyond its actual height and then move it at least three miles closer to the fort than it truly is. We will forgive the artist, however, for his creative misrepresentations because he left us the only known representation of how the lonely outpost might have appeared in the mid–19th century.

Location: On State Highway 290, 26 miles west of Ozona.
Access: A Texas Historical Commission property, the site is open daily
from 8:00 A.M. to 5:00 P.M.

BATTLE OF ADOBE WALLS
(1874)

The Battle of Adobe Walls on June 18, 1874, might easily have served as the source for Hollywood's always-popular film versions of how the West was won. Many of the now familiar elements of Western movies came into play during the siege. The scenario plays out in this way. A tiny group of white hunters have just awakened in a primitive frontier outpost when suddenly a horde of colorfully painted and feather-festooned Indians come screaming out of the half-light of a Texas dawn, clearly intent on murdering and scalping them all. Outnumbered at least 10 to 1, or maybe even 70 to 1 according to some versions, the hunters mount an epic defensive firefight and manage to lose only four men despite the heavy odds against them. The Indians, on the other hand, blinded by foolish superstition and lacking any meaningful tactical skills, suffer many casualties and fall back in shocked dismay. Later, as the Indians ponder their next move, a bullet fired from a hunter's rifle travels nearly a full mile to topple an Indian scout from his pony. Stunned and demoralized by this latest misfortune, the frustrated attackers gather their dead and wounded and slink away in defeat.

Judging from various and often conflicting eyewitness accounts related later by survivors on both sides of the battle, the above scenario at least indicates what likely occurred. All of its drama and filmscript potential aside, the result of the battle without question accelerated the course of history in the Texas Panhandle. That the Southern Plains tribes of Indians would be eventually driven from the upper reaches of Texas seemed inevitable, but the bloody incident at Adobe Walls caused it to happen much sooner than the US Army had optimistically predicted. The key factor in the army's plan to rid the Texas Panhandle of its nomadic native tribes was the total annihilation of the multitude of buffalo that were vital to the Indians' survival. The wild, shaggy beasts that literally covered the vast Texas landscape provided nearly everything essential to Native American subsistence. The Comanche, Kiowa, Cheyenne, and Arapaho alike hunted buffalo as their main source for food, clothing, and shelter.

For many years before white civilization began to encroach upon their hunting grounds, the Indians had far more than enough of the animals to provide for all the various tribes that managed to survive only by successfully hunting them. Herd size estimates of the buffalo as late as the 1870s are all but impossible to believe, particularly since the newly arrived white hunters had by then already begun to decrease the herds. Army Maj. Richard I. Dodge reported counting over 4 million buffalo in one herd in 1872. When one dry-witted plainsman was asked how it was possible to count that many animals, the reply was that all one had to do was count the number of legs and then divide that number by four. A more scientific and reliable method of grasping the enormity of the Southern Plains buffalo herd can be found in railroad freight shipping records for the years 1872 through 1874. Those figures show that 4,373,730 buffalo hides shipped east on the Santa Fe and other rail company lines. Not all skins went by freight car, of course, and estimates suggest that wagons hauled at least an additional 1 million hides to distant markets.

At first, the demands of European and US eastern fashion markets drove the need for buffalo leather. That these demands were all but insatiable is evident from the verifiable shipping records. The supply of hides, though, soon far outstripped the demands of fashion. When the herds in Kansas and elsewhere on the Northern and Central Plains dwindled to a tiny proportion of the pre-1870 level, many of the hunters who had earned excellent incomes selling hides began looking southward toward the plains of northern Texas, where Indians continued to hunt buffalo without competition from the white men.

A few years before the slaughter of the Northern Plains herd ended, the army made a rare if oblique effort to suggest that the hunting grounds south of the Arkansas River were the domain of the Southern Plains tribes. Called the Medicine Lodge Treaty, the document proved to be both vague and misleading. It was also the direct cause of the Second Battle of Adobe Walls and, eventually, the eviction of all native nomadic tribes from the Panhandle of Texas. According to its wording, the treaty gave Indians the right "to hunt on any lands south of the Arkansas River so long as the buffalo may range thereon in such numbers as to justify the chase." At the same time, the treaty ordered all nomadic Indians in the region to move to reservations in the western part of what is now Oklahoma, an area contiguous to the hunting grounds described in another of the treaty's clauses.

Unfortunately for everyone touched by the terms of the treaty, it proved to be as worthless as virtually all such treaties ever enacted between the US government and the native population it fully intended to subjugate. In the first place, the lands referred to in the treaty did not belong to the federal government at all, but rather to the State of Texas in accordance with terms inherent in the annexation of the state into the Union in 1845. As a consequence, the United States did not have the legal authority to grant hunting rights on Texas land to either the white buffalo hunters or the tribesmen of the Southern Plains. The wording of the treaty, however, somehow led the Indians to believe they had the exclusive right to hunt on the land. For some inexplicable reason, that same vague wording caused even the most avaricious of the white hunters to share the opinion of the Indians. As a result of this misconception, the Texas Panhandle remained the exclusive hunting domain of the Southern Plains tribes for another six years. Even when the white hunters' own formerly teeming hunting grounds north of the Arkansas River emptied of buffalo, they continued to abide by the inaccurately perceived tenets of the Medicine Lodge Treaty.

In the summer of 1873, however, a seasoned but increasingly disappointed buffalo man named J. Wright Mooar found the courage to challenge the army's policy on white hunters who ignored the treaty and hunted south of the Arkansas River. Maj. Richard I. Dodge stated that if he were a buffalo hunter, he would go hunt where there were buffalo. This perhaps off-the-cuff remark put in motion the events that led directly to the fight at Adobe Walls. Mooar took the major's words to be tacit permission to hunt on what nearly all hunters had believed to be a federally protected Indian domain. By late 1873, Mooar had ventured across the river to set up hunting camps and begin the profitable slaughter of the buffalo.

The Indians were understandably angered by what they believed to be an illegal incursion into their lands, particularly when they saw the animals they depended upon for their existence being brought down by the thousands by guns of the trespassing hunters. As evidence of their anger, the Indians began striking at the small encampments of the hunters, killing and scalping them. For a time, the camps represented the only available targets for the wrath of the tribesmen, but in March 1874, a handful of entrepreneurs dared to establish a somewhat substantial outpost to provide supplies to the many buffalo hunters surging into the region, and to handle the shipping of hides to the railhead at Dodge City, Kansas. The site selected for the trading post was just over a mile from the scattered old ruins some claimed had been Mexican adobe huts and later one of the Bent and St. Vrain trading posts that served local tribes in the mid-1840s. The newly built structures located close to the old adobe walls included a blacksmith shop, two stores, a corral, a saloon, and briefly, a cafe. The buildings consisted of sod, logs, or pickets, and most had roofs of only sod. Each structure faced east toward a long mesalike ridge that loomed on the horizon not quite a mile away.

The tiny settlement briefly enjoyed a brisk business and relative serenity except for an occasional altercation in the popular saloon operated by Jim Hanrahan. Buffalo men often congregated in his Adobe Walls saloon to compare notes and share concerns about the reports of increasing Indian attacks on hunter camps throughout the area. When the buffalo-hunting season reached its high level in late June 1874, the prospect for riches soon overshadowed any fear of the Indians. Early on the morning of June 27, however, any fears about Indian attacks that had been diluted by Hanrahan's rough-drinking whiskey suddenly reignited. The Battle of Adobe Walls began long before the sun rose over the ridgeline.

One historian notes the battle was a long-festering perfect storm of circumstances. "Horse thieves, buffalo hunters, poisonous whiskey, lack of warrior status, restless young (Indian) men needing trophies and coups for warrior status," wrote Donald J. Berthong, "coupled with inadequate law enforcement had finally taken their toll." In short, decades of efforts to demean, diminish, and deprive the Southern Plains tribes of their traditional way of life had at last pushed the tribes beyond their final point of no return and the white hunters to new levels of greed.

As is true in any conflict written about by the victors, there are many legends and differing opinions to be found in the story of Adobe Walls. Perhaps the most enduring of such varying accounts deals with a conveniently breaking ridgepole of the saloon. Rumors of a possible large-scale Indian raid on the outpost had been circulating in the Panhandle for days, but the preoccupation with the killing of buffalo for great profit had put such rumors out of mind. A particularly profitable hunt on June 26 prompted the hunters to celebrate during a long evening of revelry until well past midnight. Roughly two hours later, the groggy celebrants were roughly awakened by two of Hanrahan's bartenders who claimed they had themselves just been roused from sleep by what they believed to have been a "rifle shot." Upon investigation, however, the two claimed to have found that the long horizontal cottonwood ridgepole supporting the roof of the saloon had cracked. Fearing the entire saloon would be crushed by the weakened roof, Hanrahan's men decided to awaken all the hunters, most of whom had just gone to sleep.

Many historians, however, discount the cracking of the ridgepole story as being a pre-planned alert in advance of the Indian attack that came just minutes later. The later conjecture is that saloon owner Hanrahan had learned of the plans to attack the outpost from some patrons who had recently visited his bar. Some of the survivors of the attack later held that the alleged cracking was a sign of divine intervention into what otherwise would have been a total massacre of the hard-sleeping hunters. William J. "Billy" Dixon, a hero of the Adobe Walls affair, told his wife that he had seen the pole after the attack and found it to be whole in every way. Curiously, when his comments eventually made their way into a book written by his wife, the publisher expunged his claim but retained a statement allegedly made by Dixon that had the ridgepole not so loudly snapped, everyone would have fallen victim to the knives of 700 angry Indians.

Why the legend in print seemed to deny the apparent truth will likely never be determined, just as the number of braves participating in the attack will not be precisely known. J. Wright Mooar, somewhat famous for the telling of tall tales, put the number at "at least 1,500," while Billy Dixon estimated probably 700 tribesmen attacked the outpost. *The New Handbook of Texas* accepted Dixon's figure as being reasonable enough to include it in its Adobe Walls entry. Later historians and archeologists have agreed with estimates made by army officers who investigated the battle and placed the number as being more likely from 200 to 250. Archeologist J. Brett Cruse and historians Frederick Rathjen and T. Lindsay Baker each endorse this lesser figure.

The battle itself for the most part followed the movielike scenario that introduced this chapter. The Indians, frustrated by their failure to surprise a saloon full of sleeping trespassers, furiously hurled themselves in vain against the doors and walls of the outpost buildings. Further, their medicine man had told them that the white body paint given them before the attack would render them immune to the bullets from the hunters' big guns. This prophecy quickly proved to be patently false as the keen marksmanship skills of the defenders cut down the raiders in large numbers as they charged. Quanah, a young Comanche war chief who might have changed tactics to lessen the frenzy, became unhorsed and slightly injured at the beginning of the siege. It has been suggested that his more prudent leadership might have saved the day for the attackers, but he was unable to take field command.

In time, the futility of further attack against the big and accurate guns of the hunters, combined with the enormity of the loss of life already sustained, caused the tribesmen to suspend their bold if foolish charges. Those able to do so under the continuing fire risked their lives to recover the fallen warriors, both dead and wounded. Estimates of just how many Indians fell during the attack are as varied as the wild guesses about how many were in the fight. Mooar claimed from 115 to 150 killed. Bat Masterson, who survived the fight to become a legendary figure in tall tales of the Old West, put the number at "over 80 killed," while other estimates were slightly less. By all accounts, however, the ratio of loss to numbers involved in the battle remained out of all acceptable proportion, unless one prefers to believe Mooar's claims.

The final dramatic element of the battle features Billy Dixon, who was described by his wife as a "plainsman, scout, and pioneer." He was all of those in addition to being a sensationally accurate sharpshooter. When the main battle ended, the Indians remained close by, apparently contemplating yet another and hopefully more successful assault on the bullet-pocked but still standing buildings. A few days later, two scouts sat looking down on the besieged outpost from atop the ridge that loomed about a mile to the east. Encouraged by his fellow survivors, Dixon raised a borrowed .50-caliber Sharps rifle to aim at one of the scouts who appeared to be a mere fleck of color through the gunsight. To everyone's great surprise, particularly the hapless scout's, the bullet traveled nearly a mile to knock him from the back of his horse and hurl him senseless to the ground. The tribesmen who witnessed this display of marksmanship wisely turned their backs on the little buildings at Adobe Walls, but only after reaching safety behind the crest of the ridge. The Sharps rifle from then on was called by the Indians "the gun that shoots today but kills tomorrow."

With the fighting spirit of the war party at least temporarily broken by Dixon's shot, the hunters buried their dead and made a hasty exodus from the country south of the Arkansas. As word of the presence of a large party of Indians still likely on the prowl spread throughout the region, nearly all hunters joined the Adobe Walls survivors in crossing into safer territory. For a brief interlude, it appeared the Indians' failure to overcome the Adobe Walls outpost had actually accomplished their intended goal of driving the white hunters back across the Arkansas. However, the demand for buffalo hides soon resulted in an even greater influx of hunters. To protect this new wave of buffalo men, the army launched a major campaign to nullify the threat of further Indian attacks such as the one at Adobe Walls. Within a year's time, what has become known as the Red River War concluded and the people of the Southern Plains tribes moved unwillingly to reservations in the Indian Territory. In the process of that subjugation, hunters reduced the once mighty buffalo herd on the Texas Panhandle to a few pitiful animals who ranged without further restriction across the plains.

At Adobe Walls, there is nothing left of the buildings that withstood history's last great mounted, combined siege by the Comanche, Kiowa, and Cheyenne. Soon after

This rendering of the buffalo hunters' outpost at Adobe Walls is based on the actual location of the buildings that occupied the site at the time of the Indian attack in June 1874. The Meyers and Leonard Hideyard and Store are shown on the right of the painting. *John Eliot Jenkins,* Adobe Walls, *1874, 1931. Oil on canvas. Courtesy of Panhandle-Plains Historical Society Museum, Canyon, Texas.*

all the hunters fled to the north fearing for their lives, a large number of warriors returned to the battle site, perhaps to celebrate the exodus of their enemy or to destroy all visible evidence of their foiled attack. The Indians put the torch to the cluster of deserted shedlike buildings, and in doing so, they unwittingly preserved for future study many artifacts of the fight that would have likely otherwise been scattered and lost. As the buildings burned, their sod roofs fell on top of all that remained inside. Dishes, bottles, silverware, drinking glasses, tobacco pipes, coins, and cartridges were among the hundreds of items that remained buried for nearly a century. The ceaseless winds of the Texas Panhandle piled dirt just thick enough to disguise the shapes of the fallen buildings from the eyes and shovels of treasure hunters.

Professional excavations of the site led by the late archeologist Billy Harrison began in earnest in 1978. Under his watchful eye, the century-old story of Adobe Walls came to life again. As archeologists uncovered the artifacts of the brief but significant battle, it became obvious the hunters had fled the site in a virtual panic. The long-forgotten plot of land on a remote Texas ranch was for a moment in time a little like Herculaneum or Pompeii—capturing one signal event that preserved a traumatic moment in the lives of others, both white men and Indian, so long ago.

This 2009 photograph is of the Adobe Walls site looking eastward toward what is known today as Billy Dixon's Ridge. A luckless Indian was shot off his pony while on the ridge by a bullet fired from Dixon's gun well over a thousand yards away. The site is now the property of the Panhandle-Plains Historical Society Museum. *Thomas E. Alexander Collection. Entitled Looking East from Adobe Walls. Photograph by Randall Derrick, Amarillo, Texas.*

The still somehow mysterious aura of Adobe Walls is best discovered on an early morning in late June. As the sun rises above the ridge to the east where Billy Dixon's unwitting target once sat on his pony, it is possible to imagine another June day in 1874. The graves of two of the hunters slain in the attack are well marked, as is the burial place of Billy Dixon himself, who, after serving the army as a scout and receiving the Medal of Honor for that service, had settled near the adobe ruins with his wife, Olive.

The historical importance of the battle has long been argued by historians and archeologists. To some, it was a futile clash that accomplished little for the attackers, while others see it as the dying gasp of the traditional nomadic tribal way of life. In this latter view, the Battle of Adobe Walls was the last chance for the Plains Indians to strike a forceful blow.

Location: From Stinnett, take FM 207 northeast and turn east on FM 281, then follow the unpaved local road southeast to the site. Those wishing to visit the isolated site should understand that the local road may be difficult to discern, and the route can be confusing. Also, it crosses private property. Asking locally for more detailed directions is recommended.

Access: Difficult; requires driving on poorly marked gravel roads.

SOURCES

Baker, T. Lindsay, and Billy R. Harrison. *Adobe Walls: The History and Archeology of the 1874 Trading Post.* College Station: Texas A&M University Press, 1986.

Berthong, Donald J. *The Southern Cheyennes.* Norman: University of Oklahoma Press, 1963.

Boyd, Eva Jolene. *Noble Brutes: Camels on the American Frontier.* Plano: Republic of Texas Press, 1995.

Colton, Ray C. *The Civil War in the Western Territories: Arizona, Colorado, New Mexico, and Utah.* Norman: University of Oklahoma Press, 1959.

Cruse, J. Brett. *Battles of the Red River War: Archeological Perspectives on the Indian Campaign of 1874.* College Station: Texas A&M University Press, 2008.

Dixon, Olive K. *Life of "Billy" Dixon: Plainsman, Scout, and Pioneer.* Abilene, TX: State House Press (facsimile), 1987.

Duarte, Gloria. "The Fort McKavett Community in 1889: Snapshots from the Original 'Fort McKavett Breeze.'" *Journal for Big Bend Studies* 17 (2005): 83–95.

Fehrenbach, T. R. *Comanches: Destruction of a People.* New York: Alfred A. Knopf, 1974.

Frazer, Robert W. *Forts of the West: Military Forts Old Presidios and Posts Commonly Called Forts West of the Mississippi River to 1898.* Norman: University of Oklahoma Press, 1972.

Frazier, Donald S. *Blood and Treasure: Confederate Empire in the Southwest.* College Station: Texas A&M University Press, 1995.

Neeley, Bill. *Quanah Parker and His People.* Slaton, TX: Brazos Press, 1986.

———. *The Last Comanche Chief: The Life and Times of Quanah Parker.* New York: John Wiley & Sons, 1995.

Newcomb, W. W. Jr. *The Indians of Texas: From Prehistoric to Modern Times.* Austin: University of Texas Press, 1961.

Rathjen, Frederick W. *The Texas Panhandle Frontier.* Austin: University of Texas Press, 1973.

Robinson, Charles M. III. *Frontier Forts of Texas.* Houston: Lone Star Books, 1986.

———. *Bad Hand: A Biography of General Ranald S. Mackenzie.* Austin: State House Press, 1993.

Smith, Thomas T. *The US Army and the Texas Frontier Economy, 1845–1900.* College Station: Texas A&M University Press, 1999.

Tyler, Ron, ed. *The New Handbook of Texas,* 6 vols. Austin: Texas State Historical Association, 1996.

Utley, Robert M. *The Indian Frontier of the American West, 1846–1899.* Albuquerque: University of New Mexico Press, 1984.

Weeks, Philip. *Farewell My Nation.* Arlington Heights, IL: Harlan Davison, 1990.

Wellman, Paul. *Indian Wars of the West.* New York: Indian Head Books, 1992.

THE CIVIL WAR
1861–1865

*I would lay down my life
to defend any one of the
States from aggression,
which endangered peace or
threatened its institutions.
I could do more for the
union, but I wish to do
more; for the destruction
of the union would be the
destruction of all States. A
stab in the heart is worse
than a cut in a limb, for this
may be healed.*

—Sam Houston

The causes of the US Civil War stemmed from deep-seated regional issues that date back to the earliest days of the American Republic and continue to be debated to this day. These issues are varied, complex, dynamic, and open to intergenerational interpretation, but they undeniably set the nation on a course of war that by the 1860s seemed to most at the time unavoidable. In the decades leading up to the conflict there were myriad landmarks along the route, each seeming to lead the nation closer to the point of no return. They included tariffs, the Compromise of 1850, the Dred Scot case, Bleeding Kansas, John Brown's raid on Harper's Ferry, and even the "Texas question," but in all of them was the unresolved wedge issue of states' rights, especially as it pertained to slavery. With opposing sides eventually entrenched politically, the nation awaited the spark to set the powder, and that came with the presidential election of 1860. From that point, the pace toward war quickened beyond comprehension, and as historian Archie P. McDonald noted, it "crystallized Texans into a secession posture."

The election of Abraham Lincoln on a Republican platform committed to the abolition of slavery caused a number of Southern states to question immediately the

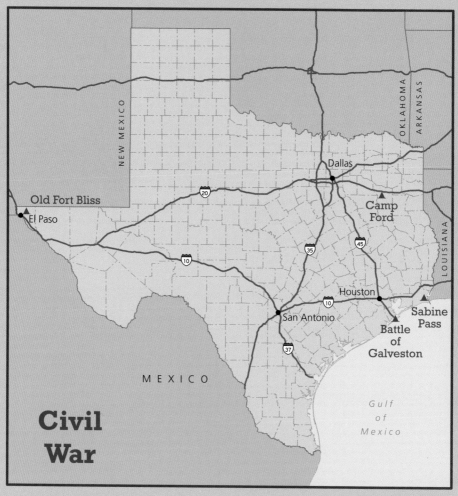

NEW MEXICO

OKLAHOMA

ARKANSAS

Dallas

Old Fort Bliss

El Paso

Camp
Ford

LOUISIANA

Houston

San Antonio

Sabine
Pass

Battle
of
Galveston

MEXICO

Gulf
of
Mexico

Civil
War

Map by Molly O'Halloran

value of continued national union. South Carolina reacted first, choosing to secede in December 1860, even before the new president took office. Other states—Alabama, Florida, Georgia, Louisiana, and Mississippi—soon followed suit, and by February 1861, Texas appeared ready to become the seventh member of the newly formed Confederate States of America. But Texas faced a unique dilemma; at the head of its government was an avowed supporter of the Union, Gov. Sam Houston. Working against his recalcitrance, state secessionists took control of the issue, forging a preliminary ordinance of secession and calling for a statewide vote on February 3. The results proved conclusive, despite limited opposition from a few counties in Central Texas and North Texas and one in deep East Texas. In March 1861, a secession convention met in Austin to confirm separation from the Union and alliance with the Confederacy, and in the process unseated Houston in favor of Lt. Gov. Edward Clark. Despite his belief that disunion would irreparably injure his beloved Texas and the other Southern states, Houston chose to reject Lincoln's offer of military intervention to overturn secession with force.

Even as the matter of secession worked its way through the political process, Texas military forces under Ben McCulloch moved on San Antonio in an effort to isolate Union forces under the command of Gen. David E. Twiggs. Without major incident, Twiggs capitulated, surrendering 160 men and all Union property in the state, but he secured the right for his forces to keep their arms as they made their way to the coast for transport back to the North. By the time it officially joined the Confederacy, Texas had control of its lands, but the hold proved tenuous at best.

Because of its size, geographic location, vast frontier, and expansive coastline, Texas faced a more stratified set of issues than other Confederate states during the war. To mitigate a possible assault from north of the Red River, W. C. Young successfully led a volunteer unit into Indian Territory to secure three strategic forts: Arbuckle, Cobb, and Washita. Responding to concerns about the seemingly defenseless frontier lands to the west, the Confederacy acted through John R. Baylor, who secured the New Mexico town of Mesilla and set up a territorial government that claimed control of the land as far west as Phoenix, and through Brig. Gen. H. H. Sibley, who led a military campaign into New Mexico and secured Albuquerque and Santa Fe before having his supply lines cut following the Battle of Glorieta Pass in 1862. The actions of Baylor and Sibley proved uneventful in the long run, but they highlighted the vulnerability of Texas along the frontier line. Of equal concern in that region was the pervasive threat of Indian attacks, and efforts to establish an effective defensive system proved problematic, having had limited success against Comanches and Kiowas at Adobe Walls and suffering a stinging defeat from the Kickapoos at Dove Creek. At no time during the Civil War did the Texans come close to securing the frontier, and many settlers thus began to draw back eastward as a result.

Texas feared that its greatest military threat would be along the Gulf Coast, and it did face occasional tests of its defenses there, most notably at Galveston, Sabine Pass, Brownsville, and Corpus Christi. The attacks were limited in scope, but the potential for invasion from the sea, coupled with the vastness and remoteness of the coastline, as well as the effectiveness of the federal blockade, served to keep the attention of forces stationed in Texas.

The state also had to worry about its boundary along the Rio Grande, and its concerns in that regard were twofold. First, the Confederacy needed to keep the border with Mexico open in order to provide an outlet for the commercial trade of cotton. Through a complex system that resulted in monetary returns directly to the government, cotton proved to be a viable means of funding Southern military supplies. But the border also represented a possible escape route for runaway slaves. Later, after French intervention brought new concerns about European expansion and possible recognition of a revived Texas republic, the border became a continual problem for the Union as well.

Internally, Texas had to contend with pro-Union groups and the often violent reactions against them from citizens loyal to the Southern cause. Retaliation ranged from military action against Central Texas Germans seeking to reach safe haven in Mexico to the widespread hanging of supposed Peace Party sympathizers in North Texas. In far Northeast Texas, military deserters established a vigilante form of social control, while East Texas had to contend with overwhelming numbers of refugees fleeing the fighting in Louisiana, Mississippi, Arkansas, and Missouri. Across the state, farm families struggled to maintain sustainable production levels as large numbers of men went off to war, and home guard units vigilantly tried to maintain local peace and protect against invasion. Texans also supported the Confederacy through industrial production of guns and ammunition, clothing and shoes, wagons and carriages, and other vital materiel. In addition, with limited resources they supported local conscription and training stations, as well as prisoner-of-war camps.

Externally, Texas made significant contributions to the war effort by supplying soldiers, sailors, and military leaders for battlefields far outside its borders. Texas forces served under such legendary leaders as Albert Sidney Johnston, John Bell Hood, Sam Bell Maxey, Lawrence Sullivan Ross, Santos Benavides, and Benjamin F. Terry. And they served with distinction in such strategic battles as Gettysburg, Shiloh, Chickamauga, Mansfield, Bentonville, the Wilderness, Antietam, and Vicksburg. But Texans not only fought for the South; there were Texas Union forces under the command of E. J. Davis, and their presence proved central to Northern plans to stabilize the state in the event it should be wrested from the Confederacy.

In effect, the US Civil War came to a close in Texas in 1865. In May 1865, a month after Gen. Robert E. Lee surrendered the forces under his command to Gen. Ulysses

S. Grant at Appomattox, Virginia, Confederates under Gen. John S. "Rip" Ford prevailed against Union forces, including African American soldiers, at the Battle of Palmito Ranch near Brownsville. It was the last land battle of the Civil War and therefore a meaningless victory for the South. The following month, Gen. Edmund Kirby Smith surrendered his Confederate troops at Galveston. There, on June 19, 1865—a date since celebrated as Juneteenth—enslaved African Americans in Texas learned of their emancipation. What followed for all Texans, regardless of their race or involvement in the war effort, was a period of great uncertainty and confusion. As a result, the impact of the Civil War continued for generations.

OLD FORT BLISS
(1854–1867)

El Paso, strategically situated on the banks of the Rio Grande at the extreme western edge of Texas, has been the location of six US military installations from 1849 to the present. Five of those army posts, each at a different site, bore the name Fort Bliss in honor of Lt. Col. William Wallace Smith Bliss, who was not only Gen. Zachary Taylor's chief of staff during the Mexican War but his son-in-law as well. While today, Fort Bliss is the nation's largest military post, all but one of the previous forts under the same name have virtually disappeared from the pages of history. The exception is the tiny Civil War–era Fort Bliss, then located on a three-acre plot as contrasted to the modern-day facility's 1.3 million acre sprawl. The historical importance of the tiny 1854 fort stems from its pivotal role in what was likely among the more grandiose dreams of glory envisioned by the leaders of the Confederacy at the outset of the Civil War in 1861. In February of that year, nearly two months before the war's first shot had been fired, the Union commander of the fort, Brig. Gen. David E. Twiggs, ordered the post abandoned. Twiggs's obviously premature order earned him not only the immediate wrath of his superior officers in the War Department in Washington, but soon thereafter a commission and a promotion as a major general in the Confederate Army. The suddenly deserted former Union post transferred to Confederate Lt. Col. John Robert Baylor on July 5, 1861.

At the same time as Fort Bliss changed its national allegiance, most US Army officers also chose which side to serve as the inevitable full outbreak of the Civil War drew closer. Among these officers was 45-year-old Capt. Henry Hopkins Sibley. Although the federal army in which he served for 23 years finally offered him a promotion to major in May 1861, Sibley, a Louisianan by birth, resigned the well-deserved if belated new rank in order to cast his lot with the Confederate cause. When he made his decision, Sibley served as the commanding officer of Fort Union, located in New Mexico Territory, northeast of Santa Fe and some 400 miles north of Fort Bliss. Sibley was personally acquainted with the rugged western reaches of the United States. After being brevetted for gallantry in the 1848 war with Mexico, which directly brought about America's acquisition of much of the western territory, Sibley saw action in Utah and in the Navajo Campaign of 1860. He had been serving at various outposts in New Mexico when ordered to march with his troops to assume command of Fort Union. He arrived there on May 17, 1861, just two weeks before he resigned from the US Army. Still a disciplined and professional soldier, Sibley remained at the fort until June 13, awaiting official notification from the War Department that his resignation had been accepted. For all intents and purposes, this West Point–trained officer was a man without a country and momentarily without an army to serve. Then Sibley took a stagecoach south to Fort Bliss before heading east to offer his services to the Confederate Army at its headquarters in Richmond, Virginia.

It is apparent that Sibley had a brilliant and inventive mind, at least in his earlier years, despite the clouded reputation many historians later ascribed to him. That mind conceived of the design for a field tent used by the US Army for decades. He also drew upon his experience gained from military campaigns to create a reliable camp stove for use on the march. Although these two early ideas proved to be practical, Sibley's much later grand scheme for a sweeping Confederate campaign to capture and occupy vast quantities of western America appeared destined to fail, in large part due to his own inadequacies as a field commander. It is not certain at what point in his journey from Fort Union to Richmond via Fort Bliss that he formulated his plan, but by the time he reached the office of Confederate president Jefferson Davis in late June, he had a well-developed and compelling strategy. It called for an invasion of the Union-held Territory of New Mexico, including lands in Arizona and Colorado, in order to position the Confederacy as a serious player on the stage of world politics rather than a regional power disenchanted with the nation from which it had just bolted. If the strategy proved successful, the Confederacy would gain access to the gold riches of Colorado as well as those in California, the acquisition of which was among the main objectives of Sibley's plan. If it could attain all the objectives, the Confederacy, thus greatly enriched and spectacularly expanded, would reach from the Atlantic to the Pacific, with the Gulf of Mexico already in the maritime fold of the Southern states. That reach of empire, manned in part by the slave labor so vital to the heart of the Confederacy, might then perhaps be expanded to include much of northern Mexico and possibly even parts of Central America. The plan, so sweeping and exciting to a young nation still confident of its untested military might, was a Southern-driven version of manifest destiny as embraced by US president James A. Polk and other leaders before him. Were it to succeed, the North American continent would then be comprised of Canada, what remained of Mexico, and two other nations sandwiched in between, namely the United States and the Confederate States of America.

While President Davis already knew and liked Sibley, he was even more fond of the Sibley's wildly ambitious scheme to invade New Mexico. Indeed, there was nothing in it for Davis to dislike because it matched identically his own thinking and his dreams of a Confederate empire in the West. With nothing to lose and literally everything to gain, Davis enthusiastically endorsed Sibley's glorious plan and gave its author a brigadier's rank in the Confederate Army. Although overjoyed at his president's acceptance of his plan and his rapid improvement in military rank, the new general must have been at least slightly troubled by one aspect of Davis's approval. While the sheer beauty of Sibley's plan seemed undeniable, it appeared equally undeniable that there were no troops available to make the plan viable. It would be up to Sibley himself to raise the brigade which he would then command. Further, there were no arms available for his brigade once the unit formed, and no provisions or basic supplies could be diverted from the Confederate legions already fighting the Union Army in Virginia and elsewhere.

In short, the new general had a star, a plan, and an enthusiastic presidential approval, but nothing more. Undaunted, he set out on his mission at once and raced westward to San Antonio. His proposal to Davis included a bold statement attesting to his ability to raise a unit of brigade strength in the Alamo City by catering to those Texans who traditionally strongly disliked anything about New Mexico. Sibley rightly sensed that given the rare opportunity to do battle with their neighbors to the west in a righteous cause, all the while striking a blow for the Confederacy, Texans would swiftly respond to his call to arms from across the Lone Star State. Indeed, Texans of all ages eagerly signed up to learn the basics of drill and at least the fundamental tenets of military courtesy. For the most part, their uniforms consisted of what was on their backs when they arrived to swear an oath to the Confederacy. Their weapons were every bit as eclectic as their wearing apparel, but their excellent marksmanship required no improvement. To add a bit of Continental-like flair to his brigade's weaponry assortment, Sibley ordered nine-foot-long lances to be made for issue to some of his companies. The weapons would prove worthless in combat but thrilling to observers of the drilling formations.

After nearly four months of basic training, the men known as Sibley's Brigade proved themselves worthy of combat by their commander. The general then gave orders to march westward to Fort Bliss and on to battles with the federals and, he hoped, a glorious victory that would more than treble the size of the Confederacy and ensure its future. The brigade left San Antonio on a staggered schedule that allowed waterholes along the route of march time to recharge between passages of troop units. The first regiment decamped on October 23, and after most of the other regiments had marched away, Sibley and his staff left the city on November 18, 1861, almost three weeks later. In all, nearly 3,000 Confederates moved west along the general route of what is now US Highway 90, accompanied by herds of beef cattle, supply wagons, and artillery caissons. It was not long before the inadequacies of the supply train became dangerously apparent. Both the men and their animals soon had to live off the land, frequently at the expense and dismay of those settlers who farmed or raised livestock along the route of march. Long stretches of rough, dry trail between the few reliable sources of water made thirst a daily companion. The well-planned staggered departure schedule actually did little to replenish the levels of the waterholes or recharge the flow of quickly diminished springs. Despite the hardships of the march, and spurred on by the fervor of their early-war patriotism, Sibley's Brigade of ill-clothed and poorly shod Texans advanced doggedly over the 800 miles to Fort Bliss.

Sibley and his staff arrived at the fort on December 13, a few days ahead of his brigade. The tiny fort appeared much as he remembered it six months earlier, before his successful journey to Richmond. The same Col. John R. Baylor who had accepted the surrender of the fort by federal forces was still there. He had, in fact, already launched several attacks against Union positions up the Rio Grande with moderate success. As soon as all Sibley's troops had successfully battled Texas weather and the equally unpredictable Texas terrain to arrive safely at Fort Bliss, the general made rapid preparations to push north up the Rio Grande to attack and subdue Union forts along the river and then to march on to Albuquerque and Santa Fe. From there, the plan was to move along the Santa Fe Trail to Las Vegas, and following that forty-year-old trade route, attack Fort Union. Having just served in the region prior to his resignation, Sibley knew a great deal about the terrain, the strength of such Union outposts as Fort Craig and Fort Fillmore, and the layouts of the major cities of Albuquerque and Santa Fe. Most important, however, the general also recognized that Fort Union, his last command while in federal service, was the key to the capture of Colorado and its gold mines.

As Sibley refined his invasion tactics and further pondered his strategy of empire, his men quickly managed to transform the El Paso villagers from cordial welcomers into disgruntled, often hostile antagonists. Although the fort itself was unusually small for a mid-nineteenth-century US Army post, the amount of land temporarily confiscated to accommodate Sibley's Brigade was immense. Long rows of tents snaked their way along established village streets and up onto the slopes of the Franklin Mountains. The few adobe buildings at the fort soon overflowed with Sibley's headquarters staff. Once the thousands of long-starved, whiskey-and-women-deprived soldiers established their campgrounds, they turned upon the hapless and largely Hispanic local citizenry in what became a lawless rampage. Nothing appeared either sacred or safe from these undisciplined and mostly young men who seemed almost viciously intent on quelling their thirst for everything denied them on the long march from San Antonio. While his soldiers created social havoc in the villages, Sibley busied himself distributing copies of his proclamation in English and Spanish to the inhabitants of the region, describing the many benefits that would accrue to them under the benevolent rule of the Confederacy. He assured them his forces came not as conquerors but as liberators to free them from the yoke of Yankee oppression.

For the most part, Sibley's message of liberation failed to generate the degree of active civilian support he envisioned. The general had told President Davis in Richmond of his confidence that the New Mexicans would welcome his brigade and eagerly cooperate in the provisioning of the soldiers as they marched up the Rio Grande and on to Fort Union. It is likely Sibley had come to believe that civilians would support his campaign when he had traveled from Fort Union to Fort Bliss several months earlier. Full of optimism about the prospects of the new Confederacy and perhaps already formulating his plans to return soon to move back up the river, the recently resigned federal officer clearly misread the situation. When the Sibley Brigade moved out of Fort Bliss in January 1862 on the first leg of the intended march to Fort Union, there was no evidence of widespread support from the citizens. Instead, wholesale pillaging and stealing became necessary in order to survive the rigors of the trail. If the citizens along the way were less than enthusiastic about the presence of the Texas troops at the outset of the campaign, they became downright antagonistic as the hungry invaders from Texas rustled their cattle and stole their crops.

Though the full story of the military misfortunes of the Sibley Brigade in New Mexico cannot be told here, suffice it to say that following some rather spectacular victories on its way to Fort Union, the brigade's advance halted at the Battle of Glorieta Pass on March 28, 1862, just 70 miles away from Fort Union. Although Sibley's men actually won the sharp skirmish that took place that day, a Union force comprised largely of Colorado volunteers destroyed their supply train. The brigade having lost its logistical support, the Confederate threat to Fort Union, the goldfields of Colorado, and all that lay beyond came to a swift conclusion. The burning of Sibley's supply wagons also forever ended his and Davis's dream of a Confederate empire in the West. Without Colorado's gold to fund the vast undertaking, no Confederate ships would ever sail from California's ports to trade with Asian nations, Mexico's northern states would remain Mexican, and the practice of slavery would go no farther west than the Texas border.

Defeated, Sibley's Brigade turned south to follow the Rio Grande back to Fort Bliss. At one point, Union forces marched south along with them just across the river, nearly matching them step for step. No battle ensued, though, as neither side had any taste for more fighting. The Union forces only wanted Sibley's men to leave the territory and go back to Texas. For the most part, the ragtag Confederate brigade

FORT BLISS, TEXAS.

This drawing of the 1854 Fort Bliss shows it as it was when Brig. Gen. H. H. Sibley occupied it
in 1861 during the Civil War. The looming Franklin Mountains afford a visual reference to the
fort's location. Retreating Confederates burned it down in 1862. *Sketch by W. W. H. Davis.*
In El Gringo: New Mexico and Her People, *ca. 1855. Southwest Collection. Courtesy of El Paso
Public Library.*

shared that desire as they staggered southward without adequate food or water. The
shattered brigade reached Fort Bliss in late April and lingered only long enough to
supply itself for the hardships of the seven-week march back to San Antonio. Brigadier General Sibley, of course, put the best possible face on what had clearly been a
debacle owing to poor logistical planning, a stronger than expected enemy opposition, an unwelcoming citizenry, and his own inferior leadership. Although the brilliant
Southern strategist Gen. Robert E. Lee sent a congratulatory message to Sibley prais-
ing his conduct during the campaign, many men of his brigade openly faulted him for
his frequent drunkenness and questionable bravery under fire. Sibley himself blamed
the defeat of his forces on everything but his leadership abilities. The fact that a formal
inquiry was opened on his generalship during the New Mexican campaign indicates
that Sibley's views of himself were in the minority. By the time the brigade limped into
San Antonio in late July 1862, over one-third of its soldiers had been killed in battle or
had died fighting starvation and thirst. Meanwhile, Union forces reoccupied Fort Bliss,
although the retreating Confederates burned most of the buildings. What had been

This intersection of El Paso's Myrtle and Willow Streets marks the approximate site of the center of the 1854 Fort Bliss. Compare this 2009 view of the Franklin Mountains with the sketch made in 1855. *Thomas E. Alexander Collection.*

the third military installation in El Paso to be called Fort Bliss was never to be occupied by any army again.

Today, the site of the Civil War–era Fort Bliss is an El Paso business district filled with shops and cantinas. Only the Franklin Mountains that appear on an old engraving of the fort remain to give a visual sense of the fort's location. At modern-day Fort Bliss, however, a reproduction of the old installation does give one a good idea of how it looked when General Sibley arrived with his brigade of empire builders. The actual site of the fort does not even hint at the importance of what took place there in 1861 and 1862. Then it was the gateway to a radical dream of expansion of the Confederacy, what might well have been a hugely significant event in North American History had not that dream of empire ground to a bitter halt in the mountains of New Mexico, never to be taken up again.

Location: The site of Old Fort Bliss was within a small area now centered at the present-day intersection of Bassett Avenue and Willow Street in El Paso.

Access: Unlimited.

BATTLE OF GALVESTON
(JANUARY 1, 1863)

From the onset of the Civil War, those charged with developing defenses for the Texas coast knew they faced an impossible task. Not only did they have 1,000 miles of often-inaccessible coastline, barrier islands, and inlets to protect, but they also had to cobble together viable defenses utilizing scavenged ordnance, inadequate numbers of retrofitted, shallow-water craft, hastily constructed earthworks—and deception. Within the vast lines of defense, though, the key strategic point was the port of Galveston. Not only did it provide extensive harbor facilities set back from the main coastline, but it also provided vital rail connections, a limiting factor in wartime Texas. By establishing a beachhead at Galveston, the North could funnel troops to the mainland, quickly sweep into the interior of the state, and effectively separate it from the other states of the Confederacy while also disrupting vital cotton trade routes and routing the commodity to Northern mills. As the war began, Galveston was the state's largest city and one of the top three ports along the Gulf of Mexico. With New Orleans in Union control by 1862, though, Northern military leaders began turning their sights toward Texas.

Feverishly working to design a defensive strategy for Galveston and the Texas coast early on was the Confederate brigadier general Paul Octave Hébert, who set up his temporary headquarters in the coastal city. To him fell the ultimate decision of how—or even if—to make a stand at that strategic point. The dilemma he faced grew out of his pragmatic assessment of limited resources but also his realization of how crucial the rail line to the mainland would be both defensively and offensively. Could he even hold the port city, or should he instead accede to the inevitable and focus his forces on the mainland to protect against the fall of Houston? As he weighed the dire consequences of either plan, oftentimes at odds with Texas governor Francis R. Lubbock, who believed Galveston must be held at all costs, US rear admiral David Glasgow Farragut, in charge of the Western Gulf Blockading Squadron, worked to secure a stranglehold on commerce along the coast. It was only a matter of time, and that in short order, before the North moved to control Galveston.

Early on the morning of October 4, 1862, the federal gunboat *Harriet Lane* moved forward to enter Galveston harbor under a flag of truce, drawing a warning shot from Fort Point, an installation at the easternmost tip of the island defended by only one gun and several painted logs known as "Quaker guns." While efforts ensued to open communications between the ship and the city, Cmdr. William B. Renshaw, aboard the flagship *Westfield,* watched from a distance and momentarily held the remainder of his federal flotilla in place. Despite complications that tested his patience and resulted in a brief exchange of gunfire, Renshaw managed to convey his call for immediate and unconditional surrender, eventually agreeing to a delay of four days to allow for the orderly evacuation of women and children from the city. Although the Confederates pledged not to increase their defenses during that time, they nonetheless moved to concentrate their forces at both ends of the connecting rail line: Eagle Grove on the island and Victoria Point on the mainland. Renshaw saw no need to contest the situation at the time, assured that sufficient reinforcements would soon arrive to press the advantage. Regardless, by the end of the truce, Union forces controlled the port of Galveston and symbolically celebrated that victory by briefly flying the US flag over the federal customhouse before returning to the safety of their ships. While awaiting reinforcements, Renshaw secured his ships in the harbor and sent troops ashore during the day for patrols as Confederates scouted their actions from a distance and prepared their defenses along the rail line.

Reinforcements took longer than anticipated, but on Christmas Day three companies of the 42nd Infantry Regiment landed at Galveston and took up position along Kuhn's Wharf at the end of 18th Street. Despite some concerns about the vulnerability of the site, but with assurances of support from Renshaw and additional reinforcements to come, Col. Isaac Burrell readied his forces by setting up barracks in a warehouse area and directing construction of breastworks from planks taken from the wharf.

As the Union moved to tighten its grip on Galveston and prepare for the assault into the interior of Texas, Confederate leaders in Richmond named a new commander of defenses in the Southwest, including the Texas coast. His name was Maj. Gen. John Bankhead Magruder, an enigmatic and controversial figure who garnered recognition for his successful use of the "flying artillery" technique during the Mexican War. A native of Virginia, Magruder offered great promise for the Confederacy during the opening days of the war in the Peninsula Campaign but drew the wrath of Gen. Robert E. Lee for his disappointing actions at Malvern Hill. Known by the sobriquet "Prince John" for his flamboyant style and courtly manner, Magruder was given to theatrics, independent decision-making, and heavy drinking. Despite his drawbacks, he offered forces along the western Gulf Coast the hope borne of an aggressive nature and a keen understanding of strategy. He quickly assessed unfolding developments in Galveston and determined that before Union forces could arrive there to tip the balance even further, he had to strike back to retake the island.

Magruder's ultimate plan called for attacks by both land and water, with diversionary actions by infantry and artillery allowing a surprise naval attack on the bay side of the island. It involved a high degree of coordination from various levels of local command, as well as a large degree of luck. For the naval operations, he relied on Comm. Leon Smith, who he had known earlier in California. At Magruder's request, Smith worked to outfit two gunboats—the *Bayou City* and the *Neptune*—with layers of "armor" from readily available cotton bales. The so-called cottonclads would carry field artillery pieces as well several hundred infantry sharpshooters who would provide cover and serve as a landing or boarding party as necessary. Commanding the onboard infantry was Col. Tom Green, who distinguished himself during the lengthy and ultimately ill-fated expedition into New Mexico headed by Brig. Gen. Henry Hopkins Sibley earlier in 1862.

Before unleashing his naval counterpunch, though, Magruder planned to open the battle with artillery bombardment from Virginia Point followed immediately by land actions on two fronts utilizing flying artillery emplacements throughout the city and an infantry assault on Kuhn's Wharf. Through scouting expeditions, some of which he conducted himself, Magruder knew a frontal assault on the position held by the Massachusetts troops was not possible, and so he had his troops construct scaling ladders that would allow them to access the wharf from the water. Magruder hoped to begin his assault in the days following Christmas, but work on the cottonclads delayed the implementation to the early morning hours of New Year's Day 1863. With all the elements in place, Magruder personally fired the signal shot from a battery set up adjacent to the Hendley Building along 20th Street about 4:00, and his forces quickly followed with their various assignments as planned.

The battle began with the rolling thunder of artillery, thick clouds of gunpowder smoke, the shadowy silhouettes of infantry troops running toward the wharf, and for the Union forces, momentary confusion. They quickly regrouped, though, and naval crews along the wharves manned their guns to fire at the forces in town. Meanwhile, Renshaw sought to move the *Westfield* into position near Point Bolivar to seal that area of the bay but, as had happened before, it ran aground and had to signal the *Clifton* for assistance. At Kuhn's Wharf, Burrell ordered his men into position behind the breastworks as they prepared for what they believed would be a direct online assault from the city. Meanwhile, Col. Joseph J. Cook directed the Confederate attack from underneath, albeit unsuccessfully; only as the troops plunged forward into the water to start their ascent under cover by sharpshooters did they learn that their scaling ladders were too short to reach the top of the wharf. They had no choice but to fall back as the Union troops fired down on them from above and from the nearby ships. The Confederates' light artillery also received heavy return fire, and soon troops either abandoned positions or likewise fell back, some even regrouping behind the US Custom House, which received several rounds.

For a time it seemed Magruder's plans would lead to quick defeat, but just as he faced the decision to abandon the operation, four Confederate cottonclads steamed into the bay from the north bearing down on the USS *Harriet Lane* under full steam. The Union gunboat, in an awkward left flank position along the wharf, maneuvered to reach a more open position, but before she could, the *Bayou City* struck it a glancing blow as Confederate sharpshooters scattered the crew. The initial crash, while insignificant structurally for the *Harriet Lane,* nevertheless broke the mechanism that held its anchor in place, causing it to dislodge into the bay and effectively holding it in place while the *Neptune* made a strike against its starboard side near the paddlewheel. The maneuver severely crippled the *Neptune,* however, giving the Union ship's crew time to regroup with renewed hope for evasion and escape. The *Bayou City,* crippled and taking on water, still managed to turn around in time, though, and giving off withering fire from the sharpshooters, it steamed ahead into the port paddlewheel of the *Harriet Lane,* locking the two ships together in the process. Leon Smith quickly led the assault by the boarding party, and in short order the Confederates had control.

The fighting in the harbor then focused on the USS *Owasco,* which had moved up to support the *Harriet Lane.* But with guns trained on her and backup firepower from sharpshooters, *Owasco* moved away, passing close by—but not stopping at—Kuhn's Wharf. With a white flag now flying from the *Harriet Lane,* both sides agreed to a temporary truce. Burrell used the time to assess his desperate situation, isolated on a wharf with no backup in sight. Capt. Henry S. Lubbock, the governor's brother and commander of the *Bayou City,* used the situation to press for surrender of the remaining ships, and Renshaw called them in closer for a council of war. Amazingly, he acquiesced and ordered them to fly white flags but to prepare for escape as well. With no means of carrying on the fight on land, and with Confederate forces once again moving their artillery into place for a continued assault, Burrell surrendered.

Meanwhile, Renshaw realized the *Westfield* could not be saved, and so he directed the destruction of his own ship, ordering crews to open the magazines, spread turpentine and gunpowder across the decks, and set a delaying explosive device known as a "slow match." Sources differ on what happened next—whether the detonation was too quick or whether it was too slow, causing Renshaw and his men to return for inspection—but both accounts ended with the same result: the magazines of the *Westfield* exploded with tremendous force, instantly killing the captain and his crew. In the confusion that followed, remaining Union gunships not yet under Confederate control, including the *Clifton, Sachem,* and *Owasco,* all three later involved in fighting at Sabine Pass, quickly made for open water while still flying flags of truce. Although Confederate forces aboard the *John F. Carr* gave chase, they soon broke it off but managed to capture three small ships upon return to the port. With the incomplete chase across the bar, the Battle of Galveston came to a close six hours after Magruder fired the first shot.

While the Southern forces understandably had cause for celebration, there was also cause for concern. Galveston with its inadequate defenses remained a vulnerable port and therefore subject to a concentrated effort toward reoccupation. As if to signal that vulnerability, the USS *Cambria* arrived off Galveston the morning after the battle. On board were the additional reinforcements Burrell and Renshaw had hoped for in vain. Among them was Col. Edmund J. Davis and members of the First Texas (Union) Cavalry.

Davis, later governor of Texas during Reconstruction, hoped to form an occupation government for Texas following the fall of Galveston. Magruder took deceptive precautions to indicate the city was in Union hands in an attempt to lure the *Cambria* in for capture, but the ruse failed and the ship managed to escape. Within days, though, other ships showed up off the coast to continue enforcing the naval blockade. On January 11, an unidentified ship arrived some distance from shore and the USS *Hatteras* gave chase, only to find it was the dreaded CSS *Alabama,* the bane of existence for many Union ships during much of the war. As usual for encounters of that kind, the *Hatteras* lost the contest, leaving only traces of its existence in the process.

Although there were other isolated shows of force off the coast in the ensuing years of the war, Galveston remained in Confederate control. Ever vigilant, Magruder strengthened defenses around the city, but no further attempt at an invasion occurred. When the end finally came, though, officials of the Trans-Mississippi Department, including Magruder, signed the final documents aboard the USS *Fort*

This 1861 Galveston photo shows the Hendley Building on the right along 20th Street at Avenue A. Given the structure's height and its proximity to the waterfront, both Union and Confederate forces used it for observation purposes during the Civil War. From a battery at this location on January 1, 1863, Gen. John Bankhead Magruder fired a cannon shot to rally his forces for the beginning of what would be the Battle of Galveston. *Courtesy of Rosenberg Library, Galveston.*

Jackson off Galveston on June 2, 1865. Seventeen days later, the US general Gordon Granger formally announced in Galveston that President Lincoln's 1862 Emancipation Proclamation was in effect for Texas. In the ensuing years, that date of June 19, 1865—known as Juneteenth—became an important day of celebration for the end of slavery in the United States. Now recognized worldwide, it is a celebration that also reflects the impact of the Civil War in Texas.

Location: Related historical sites in Galveston include the 1861 US Custom House (headquarters of the Galveston Historical Foundation) and Texas Civil War Monument, 502 20th Street; Galveston County Historical Museum, 123 25th Street; and the Galveston and Texas History Center, 2310 Sealy. Kuhn's Wharf no longer exists.

Access: All sites are open to the public.

The Hendley Building, 2010. Taken from along 20th Street near the intersection with Harborside, this photo shows that some of the 1861 wharf area has since been filled in for later development. In the street, near the red curb mark visible in the center of the photo, is where General Magruder fired the opening shot of the battle back in the general direction of Kuhn's Wharf (since razed) behind the photographer's position. At the time of this photo, the Hendley Building remained abandoned and unrestored. According to local tradition, a damaged pilaster capital, still visible along the 20th Street façade, dates from the Civil War battle. *Photo by Dan K. Utley.*

CAMP FORD
(JULY 21, 1863–MAY 17, 1865)

From the onset of the Civil War, Texas troops had to deal with the issue of prisoners of war. Due to the state's relative isolation and its distance from the opening engagements of the war, the matter remained insignificant early on. In the early years, incarcerations were generally limited to existing facilities such as jails, courthouses, and even warehouses. Informal exchange protocols determined some paroles, but field commanders also reserved the right to make such decisions on their own as necessary. By 1863, as the fighting moved into the Trans-Mississippi West, though, and especially into Louisiana, Arkansas, and along the Texas coast, the detainment of prisoners took on increased significance. Changes in the exchange cartel system around the same time affected the situation as well.

The best known of the Texas prisoner camps, and the largest such facility west of the Mississippi, was Camp Ford, located four miles northeast of Tyler (now within the city limits) along the Tyler-Marshall Road and adjacent to Ray's Creek. The facility opened not as a prisoner camp, though, but as a training camp for conscripts. Officially established as the Eastern Camp of Instruction in 1862, it soon bore the name of Brig. Gen. John S. "Rip" Ford, then the Confederate superintendent of conscripts in the area.

The young town of Tyler, founded in 1846 as the seat of government for Smith County, seemed a logical location for a Confederate military camp. It was relatively remote, deep in the heavily forested region of East Texas, although not too distant from the key railroad center, supply point, and riverport of Shreveport, Louisiana. Tyler also had a stable economy in 1862 with a strong agricultural base as well as wartime industrial components that included an ordnance plant, ammunition factory, iron foundry, and a nearby manufacturer of wagons and carriages. Additionally, the area had abundant groundwater, along with vast stands of timber for fuel and construction. The same factors that made Tyler an ideal training center also contributed to its suitability as a prisoner-of-war campsite, and the transition to its new purpose began only about a year into its existence.

The first prisoners, numbering 48 and made up of captives from an engagement at Brashier City, Louisiana, as well as officers from the Union gunboat *Diana,* arrived in July 1863 under escort by the Walter P. Lane Rangers of Harrison County. Initially, the guard-to-prisoner ratio proved adequate for such a small number, so there was little need for an enclosure, and the prisoners had some limited freedom to move about the area and even into town. Under an act of the Confederate Congress, prisoners received the same daily rations as the soldiers guarding them, and that consisted of generous measures of meat and meal. The detainees did their own cooking, and they often supplemented their diet with local produce from area farmers and suppliers. The camp had its own supply of freshwater from a spring as well as the creek. The situation was less than ideal but tolerable, despite the heat and humidity of the Southern summer in the Piney Woods.

Tensions mounted, though, as the war drew closer to the region. In September 1863, following the Battle of Sabine Pass, which thwarted Union plans to divide Texas from the Confederacy, Maj. Gen. Nathaniel P. Banks returned to southern Louisiana and began reinforcing his units, still intent upon moving westward across the Sabine River. Driving up Bayou Teche, his forces met considerable resistance from Confederates under the command of now brigadier general Tom Green of Texas, who captured 468 men at Stirling's Plantation near Morganza, Louisiana. The arrival of those prisoners at Camp Ford dramatically changed the situation at Tyler in terms of both security and living conditions. Soon after, rumors of a planned uprising among the detainees spread fear throughout the town, and local citizens demanded construction of a perimeter wall. With local African American slaves impressed to provide the labor, an immense stockade of split logs 18 feet high soon surrounded a core area of four acres.

The Confederates maintained Camp Ford as an open stockade facility. Interior housing, like the cooking chores, fell to the prisoners themselves. Some responded by constructing crude log huts with mudcat chimneys. Once they stripped the land of the available timber within the compound, there were occasional supervised patrols outside to gather wood. As that source also soon disappeared, the detainees turned to other means of shelters, everything from cloth tents to shebangs, in effect, small half-dugouts cut into a slope and covered with either wood or fabric as available. The shebangs were a common feature at Camp Ford, and archeological evidence of them indicates they generally held a few prisoners who often spread the floors with clay from the creek or with other materials to make them more habitable.

The growth of Camp Ford in 1863 reflected not only more fighting in the area and thus greater reliance on the site as a primary incarceration facility but also a significant change in the exchange cartel system, the result of both political and military pressures. Union officials had long known the existing exchange system did not work properly, especially since captured rebels often failed to heed the pledge not to take up arms immediately and return to fighting. As a result, the breakdown of the system only served to resupply the Southern ranks, a situation the Union could ill afford, especially in the Deep South. But an additional concern exacerbated the situation, and that was the treatment of African American Union prisoners by the Confederacy, which often failed to recognize the legality of their status as captives.

By 1863, Union officers found themselves having to balance concerns for their own captured forces against the economic realities of warfare. Large numbers of prisoners were an economic drain on the Southern economy, already strapped to sustain the South's own troops. Escapees' reports back to Union commanders told of severe hardships for the prisoners, and they also revealed a Southern society in the initial stages of collapse. As a result, Gen. Ulysses S. Grant suspended the protocols of the previous exchange cartels while also allowing his field commanders to make their own decisions regarding battlefield paroles. It was no doubt a vexing decision to make, given the extra prison time it would mean for some Union soldiers, but one tempered in part by the North's belief that in the summer of 1863 it had gained the upper hand in the war following significant battlefield victories. Grant and other Union leaders gambled that time was on their side.

The number of prisoners at Camp Ford continued to increase through the end of 1863 with the temporary closing of Camp Groce near Hempstead, but a more pronounced and ultimately debilitating acceleration began in the spring of 1864 with the advent of Banks's Red River Campaign, another of his attempts to split the Trans-Mississippi area. Confederates captured about 4,000 Union forces during key battles at Mansfield and Pleasant Hill, Louisiana, and Marks's Mills, Arkansas, and most of those soon made their way to Tyler. As fighting intensified around northwestern Louisiana, officials also transferred prisoners over from Shreveport. The population at Camp Ford soon reached nearly 5,000, and slave crews once again worked on the stockade, expanding the interior space to more than 11 acres. As the number of prisoners increased and supplies drastically declined, disease and death rates soared. The death counts, approximated by month, showed alarming increases beginning in July, rising to a peak in October, and tapering off by November 1864, when the resumption of transfers began to ease the pressure on Camp Ford.

Living conditions at the camp were never ideal, given the lack of sanitary procedures and medical supplies, and the paucity of fresh clothing and food, but it became a scene of abject squalor in 1864. Mounting tensions within the camp populace also affected the guards, and there were concomitant increases in attempted prisoner escapes as well as harsh punishment. While prisoners recalled some measure of respect for Cmdr. Robert Thomas Pritchard Allen, who served from late 1863 to May 1864, they felt nothing but contempt and loathing for his successor, Col. J. P. Border. Allen, and especially his wife, tried as best they could to improve conditions at Camp Ford, but Border, who took over at the onset of its decline, chose to enforce his policies with an iron hand.

Life within Camp Ford was typical of that in any Civil War prison, and in many ways it reflected the best and worst of the greater society. Within its walls were countless incidents of greed, deception, gang violence, bribery, petty theft, and organized crime, but even as the prisoners endured overwhelming adversity, there was the abiding hope and strength of the human spirit as expressed in the arts, sports, friendships, and community structure. Prisoners cooked, worked on their housing, gardened as practicable, practiced rudimentary free enterprise, and crafted equipment, tools, weapons, musical instruments, a camp newspaper, and articles of clothing. Overall, however, they had to fight excruciating and debilitating boredom on a daily basis, and some fared better than others in that regard.

Escape was always a key objective for the prisoners, and they used a variety of means to break free of the stockade. While the guards instituted a *deadline*—a physical boundary inside the compound beyond which any would-be escapee faced immediate death—there were always those who challenged the system. Some dug lengthy tunnels, only to have them discovered or to find they came up short of their mark, while others hid in refuse carts awaiting escape at the garbage dump outside the walls. And there were those who schemed with local Union sympathizers, bribed guards, scurried under loosened logs, and simply ran away while on work details. Rainy days in particular were considered ideal for planned escapes, since downpours erased footprints and foiled the hounds and trackers inevitably sent in pursuit. While many were successful in their endeavors, many also failed to make it far from the camp, sometimes inadvertently circling back to the area, confused by the thick woods. Escape remained a continual effort throughout the camp's existence.

Rumors of the war's end always brought hope to the prisoners, but by the spring of 1865 the rumors seemed to come with more details than usual. When news of Gen. Robert E. Lee's surrender in Virginia reached the camp, it should have been a time of great celebration for the prisoners, but instead quickly came the speculation—with some degree of validity—that the war might continue on in the Trans-Mississippi. On May 13, 1865, though, official word came to those in charge that the prisoners would be exchanged in Shreveport. Most of the guards left the site that night to return home, and on the morning of the 15th, open gates greeted the detainees at daybreak. Rather than make a break for the surrounding woods, though, the prisoners remained on the grounds or in the immediate vicinity, sharing whiskey and tobacco with their former guards. Together, they faced an uneasy and uncertain future. Meanwhile, lawlessness prevailed in the surrounding area, as looters and deserters scavenged for food, clothing, and weapons. The prisoners felt safer in the camp, and so they remained to await the formal transfer, which came two days later. Then, riding in wagons under military escort by the 15th Texas Cavalry, some 1,200 former prisoners of war began their journey to Shreveport and eventual release. The following month a detail of the 10th Illinois Cavalry, including former inmates of Camp Ford, visited the site and destroyed the remaining structures, thus allowing the land to eventually be reclaimed by the surrounding woods. Today, a highway cuts

This 1865 lithograph depicts life at Camp Ford and provides a representation of the various types of shelters constructed by the prisoners. The scene also indicates how the formerly wooded site had been cleared of all standing timber. *From* Harper's Weekly, *March 4, 1865. Courtesy of Texas State Library and Archives Commission.*

through a portion of the site, and a 1962 Official Texas Historical Marker—the first placed by the Texas State Historical Survey Committee (now Texas Historical Commission)—marks the site. In recent years, local preservationists have worked to interpret the camp through informational kiosks and replica structures. There have also been extensive archeological investigations of the site under the direction of Texas A&M University.

Exact numbers for Camp Ford are unknown, but careful estimates of those incarcerated there indicate it housed about 6,000 men overall. Of that number, 286 are known to have died while in prison. In the years following the war, officials relocated the existing graves, with many reinterred at the Alexandria National Cemetery in Louisiana. The death total at Camp Ford was far below the average for prisoner camps in the South, and despite later official reports of harsh living conditions and

In 1998, Alston Thoms led Texas A&M University students in an intensive archeology investigation of the Camp Ford site. Despite sandy acidic soils, extensive woodland growth, and postwar agricultural use of the property, the survey crew was able to map important aspects of the prisoner-of-war camp through careful analysis of subsurface features and comparison of the archeological findings with archival records. *Courtesy of Stephen L. Black, PhD, Texas State University–San Marcos.*

treatment, especially in the latter years, the camp did not rival infamous places like Andersonville, Georgia, or Elmira, New York. In existence only a brief time, Camp Ford nonetheless served as the largest prisoner-of-war facility in the Trans-Mississippi Department of the Confederacy. The site remains an important reminder of the terrible human sacrifices associated with war and of the pivotal role Texas played in the conflict.

Location: Northeast of Tyler on US Highway 271, just north of Loop 323 on the east side of the road.

Access: Marker site and informational kiosks open to the public.

BATTLE OF SABINE PASS
(SEPTEMBER 8, 1863)

Visually, the Battle of Sabine Pass is difficult to comprehend in the modern context, and historians find it a challenging place to interpret for the general public. Massive, multistory drilling platforms under construction or repair dot the surrounding landscape while marine vessels of varying sizes ply the nearby waters of the pass. No longer do coastal marshes and low prairies dominate the immediate area, although they abound farther afield. As visitors to a small commemorative park read historical markers or photograph the central monument, they stand nine feet or more above the historic battlefield horizon, which has subsided over the years to be replaced with dredging spoil from the channel. The site of the historic fort that was the focal point of the Civil War battle now lies underneath the water several yards offshore. And across the park are newer intrusions: parking lots and picnic pavilions, ammunition magazines from later military campaigns, and a modern fishing pier. Most of the people who visit Sabine Battlefield State Historic Site these days come to fish or to spot birds and not to contemplate history.

Historically, the Battle of Sabine Pass is equally difficult to comprehend because of the complex human element it represents. Those who study the battle are often bewildered by the vagaries of the events that unfolded on September 8, 1863, and some come away with more questions than answers. The Battle of Sabine Pass offers one of the most compelling stories of the Civil War, involving a number of colorful characters and a grand scheme to hasten the end of the war, yet that story remains relatively obscure to this day. Today, the battlefield's remote location within an industrial complex not particularly conducive to heritage tourism only adds to that obscurity.

To understand the battle, it is first important to understand the underlying strategies that went into the planning. On the Union side was a stratified set of concerns that included the commodity demands of Northern textile mills, an interest in disrupting Southern commerce and blockade running, and a growing fear that failure to move on Texas immediately following a summer of victories at places like Gettysburg and Vicksburg would leave it vulnerable to outside influences from France, which then controlled Mexico. And it should be added that the future political and military concerns of those involved played into the decision-making as well. President Lincoln believed the Texas matter was more significant at the time than the securing of Mobile Bay, and he called on Maj. Gen. Henry Wager Halleck to devise a plan that would, in effect, quickly separate the state from the Confederacy. Halleck turned the operation over to a political military leader, Maj. Gen. Nathaniel Prentiss Banks, former governor of Massachusetts, and gave him considerable leeway in determining the point of attack. While Galveston, Indianola, and Brownsville were all under consideration, Banks instead chose to focus on Sabine Pass, believing the lightly guarded area would produce little resistance and that access to a natural harbor and the state's only railroads at the time would allow troops to move quickly on Beaumont, Houston, and Galveston, sealing those significant ports for the Union. From there, actions could be directed northeast to Shreveport or southwest to the Rio Grande. Banks relied on Comm. Henry Bell, a Southerner by birth and known for his aggressive tactics, to assist him with the overall planning.

In Texas, Maj. Gen. John Bankhead Magruder, the flamboyant hero of the Battle of Galveston, directed Confederate defenses. Acutely aware of the vulnerability of Sabine Pass, he called on his trusted engineers, Polish native Valery Sulakowski and Swiss native Julius Kellersberg, to design and construct an earthwork fortification farther up the pass from the earlier Fort Sabine, the site of a brief and insignificant attack in 1862. The site was at the head of a massive oyster reef that divided the pass into two narrow channels, one that ran along the Louisiana side and the other on the Texas side. African American slaves were impressed locally to build the fort. The new installation, dubbed Fort Griffin for Lt. Col. William H. Griffin, commander of the 21st Texas Infantry, would be on higher ground and closer to Sabine City. Six cannon, including two reconditioned pieces retrieved from the ruins of Fort Sabine, provided the only artillery power, but Sulakowski's plan allowed them to rake both south and east across the pass. Gun emplacements were in the military manner known as *en barbette,* an exposed arrangement that allowed greater flexibility than an enclosed portal configuration. The greatest vulnerability of the design was on the north face, but the likelihood of an enemy attack, the Southerners realized, was from the south.

By late August the Union plan under command of Maj. Gen. William Buel Franklin began to coalesce. It called for a joint army-navy amphibious assault through the pass, with navy gunboats providing cover for an initial landing of infantry forces numbering more than 5,000. More would later pour into the area once it had been secured. Capt. Frederick Crocker oversaw the naval operations and Brig. Gen. Godfrey Weitzel commanded the army's landing party. As preparations moved forward, the plan evolved decidedly in favor of the navy, with the army taking a secondary role, despite the fact that the army apparently could have landed at a more secure site along the coast. Union military leaders would later disagree on whether that option received serious consideration. Regardless, the eventual development of an all-or-nothing, navy-centric plan proved to be the crux of the joint operation.

The final battle plan called for a surprise attack to commence late on September 7, but as an advance party aboard the USS *Granite City* arrived off the Texas coast on the 6th to convey operational plans to the blockading force, the ship assigned to that locale was instead away refueling near Galveston. Fearing the worst and even reportedly sensing the presence of a ghost ship, the captain of the *Granite City* ordered the crew to fall back to Calcasieu Pass off the Louisiana coast, leaving Sabine Pass unguarded until other ships in the operation began to arrive. In the confusion that followed, the navy lost its element of surprise, but Crocker chose to regroup and proceed regardless on the 8th.

At the time of the attack, Capt. Frederick Odlum had temporary responsibility for Confederate forces around Beaumont and Sabine City, and he busied himself recruiting reinforcements. While he was away, Fort Griffin remained under the direct field command of Lt. Richard W. "Dick" Dowling, a popular saloon owner in Houston married to Odlum's niece, Annie. A native of Ireland, Dowling commanded a group of less than 50 men known as the Davis Guard, named for Confederate president Jefferson Davis and seasoned in service with John S. "Rip" Ford along the Rio Grande and with Magruder at the Battle of Galveston. Comprised of men of Irish heritage, the unit was officially commissioned as Company F of the 1st Texas Heavy Artillery under the command of Col. Joseph J. Cook, who provided extensive training in the principals of cannoneering. As the Davis Guard readied its station along the Sabine River in the days leading up to the battle, they regularly measured the effective range of their guns by placing large wooden stakes or posts along the far channel. These stakes would be a factor during the battle.

By September 7, Dowling and his men clearly knew they faced overwhelming odds. Their own reconnaissance, as well as observations from the CSS *Uncle Ben* anchored off Sabine City, indicated that more than two dozen ships—gunboats and transports—had massed outside the pass. As Magruder and Odlum considered the option of falling back to a more defensible position between Sabine City and Beaumont, Dowling ascertained that his men instead preferred the chance to hold the position as best they could. Upon learning of their resolve, Odlum concurred, issuing an order to "Hold the fort at all hazards."

The Union plan of attack in the pass called for four gunboats to cross the bar and make the initial assault. The gunboats selected were shallow-draft vessels valued for their ability to maneuver in the tight areas that characterized many of the Southern coastal waterways. Upon entry into the pass, the four gunboats would split into pairs, with the USS *Clifton,* a converted Staten Island ferryboat, taking the westernmost channel and heading directly toward the fort, followed by the USS *Granite City,* laden with sharpshooters who would be put ashore near the site of old Fort Sabine and from there would make an overland assault on the fort, providing cover to scatter the cannoneers. A diversionary tactic, though, would center on the two ships in the easternmost channel—the USS *Sachem* and the USS *Arizona*. As they made what appeared to be an attempt to pass the fort at full steam, they hoped to draw the guns in their direction, thus allowing the *Clifton* the opportunity to charge forward for a frontal assault and providing cover for the *Granite City* to the rear. If the *Clifton* were to be sacrificed, as anticipated, Union leaders believed either the infantry or the ships in the easternmost channel would eventually prevail, quickly overrunning the fort's limited defenses. With the site secure, the deeper-draft transports could then offload the troops along the coast without having to deal with the channel's sandbar. No one on the Northern side anticipated either intense resistance or a lengthy battle.

The Union gunboats drew their anchors at approximately 3:30 P.M., and the assault got underway 10 minutes later with opening rounds from the *Clifton* that surprisingly drew no response from the fort. Despite continued shelling, which either caused little damage or missed the mark entirely, the Confederate guns remained silent, leading some Union leaders to speculate they might be facing fake "Quaker guns."

Within minutes the *Arizona* ran aground on the reef, requiring assistance to break free, but the diversion of the faster vessels in the far channel allowed Dowling's men time to train their cannon in their direction. When the *Sachem* came within range, as marked by the poles she passed, the Confederates opened fire for the first time. Almost immediately, the boat ran aground in the mud, becoming a sitting target for the trained artillerymen of the fort. In short order, a round pierced her steam chamber, causing a cloud of scalding steam to envelop the boat and its crew. Efforts to continue firing the boat's guns in support of the *Clifton* proved fruitless as survivors abandoned the ship to save their lives. Given the general confusion of the moment and the narrow width of the channel, the captain of the *Arizona* abandoned his own route to provide rescue efforts for the *Sachem* and began trying to back down the channel out of the range of the fort's guns. Meanwhile, as planned, the *Clifton* began moving directly toward the fort under a full head of steam, but in that assault position the only armament it could utilize was the forward pivot gun, which not surprisingly proved ineffective. The boat also failed to gather the speed it needed, allowing the Davis Guard, now no longer distracted along the Louisiana channel, to train its remaining five guns—one fell from its position during the opening shots—on the Texas channel. A round quickly severed the boat's tiller rope, causing her to drift sideways in the channel, despite evasive efforts by the captain. While this broadside (starboard) position just 500 yards from the fort brought three more of the boat's guns to bear, it proved to be too late. A Confederate shot soon pierced the *Clifton*'s steam chest, with the same result as on the *Sachem* earlier. In the confusion that followed, even as Crocker ordered the operating guns to keep firing, the *Granite City* held back and neither offloaded the infantry nor moved up to provide cover. With both channels

The artist's depiction of the opening moments of the Battle of Sabine Pass shows the Union ships moving into position for the assault on the Confederate fortification. The view is to the north from the pass, with Texas on the left and Louisiana to the right. *Courtesy of Texas Parks and Wildlife Department.*

blocked, the *Arizona* in retreat, and no signs of immediate support, the commander finally accepted defeat and surrendered.

Unquestionably, the attack could have proceeded despite the setbacks of the initial assault. There were still thousands of armed soldiers just off the bar who could have gone ashore farther down the coast and worked back to the fort, even perhaps attacking it from the most vulnerable, northerly side. But as Banks and others would later argue, naval leaders ultimately made the decision to call off the operation. Soon, without further military action, the ships headed back to New Orleans.

An ironic dilemma faced Dowling and his Davis Guard following their unlikely victory against overwhelming odds. With less than 50 men at the site, how could they effectively round up and secure the hundreds of prisoners? If their small numbers became known immediately, they risked the possibility of a renewed assault from the infantry. Eventually, leaving a few men exposed on the ramparts to represent leaders

Visible in this recent photo of the Sabine Pass Battleground State Historic Site is the 1930s Dick Dowling monument (left center) and an ammunition magazine (right center) that dates from World War II. *Photo by William A. McWhorter. Courtesy of Texas Historical Commission.*

of available reserves, Dowling and others moved forward to effect surrender, and the Union offered no resistance.

The Battle of Sabine Pass lasted an hour and a half. During that time the Davis Guard discharged over 130 rounds from essentially five cannon, overworking them to such a degree that their heat scorched skin to the bone upon touch and remained too hot to handle well into the following day. Against unbelievable odds Dowling and his men also grounded two heavily armed gunboats and chased two away, diverted a planned amphibious assault by thousands of soldiers, captured approximately 350 prisoners, and ended the immediate threat of Union invasion along the upper Texas coast. Understandably, the Davis Guard members quickly achieved hero status in Texas. Union officers Banks, Franklin, Crocker, Bell, and others who planned the attack at Sabine Pass did not fare as well, though, having to defend their controversial decisions throughout their careers.

Despite setbacks at Galveston and Sabine Pass in 1863, the Union command nonetheless continued efforts to make a stand in Texas, primarily due to the intervention of France in Mexico and the need to disrupt the Confederate cotton trade. To those ends, the focus soon turned farther south to the Rio Grande and the occupation of Brownsville. Successes there, however, ultimately did little to address either objective. Never again, though, did Texas face a major invasion during the war, and Sabine Pass remained an open port, although the Union operated a continual though limited blockade against it.

While the fight at Sabine Pass remains one of the lesser known events of the Civil War, it was celebrated at the time as a key Confederate victory following a summer of significant setbacks for the South. Years after the close of the war, as military historian Edward T. Cotham Jr. noted, Jefferson Davis was among those who worked to keep the story alive. At an 1882 gathering of the Southern Historical Society in New Orleans, the former president of the Confederacy compared the bravery of the Davis Guard to the heroic stand by Spartans who defiantly guarded a key pass against an overwhelming Persian force in 480 BC. Observing that few people even at the time of his speech could recall the name of the Fort Griffin commander, Davis added, "And yet, that battle at Sabine Pass was more remarkable than the battle of Thermopylae, and when it has orators and poets to celebrate it, will be so esteemed by mankind."

Location: Sabine Pass Battleground State Historic Site, administered by the Texas Historical Commission, is 1.5 miles south of the town of Sabine Pass, Jefferson County, on Dick Dowling Road. Historical exhibits related to the battle are housed in the Museum of the Gulf Coast, 700 Procter Street, Port Arthur.

Access: Both the battleground park and the museum are open to the public.

SOURCES

Boyd, Eva Jolene. *Noble Brutes: Camels on the Western Frontier.* Plano: Republic of Texas Press, 1995.

Casdorph, Paul D. *Prince John Magruder: His Life and Campaigns.* New York: John Wiley & Sons, 1996.

Colton, Ray C. *The Civil War in the Western Territories: Arizona, Colorado, New Mexico, and Utah.* Norman: University of Oklahoma Press, 1959.

Cotham, Edward T. Jr. *Battle on the Bay: The Civil War Struggle for Galveston.* Austin: University of Texas Press, 1998.

———. *Sabine Pass: The Confederacy's Thermopylae.* Austin: University of Texas Press, 2004.

Dupree, Stephen A. *Planting the Union Flag in Texas: The Campaigns of Major General Nathaniel P. Banks.* College Station: Texas A&M University Press, 2008.

Foote, Shelby. *The Civil War: A Narrative: Fort Sumter to Perryville.* New York: Vintage Books, 1958.

Frazier, Donald S. *Blood and Treasure: Confederate Empire in the Southwest.* College Station: Texas A&M University Press, 1995.

———. *Cottonclads! The Battle of Galveston and the Defense of the Texas Coast.* Abilene: McWhiney Foundation Press, 1998.

Glover, Robert W., and Randal B. Gilbert. *Camp Ford, Tyler, Texas: The Largest Confederate Prison Camp West of the Mississippi River.* Tyler: Smith County Historical Society, 1989.

Grear, Charles David. *Why Texans Fought in the Civil War.* College Station: Texas A&M University Press, 2010.

Lawrence, F. Lee and Robert W. Glover. *Camp Ford, C.S.A.: The Story of Union Prisoners in Texas.* Austin: Texas Civil War Advisory Committee, 1964.

McDonald, Archie P. "The Civil War and the Lone Star State: A Brief Overview," *The Seventh Star of the Confederacy: Texas during the Civil War,* ed. Kenneth W. Howell. Denton: University of North Texas Press, 2009.

Mitchell, Leon Jr. "Camp Ford: Confederate Military Prison." *Southwestern Historical Quarterly* 66, no. 1 (July 1962): 1–16.

Settles, Thomas M. *John Bankhead Magruder: A Military Reappraisal.* Baton Rouge: Louisiana State University Press, 2009.

Smallwood, James M. "Prison City, Camp Ford: Largest Confederate Prisoner-of-war Camp in the Trans-Mississippi," in *The Seventh Star of the Confederacy: Texas during the Civil War,* ed. Kenneth W. Howell. Denton: University of North Texas Press, 2009.

Thompson, Jerry. *Confederate General of the West: Henry Hopkins Sibley.* College Station: Texas A&M University Press, 1996.

Tolbert, Frank X. *Dick Dowling at Sabine Pass.* New York: McGraw-Hill, 1962.

Townsend, Stephen A. *The Yankee Invasion of Texas.* College Station: Texas A&M University Press, 2006.

Utley, Robert M. *Fort Union National Monument.* Washington, DC: National Park Service, US Department of the Interior, 1962.

Wooster, Ralph A. *Civil War Texas.* Austin: Texas State Historical Association, 1999.

———. *Texas and Texans in the Civil War.* Austin: Eakin Press, 1995.

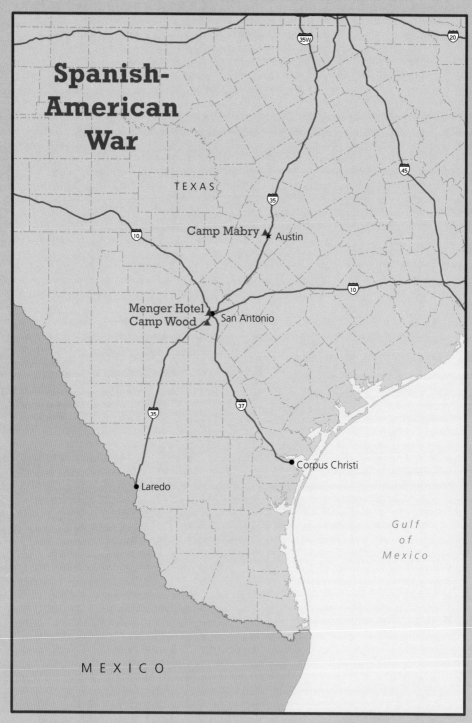

Spanish-
American
War

TEXAS

Camp Mabry ▲ Austin

Menger Hotel
Camp Wood ▲ San Antonio

Laredo

Corpus Christi

Gulf
of
Mexico

MEXICO

Map by Molly O'Halloran

THE SPANISH-AMERICAN WAR 1898

These men are wild. If we don't get them to Cuba quickly to fight the Spanish there is a real danger they'll be fighting themselves.

—Col. Leonard Wood

The Spanish-American War of 1898 marked both a turning point in American foreign policy and a maturation of a new national vision of the United States as a rising global power. It was a conflict Americans engaged in not because of an imminent threat to national security, as in past disputes, but rather out of a collective sense of moral obligation. But there were also underlying currents of expansionism and imperialism, despite a long-standing trend toward isolationism. In the decades following the Civil War, the United States increasingly found itself on the periphery of complex foreign affairs in such locales as the West Indies, Samoa, Hawaii, and Venezuela, among others. By the mid-1890s it also had to deal with the matter of Cuba.

For years Spain had dealt with its role as a declining empire, in large part because of unrest in Latin America, but through it all Cuba remained loyal to the crown and therefore received favored status. But a spirit of independence grew there nonetheless and spilled over in the 1870s and again in the 1890s. By the time of the second major rebellion, Spain began implementing stronger measures to quell any further disturbances. Under Gen. Valeriano Weyler, the Spanish government instituted concentration camps and cast a wide net for what it loosely defined as insurrectionists and revolutionary sympathizers. Word of atrocities in the camps and in the rural areas of the territory spread to the United States, where the "yellow press" of the time took up the cause and through its sensationalist reporting pressured the American people and political leadership to intervene in support of the rebels.

In the ensuing debate, Pres. Grover Cleveland and his successor, Pres. William McKinley, were reluctant to get involved in the war. Committed as past presidents were to upholding the Monroe Doctrine which discouraged foreign involvement in the Western Hemisphere, they were also aware that existing foreign ties were, in effect, exempt. While the United States had used its power to support in principle earlier Latin American struggles for independence and had even sent its ships into harm's way to protect its citizens in times of revolution, it had never unleashed its power in support of any warring nation. By the late 1890s, though, a changing national vision of its military strength and moral obligations changed the way the United States reacted to such matters.

Following a particularly intense riot at Havana in January 1898, the US government sent the battleship *Maine* to provide protection for American citizens and also American business interests. While anchored in Havana harbor on the evening of February 15, an explosion ripped through the ship, sinking it and killing 260 crewmen. Although a Navy Department board of inquiry determined the cause to be a mine, it failed to identify the parties responsible for the incident. Regardless, the yellow press intensified the call for action against Spain. In late March, President McKinley sought first a diplomatic solution, calling on the Spanish government to declare a temporary armistice and to end its policy of concentration camps. But quickly giving in to mounting pressures for military intervention, he decided to forego diplomacy in favor of a war resolution from Congress, which he received on April 20. In the resolution, Congress stated its recognition of an independent Cuba, emphasizing that the United States sought no territorial claims on the island. It called on Spain to withdraw its forces immediately and authorized the president to utilize military power to prosecute the demands. In quick succession, Spain withdrew its diplomats from the United States, which in return instituted a blockade of prime Cuban ports. Spain followed that action with a declaration of war, and the United States reciprocated, marking the start of the intense and pivotal, but short-lived, Spanish-American War.

At the opening of the conflict, U.S. military strength rested with the navy, because the army was ill prepared in terms of both personnel and supplies to wage an overseas assault against entrenched forces in a tropical locale. Congress acted immediately to address the weakness, authorizing a major call-up of both regulars and volunteers. American citizens, primed for action against what they perceived as an evil empire, quickly filled the ranks, and "Remember the *Maine*" became the rallying cry for an unprecedented war. Naval actions at Manila Bay under Comm. George Dewey and along the Cuban coast under R. Adm. William T. Sampson and Comm. Winfield S.

Schley gave the United States the upper hand in the war. Among the warships included in the decisive movements against Cuba was the USS *Texas*. Army forces under Maj. Gen. William Shafter, most notably the Rough Riders, led by Leonard Wood and Teddy Roosevelt and trained at San Antonio, provided the pressure by land that in turn led to the demise of the remaining Spanish naval fleet in Cuba. By August the war was over, but resulting foreign policy questions lingered for generations, carrying over to future conflicts. But for the moment, the hostilities formally ended with the Treaty of Paris on December 10, 1898. Under its provisions, Spain renounced claims on Cuba and ceded Puerto Rico and Guam to the United States. Additionally, giving into McKinley's demands, Spain also ceded the Philippines in return for a payment of $20 million and agreeing to assume liability for Cuba's considerable debts.

MENGER HOTEL
(1852–PRESENT)

Located immediately adjacent to the Alamo compound in downtown San Antonio, the Menger Hotel is certainly not a typical military site. Neither is it a typical hotel, having remained in operation since before the Civil War. Given its prominent location at the commercial center of San Antonio, one of the nation's leading military towns, it is not surprising its history includes a strong military connection. Among the noteworthy individuals who reportedly stayed there are several with distinguished careers in the armed forces, including Robert E. Lee, Ulysses S. Grant, Sam Houston, and John J. Pershing. But perhaps the most compelling and enduring military association involves an oft-told tale from the time of the Spanish-American War and a visit by Theodore Roosevelt.

To place the story in its proper context, it is important to understand the role the Menger Hotel played in the early development of San Antonio's commercial core in the decades following the Texas Revolution. German-native William Achatius Menger, a cooper by trade, immigrated to the city in 1847 and soon after met and married Mary Baumschleuter Guenther, also of Germany. In 1855, William started a small brewery on his property adjacent to the Alamo. As the business grew he added a tavern and Mary opened a boardinghouse. Within a few short years, the couple decided to expand the operation to include a 50-room inn, and they hired John M. Fries and builder J. H. Kampmann to oversee the work. The inn opened in 1859, and within a year the Mengers embarked on the first of what would be many additions to the thriving enterprise over the years. Adding to the significance of the Menger Hotel as a successful business venture were the numerous civic contributions of its owners. William Menger served as a city alderman and a member of the fire department, and together the couple supported a number of worthy causes, including the Santa Rosa Hospital. They were also instrumental in promoting the role of the US Army in the city's growth. William died at an early age in 1871, but Mary and her son, Louis William, continued the hotel operation for 10 years, eventually selling to Maj. John H. Kampmann, the hotel's builder. A native of Prussia who studied architecture as well as the building trades, Kampmann came to San Antonio in 1848 and wed Caroline Bonnet the next year. Following military service with other German Texans during the Civil War, he became a prominent businessman in San Antonio, establishing several enterprises, including a sash, blind, and door factory, and constructing a number of prominent structures in the city.

Several years prior to his death in 1885, Kampmann began turning over business operations, including the Menger Hotel, to his son, Hermann D. Kampmann. A savvy and influential business leader in his own right, with interests in banking and real estate, Hermann quickly made his own mark on the hotel. Continuing his father's efforts to enlarge the facility, he further sought to introduce greater sophistication in the design and furnishings. To that end, he reportedly sent an architect to London to study the elaborate detailings of the pub at the House of Lords, which served to influence the style of the Menger's new tap room that is the focal point of the Spanish-American War story. As originally built, the bar was larger than the present facility and included a poolroom with two tables and an assembly room furnished with ornate mahogany tables and chairs. Additional details included large mirrors, a paneled wood ceiling, glass-front cabinets, and brass footrests. Service ware of fine crystal and sterling silver complemented the setting, reflecting a European gentleman's club of high design.

With the onset of the Spanish-American War in April 1898, Congress authorized the War Department to quickly recruit three volunteer regiments of cavalry. The 1st Regiment, which came to be known more informally as the Rough Riders, was initially to be drawn from the nation's western territories. Secretary of War Russell A. Alger offered the command to Theodore Roosevelt, then the assistant secretary of the navy, but Roosevelt fully realized his limitations as a military leader and thus declined in favor of his friend, Leonard Wood, an experienced commander and President McKinley's personal physician. Wood accepted the command and received an appointment as colonel, while Roosevelt signed on as the second in command with the rank of lieutenant colonel.

Soldiers recruited primarily in the West soon made plans to rendezvous in San Antonio for training. Wood arrived in the Alamo City on May 5 and, after visiting Fort Sam Houston to secure equipment and horses, made his way several miles south of town to Riverside Park to oversee development of the training camp called Camp Wood (see chapter 5 for more discussion of the camp). Roosevelt remained behind in Washington to finalize his assignments with the navy and to make supply arrangements on behalf of the 1st Regiment, but he finally arrived in San Antonio on May 16. According to the story handed down over the years, Roosevelt personally recruited members of the Rough Riders in the hotel bar (or courtyard, depending on the version). Whether or not that happened is open to speculation, but regardless, there were other associations between the hotel establishment and the Rough Riders that can be adequately documented.

Roosevelt first stayed in the Menger Hotel during an 1892 visit to the San Antonio area. Six years later, when he arrived by train to join the Rough Riders at Camp Wood, he made his way to the hotel for breakfast and there met with regimental leaders, including Colonel Wood, who escorted him to the training camp that morning. There, Roosevelt set up his office in a tent adjacent to Wood's, and in the days to follow he busied himself with matters related to troop drills, discipline, and morale, and also visited with newspaper reporters wanting to know more about his association with the unit. While Wood remained the official commander, he could not compete in terms of public interest with the more colorful and dynamic Roosevelt. While TR's presence no doubt continued to attract curious bystanders and would-be recruits who frequented the campground trying to catch a glimpse of him, the Rough Riders had reached allowable limits by the time he arrived in San Antonio. It is known, though, that he made exceptions, so it is possible he may have done so at the Menger Bar. A more likely scenario is that Colonel Wood recruited the last of the unit members there, as he was in town much earlier. At least a few of those Roosevelt is known to have personally recruited prior to reaching San Antonio—the so-called Fifth Avenue Boys (or Crowd) among them—enjoyed a final night of luxury at the Menger upon arrival in San Antonio before committing to the rustic realities of camp life.

Another association with the Rough Riders occurred after the war, in 1905, when then Pres. Theodore Roosevelt participated in a unit reunion at the Menger Hotel. Only three years later, though, as part of the continual renovations that marked the evolutionary history of the hotel, the owners relocated the historic bar to a new site within the complex. The tap room closed altogether in 1918 with the advent of Prohibition, although the owners retained the furnishings and reopened it years later after the amendment's repeal. In 1948, new owners moved the bar to its current, smaller site, where it remains an important feature for hotel patrons and heritage tourists. Despite numerous changes to the bar and to the hotel over the years, the Texas State Historical Survey Committee (now the Texas Historical Commission) designated the structure a Recorded Texas Historic Landmark in 1965 due to its architectural integrity and historical significance.

Location: 204 Alamo Plaza, San Antonio.
Access: Bar and hotel open to the public.

The Menger Hotel, ca. 1890s. This photo depicts the historic hotel as it would have looked at the time Col. Theodore Roosevelt and Col. Leonard Wood began assembling the Rough Riders in San Antonio. *Institute of Texan Cultures, University of Texas at San Antonio, #095–0503. Courtesy of Hall Hammond.*

CAMP MABRY
(1892–PRESENT)

Located on the near west side of downtown Austin and immediately adjacent to busy Loop 1 (Mopac Expressway) is a military installation that today houses offices of the Adjutant General of Texas, the Texas Army National Guard, the Texas Air National Guard, and the Texas State Guard, as well as the Texas Military Forces Museum. The collection of distinctive limestone, brick, and metal structures, now listed in the National Register of Historic Places, is evocative of earlier military eras, most notably World Wars I and II, but Camp Mabry has historic ties to the Spanish-American War.

In 1892, at the height of the Gilded Age marked by unprecedented industrial

This 2010 photo shows the historic section of the Menger Hotel within the context of the urban cultural landscape that has developed around the site. *Photo by Dan K. Utley.*

growth, economic expansion, and global unrest, a group of interested Austin citizens donated a tract of land to the State of Texas to serve as an encampment and maneuver site for the Texas Volunteer Guard, as the state militia was then known. Located three miles north-northwest of the Capitol, it opened for guard training operations the same year. There were no permanent military buildings on the property at the time, and for years the guard stored much of its equipment in the Capitol basement. Local citizens helped clear part of the site for a drill field (later parade ground) and small dam with a nearby picnic area. They also raised funds for construction of a grandstand adjacent to the drill field which provided space for viewing military maneuvers and also housed the base commander's office during the initial encampments. The grandstand burned in 1902 and a new dam replaced the original one in the 1930s, but the parade ground (now reduced from its original configuration) and picnic area remain as historical evidence of the site's earliest days.

Shortly after it opened, guard members voted to name the camp for Woodford Haywood Mabry, appointed adjutant general of Texas by Gov. James Stephen Hogg

(1.)

(3.)

(2.)

(4.) One of the earliest known photos of Camp Mabry, this scene of troops gathered on the parade ground dates from 1911 but depicts the camp much as it would have looked during preparations for the Spanish-American War several years before. The view to the west shows the Mount Bonnell ridge line along the Colorado River. *Courtesy of Texas Military Forces Museum, Austin.*

(5.) Camp Mabry then *(Continued)*

in 1891. In that capacity, Mabry also served on the site selection committee. A native of Jefferson, Texas, and the son of a celebrated Confederate colonel, Mabry attended Virginia Military Institute, where one of his classmates and friends was Charles A. Culberson, later governor of Texas during the Spanish-American War. Upon graduation, Mabry served on the staff of Brig. Gen. Lawrence Sullivan Ross and enjoyed success as a merchant prior to his state appointment. When the war against Spain broke out, Mabry resigned as adjutant general and accepted commission as a colonel with the 1st Texas Infantry. Soon after arriving in Havana, he contracted cerebral meningitis (or cerebral malaria) and died there at Camp Columbia in January 1899. His body was returned to Jefferson for burial beside his father's grave.

As the war got underway, Governor Culberson called for volunteers to be mustered into service at Camp Mabry, marking its first use in a national war effort. An estimated 4,200 men answered the call. As there were no permanent structures on the grounds at the time, a tent city sprang up when training operations got underway. A nearby rail line, a key element of the initial site selection, provided necessary transportation for both materiel and soldiers. As the war concluded in 1899, Camp Mabry remained in operation, with new facilities and tracts of land added soon after. During World War I, the University of Texas contracted with the US Army to run an automobile mechanics training facility there, and buildings of that era included barracks and workshops. In the ensuing years, other organizations became temporary tenants, including the Texas Rangers, the Texas Department of Highways, and the Department

Camp Mabry's historic parade ground is rimmed with static displays that depict the installation's continuing role in military preparedness through the years. *Photo by Dan K. Utley.*

of Public Safety. Beginning in the 1930s, work programs associated with the New Deal under Pres. Franklin D. Roosevelt resulted in significant improvements to the infrastructure. More construction, including both temporary and permanent structures, went on during the World War II years as the site's scope of service expanded.

Camp Mabry has remained in continuous operation through subsequent military campaigns and the Cold War era. In the years following the terrorist attacks on New York and Washington in 2001, heightened security concerns resulted in restrictions to public access, but the Brig. Gen. John C. L. Scribner Texas Military Forces Museum, adjacent to the historic parade ground, remains open to the public, providing exhibits and static displays depicting the role of the state guard throughout its history. Camp Mabry is now the third-oldest active military installation in the state, behind only Fort Bliss and Fort Sam Houston, and it serves as one of the few reminders of the role Texas forces played in preparedness for the Spanish-American War.

Location: 2200 West 35th Street, Austin.

Access: Although visitation to the camp is limited and subject to security procedures, the museum is open to the public. Photo identification is required at the main gate.

CAMP WOOD (SAN ANTONIO)
(MAY 5–30, 1892)

When the United States entered into war against Spain in the spring of 1898, Theodore Roosevelt and Leonard Wood were in Washington, DC, at the epicenter of political activity and national military preparedness, and both seemed destined to assume command positions for troops headed off to Cuba. The two friends felt strongly about the justification for war but also understood their involvement could serve to further their own personal objectives, Roosevelt's in politics and Wood's in the military. Despite their early efforts to secure line commands even before the formal onset of war, they found themselves passed over in favor of more experienced military men. That changed in April, with congressional approval of three new western regiments, and they were soon working in tandem to plan for creation of the 1st US Volunteer Cavalry.

From the beginning of their efforts, Wood and Roosevelt seemed to understand clearly their individual leadership strengths. Wood, the only one of the two with actual military command experience through limited but distinguished service in the Indian Wars against Geronimo's forces in Arizona, for which he received the Medal of Honor, was a devoted student of modern military tactics. Skillful as a rifleman and horseman, and a proponent of new technologies, he had a reputation for clear judgment and executive decision-making. To him would fall the responsibility for the comprehensive regimental structure from the ground up, with due attention to maps, lines of communication, and adherence to general orders.

By contrast, Roosevelt was charismatic and motivational, and therefore charged with direct oversight of troop training and morale. Because he was by far the better known of the two by the general public through his writings, adventures, and political career, he enjoyed something of a celebrity's status, and the public quickly associated his name with the cavalry unit, even though he was at the time second in command. Roosevelt also had political connections which he used early on to the regiment's benefit. Despite the volunteer status of his regiment, Wood pressed for the same equipment procurements as the regulars, and Roosevelt worked through the inner circles in Washington to make it happen. Most significantly, that came in the form of armaments. Rather than depending on outmoded single-shot, black powder Springfield rifles, as other volunteer units did, Roosevelt successfully pushed for the more advanced foreign design of .30-.40 caliber, bolt action, five-shot Krag-Jørgenson rifles that fired smokeless ammunition. Completing the individual weaponry were .45-caliber pistols and machetes.

As planning for the regiment got underway, Wood was the first to make his way to San Antonio. As he did, recruits assembled in the territories at Prescott, Arizona; Santa Fe, New Mexico; Guthrie, Oklahoma; and Muskogee, Indian Territory, before heading to the Alamo City. While the initial intent was to limit the unit to 780, mostly cowboys, miners, railroaders, hunters, lawmen, and similar frontier stock from the territories, others—including Texans—soon joined up as well, resulting in an increase to 1,000 and providing a broader measure of diversity. Roosevelt, giving in to the influence of longtime friends and political colleagues, also recruited a number of individuals from the eastern United States who were aristocrats, Ivy League graduates, young urban professionals, society club members, and even polo players. Designated Company K but informally known as the Fifth Avenue Crowd or the "lah-de-dah boys," the elite corps quickly adjusted to the rigors of military life. In all, the Rough Riders were an odd mixture held together in large part by the steady leadership of Wood and the military vision of Roosevelt.

Colonel Wood reached San Antonio early on the morning of May 5, 1898, and by the afternoon was at Riverside Park, the site of Camp Wood. Within days, recruits from Arizona and the Indian Territory joined him, and supplies and animals began reaching the camp as well. Most of the integral elements of the unit, including the remaining companies, were in place by the time Roosevelt arrived at the Southern Pacific depot on May 15 wearing his specially designed Brooks Brothers uniform. The uniforms of the volunteers proved to be less elaborate, but they nonetheless reflected the design considerations of the regimental leaders. As Roosevelt observed, "In their slouch hats, blue flannel shirts, brown trousers, leggings and boots, with handkerchiefs knotted loosely around their necks, they looked exactly as a body of cowboy cavalry should look."

Riverside Park provided an ideal setting for Camp Wood. The San Antonio and Aransas Pass Railway developed the site in the 1880s as a means of promoting local land sales and also attracting tourists to the mission area south of downtown. Comprising more than 300 acres and located adjacent to the grounds of the San Antonio International Fair and Exposition (to the east), which ran seasonally from 1888 to the early 1900s, it was at one time the largest tract of parkland in the city—albeit privately owned—and a popular destination for picnics and weekend excursions. A funeral director purchased the property in 1892 to develop it as a cemetery, but local opposition forced him to abandon the plan, and it remained an informal park. A trolley line served the area at the time of Camp Wood, providing a way for the crowds to come and watch the soldiers train, observe their mock battles, and perhaps catch a glimpse of Teddy Roosevelt.

City leaders were understandably proud of their important role in the military preparedness for the war. One symbol of that pride was a local brass and drum corps under the direction of "Professor" Carl Beck that performed concerts on occasion

While the Rough Riders trained at Camp Wood, they conducted some exercises and public reviews at nearby Mission Concepción, where this photo was taken. Col. Theodore Roosevelt is in the center. *San Antonio Light Collection, Institute of Texan Cultures, University of Texas at San Antonio, #L-0066-B. Courtesy of Hearst Corporation.*

for the soldiers, including one on May 14 on the eve of Roosevelt's arrival. Among the more popular pieces the band performed were the "Star Spangled Banner," "Dixie," "La Paloma," "Manhattan Beach," and the number that became the unofficial theme song for the Rough Riders, "There'll Be a Hot Time in the Old Town Tonight." The latter proved particularly appropriate for a concert later that month when a rousing cavalry charge from the band, coupled with the firing of a weapon (sources differ on whether it was a pistol or a ceremonial cannon), set off a brief but intense stampede and ensuing fusillade from the startled soldiers as spectators dove for cover behind trees and under park benches or ran for the gateway.

In general, the daily routine at Camp Wood began at 5:30 A.M. with the sounding of reveille, followed by the feeding and care of the horses. Mounted drills (which began May 23) or marching got underway by 8:30, with dinner (lunch) at 1:30 and then afternoons and early evenings devoted to marksmanship training, additional drills, marching, inspections, and the occasional dress parade, some conducted at nearby Mission San José. Evening meals occurred at 7:00 P.M., followed by "Tattoo" at 8:30 and "Taps" 30 minutes later. Although the earliest soldiers reporting to the camp

A neglected stone monument along South Roosevelt Avenue in San Antonio commemorates the site of Camp Wood, where the Rough Riders trained in 1898. Visible through the fence in the background is Riverside Golf Course, which encompasses much of the temporary camp. Not visible are a series of companion stones to this central monument that are inscribed "No North, No South, No East, No West," a reference to the unified action of the first major national military campaign following the Civil War. At the time of this photo in 2010, local preservationists were discussing preliminary plans to restore the monument at a location nearer the golf course where it would be more accessible to the public. *Photo by Dan K. Utley.*

stayed in Exposition Hall, all the companies relocated to so-called dog tents when they became available. As the tent city took shape, so too did informal interior streets with names such as (Commodore George) Dewey Avenue, Manila Avenue, and Arizona Avenue. Heat, blowing sand, mosquitoes, and the occasional tarantula contributed to daily camp life, as did sporadic fights and confrontations. Overall, though, there were few complications in the training process, and in short order the unit appeared ready for battle.

On May 23, Colonel Wood received an official communiqué inquiring about when he would be ready for shipping out, to which he replied "at once." Four days later came the word to prepare the troop train, and he duly notified Southern Pacific officials the regiment would require 25 coaches for personnel, two Pullmans, several boxcars and baggage cars, and 60 livestock cars. Quickly, the troops packed equipment and transported it to the Union Stockyards southwest of downtown. Reveille sounded at 3:00 A.M. on the morning of May 29, and soldiers soon began striking the camp and policing the grounds. The first group reportedly mounted up and headed out just after daybreak for the three-mile trek to the rail line, but despite the preparations the loading did not go as planned due to a lack of feed and an inadequate number of loading chutes for the animals, and then a shortage of coaches for the troops. As some soldiers worked to construct new ramps, others wandered off to nearby bars, necessitating a widespread roundup later that evening as the loading neared completion. With all supplies, stock, and personnel finally on board early on the morning of May 30, the troop train finally pulled out of San Antonio before daybreak. The route to Tampa, Florida, where the unit would join up with the Fifth Army Corps under Maj. Gen. William R. "Pecos Bill" Shafter, took the train through Houston, New Orleans, Mobile, and Tallahassee, and all along the way large crowds gathered to cheer on the Rough Riders.

Despite intensive training in cavalry maneuvers during their stay in Texas, the Rough Riders ultimately went ashore at Daiquiri, Cuba, as a smaller dismounted unit on June 22. Two days later they experienced their first battle at Las Guásimas, and by the end of the month they joined other US forces closing in on the fortified city of Santiago. Prior to reaching the objective, Colonel Wood received promotion to brigadier general and Roosevelt became colonel of the Rough Riders. At Santiago, on July 1, his men displayed uncommon valor and determination in the successful assault on the San Juan Heights, an episode remembered in history as the Battle of San Juan Hill despite the fact it occurred on Kettle Hill. The actions of the Rough Riders proved to be a pivotal point in the war, breaking key defenses and causing the Spanish navy to retreat toward eventual destruction by American naval forces. For his bravery as commander of the Rough Riders on that eventful day, Roosevelt eventually received the Medal of Honor.

The Spanish-American War officially ended on August 12, 1898, resulting in a new role for the United States as a global power and the protector of far-flung lands. Two days later, the Rough Riders who served in Cuba arrived at Montauk Point on Long Island, New York, joining up with the companies they left behind at Tampa. After days marked by celebrations, congratulatory speeches, special presentations, transfer of supplies, and for some, medical treatment, the Rough Riders formally disbanded on September 15. In a brief history that spanned less than half a year, the unit achieved much, securing legendary status and a revered role in US military history, and it all began with the training at Camp Wood, in existence for less than 30 days.

As the war overseas moved steadily toward its ultimate conclusion, Riverside Park reverted temporarily to its former role as a privately owned recreation point for the community. With the opening of the much larger Brackenridge Park on the north side of the city in 1901, though, Riverside declined in popularity, resulting in its eventual abandonment. By the 1920s, however, responding to renewed interest in a park for the area, the City of San Antonio purchased 90 acres and initially named it in honor of its favored adopted son, Theodore Roosevelt. Later, it became known once again as Riverside Park upon the dedication of a new Roosevelt Park closer to town. Today, the east side of the public golf course at Riverside—located adjacent to Roosevelt Avenue—covers part of the historic footprint of what was Camp Wood. Few people today know of the site's connection with a legendary military unit, an international war, and a future US president, but those seeking the link (no pun intended) can find it in the words of Roosevelt, who never forgot his connection with the Alamo City. Writing about his days as a Rough Rider in training, he noted fondly, "We had enjoyed San Antonio, and were glad that our regiment had been organized in the city where the Alamo commemorates the death fight of Crockett, Bowie, and their famous band of frontier heroes."

Location: Roosevelt Drive, south of downtown San Antonio, in the general vicinity of Riverside Golf Course.
Access: Residential and commercial areas accessed via city streets.

SOURCES

Bradford, James C., ed. *Crucible of Empire: The Spanish-American War and Its Aftermath.* Annapolis, MD: Naval Institute Press, 1993.

Brinkley, Douglas. *The Wilderness Warrior: Theodore Roosevelt and the Crusade for America.* New York: Harper Collins, 2009.

Camp Mabry vertical files, Brig. Gen. John C.L. Scribner Texas Military Forces Museum, Austin.

Hendrickson, Kenneth E. Jr. *The Spanish-American War.* Westport, CT: Greenwood Press, 2003.

Jones, Virgil Carrington. *Roosevelt's Rough Riders.* Garden City, NY: Doubleday, 1971.

Lane, Jack C. *Armed Progressive: General Leonard Wood.* San Rafael, CA: Presidio Press, 1978.

Miller, Nathan. *Theodore Roosevelt: A Life.* New York: William Morrow, 1992.

Rayburn, John C. "The Rough Riders in San Antonio, 1898." *Arizona and the West* 3, no. 2 (Summer 1961): 113–28.

Roosevelt, Theodore. *The Rough Riders.* New York: Library of America, 2004.

Smith, Joseph. *The Spanish-American War: Conflict in the Caribbean and the Pacific, 1895–1902.* New York: Longman, 1994.

Texas Historical Commission marker files, Bexar County.

Walker, Dale L. *The Boys of '98: Theodore Roosevelt and the Rough Riders.* New York: Tom Doherty Associates Book, 1998.

Williams, Docia Schultz. The *History and Mystery of the Menger Hotel.* Plano: Republic of Texas Press, 2000.

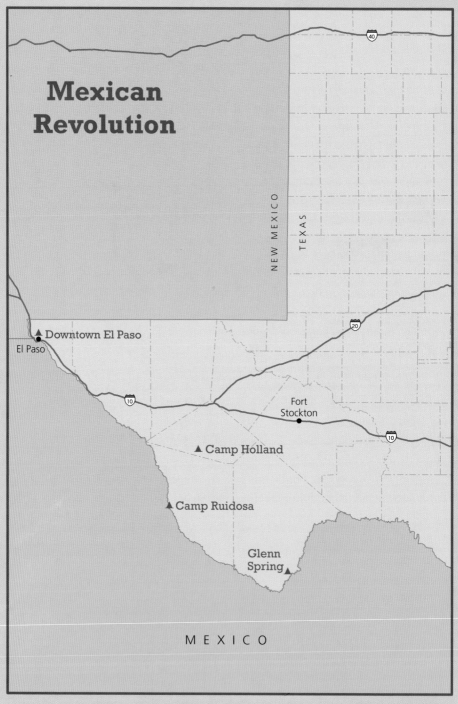

Mexican Revolution

NEW MEXICO

TEXAS

▲ Downtown El Paso
El Paso

Fort
Stockton

▲ Camp Holland

▲ Camp Ruidosa

Glenn
Spring ▲

MEXICO

Map by Molly O'Halloran

THE MEXICAN REVOLUTION 1910–1920

There can no longer be any doubt about it. The bloody Revolution that has long inundated all of Mexico with murder and mayhem has now flowed across the Rio Grande to lap at our very doorstep.

—Alpine Avalanche, Alpine, Texas, May 12, 1916

Although no formally declared state of war existed between Mexico and the United States during the Mexican Revolution of 1910, armed conflicts between military forces of both nations took place. The best known of these clashes was the attack on Columbus, New Mexico, by the Revolution's Gen. Francisco "Pancho" Villa on March 9, 1916. This unprovoked and still largely unfathomable invasion of American territory by a foreign military force was the first since the return of the British in the War of 1812. The Columbus Raid in turn immediately prompted Brig. Gen. John "Black Jack" Pershing's ill-fated Punitive Expedition, which marked the first formal invasion of foreign territory by the American army since the Mexican War of 1846.

Because it shares as a border with Mexico more than 1,000 miles of the Rio Grande, Texas was directly involved in many aspects of the Revolution. When a Mexican force of indeterminate allegiance struck the remote village of Glenn Spring on the Texas side of the border two months after the Columbus Raid, the War Department ordered a full-scale mobilization of National Guard units. Within two months of the raid, well over 160,000 troops from across the nation had been deployed to a series of outposts hurriedly constructed along the river. Texas towns relatively close to the border formed civilian home guard companies to stand watch around the clock to repel any further Mexican incursions that ceaseless rumors held to be imminent. The Alpine, Texas, newspaper reported in late April 1916 that the first surprise practice alert was a total failure when not one of the home guard volunteers responded to the call to muster. As a result, officials soon abandoned the entire project.

What eventually became known as the Mexican Revolution had a long and fit-fully sputtering fuse that ignited years before the shooting began. The basic cause of it all was the increasingly harsh rule of Gen. Porfirio Díaz, president of Mexico from 1876 to 1911. As president, Díaz was a paradox. A visionary, he literally prodded his traditionally backward nation toward a belated industrial revolution. He warmly welcomed foreign investors in the development of an infrastructure that he believed would move Mexico into the future and away from her dark agrarian past. His actions led to establishment of a national railroad system, the encouragement of manufacturing, and the expansion of exploration efforts to tap into Mexico's vast petroleum resources. After the president's first decade in office, the new Porfirian-era Mexico seemed poised on the threshold of modernity. While his accomplishments were many, his methods were dictatorial. In his haste to break the centuries-old pattern of subsistence farming, Díaz illegally took the agricultural lands historically tended by small families and gave them to the wealthy, powerful land barons who reciprocated his generosity with their loyalty. At the peak of the Porfirian era, only 800 families owned all of Mexico's 761,000 square miles of land. Under Díaz, the rich became richer and the lower classes, deprived of their land and status, sank into relative pe-onage. All attempts to undo or even publically protest the inequities and outright corruption rampant in the Porfirian administration proved both futile and dangerous. Those who dared to speak out and seek justice faced imprisonment, torture, execution, or in a few cases, forcible expulsion from the country. Fearing these harsh prob-abilities, countless numbers of imperiled Mexicans began a mass exodus to Texas as early as 1900, a decade before the actual revolution erupted.

Somewhat sketchy U S census statistics indicate that nearly 500,000 Mexicans legally migrated to Texas between 1900 and 1920. As it is unlikely that all who crossed the Rio Grande during that period dared to seek official US documentation, it seems almost certain the actual number of dispossessed newcomers was much greater. A perhaps more accurate 1930 census report placed the number of Texans who de-clared themselves to be "of Mexican descent" at nearly 630,000, or some 10 percent of the total population at the time. Over one-half of all Mexicans counted in 1930 claimed to be "foreign born." This rapid infusion of immigrants, both legal and un-documented, formed the foundation for the strong Mexican American influence on modern-day Texas demographics. The tidal wave of angry immigrants that surged into Texas from 1900 onward created a volatile hotbed of anti-Porfirian dissent throughout the state, particularly in its southern region. Newspapers published in San Antonio by fiery expatriates constantly railed against the tyrannical conditions that prevailed in their homeland. Even though his policies were being widely criticized, the culpable Díaz retracted a pledge to step down by announcing that he would instead seek another term of office in 1910.

Although the revolutionary fuse had long been smoldering, the president's unexpected announcement caused it to finally burst into open flame. Seizing the moment, Francisco Madero, the first overt challenger to the Porfirian dictatorship, issued a bold call for revolution from his temporary home in San Antonio in October 1910. Madero, the American-educated scion of a wealthy Mexican family, then launched a crusade that shortly brought about the downfall of Díaz on May 25, 1911. Six months later, Madero became the president of a Mexico he had sworn to free from its shackles of oppression and injustice. Briefly triumphant, the relatively weak new president discovered the fires of the revolution he had so successfully fanned were far too intense to be easily quelled by the simple ouster of Díaz. Within 16 months after he assumed the presidency, Madero himself was turned out of office through political intrigue. On February 22, 1913, agents of his eventual successor, Gen. Victoriano Huerta, assassinated him.

For the next 10 years, counterrevolution bred even more counterrevolution as assassinations and forced exiles featured a succession of ambitious and ruthless pretenders to, and occasional occupants of, the presidential palace in Mexico City. The cast of characters in this violent game of musical chairs included Pancho Villa, Victoriano Huerta, Pascual Orozco, Emiliano Zapata, Álvaro Obregón, and the ultimate survivor, at least for a time, Venustiano Carranza. During the course of the revolution, the nation spiraled out of civil control and into a state of virtual anarchy fueled by the rapacious egos of ruthless men who sought everything for themselves and nothing for the nation they wished to rule. In the process, an estimated 2 million of their fellow countrymen died, all victims of the crossfire created by various vying factions.

As the struggle for power raged on, Texas continued to be both safe haven for the oppressed and breeding ground for further intrigue. The International Bridge that connects El Paso with Juarez became a free-flowing conduit of supply, funding, and revolutionary mischief. Leaders of the various factions frequently crossed the bridge to arrange delivery of arms and to solicit American banks for the money to buy the guns. The colorful Villa even moved his wife and son to the Texas city to protect them from his many enemies. Meanwhile, along the border, bands of raiders frequently struck Texas ranches. Most of such raids occurred under the direction of bandits who used the well-publicized revolution as a handy diversion for their nonpolitical, self-enriching attacks. No matter the real purpose of the incidents, it seemed Pancho Villa usually took the blame. Eyewitnesses persisted in their claims that it was the legendary

Villa who had personally ransacked their ranches from Brownsville, through the Big Bend, and on up the Rio Grande. As one historian put it, "Villa seemed to be everywhere and nowhere all at once." That he did attack Columbus and then led Brigadier General Pershing on a fruitless and embarrassing trek through northern Mexico is, however, a substantiated historical fact. Although Pershing's Punitive Expedition failed to find Villa, it did establish San Antonio as a preeminent military center in the Southwest. Overall direction of the campaign came from army headquarters at Fort Sam Houston, and Capt. Benjamin Foulois's 1st Aero Squadron left for northern Mexico from the fort. It marked the first use of American airpower in combat.

It was Carranza, the self-styled "First Chief of Mexico," who finally brought at least a semblance of peace to his nation with great support from the United States. He later joined the list of those whose lives were cut short by an assassin's bullet. Pancho Villa was also gunned down by a virtual battery of assailants on July 20, 1923. An annual event at the assassination site in Parral, Mexico, recreates the bloody event for the edification and entertainment of tourists.

It is clear the Mexican Revolution was closely tied to Texas and that legacies from it still remain. Madero launched it from San Antonio, but along with Villa and countless others, he used El Paso as both haven and logistical center, and Huerta came to the state to die. The violence often spilled across the river, causing hardship throughout the Rio Grande Valley and beyond. The Mexico that emerged from its bloody Revolution has been in flux ever since. Perhaps, as some scholars suggest, the violent event was in fact just the beginning of a social, economic, and political struggle that has yet to be fully resolved.

DOWNTOWN EL PASO
(1910–1920)

During the bloody years of the Mexican Revolution, the city of El Paso, Texas, served as the key gateway for many competing elements of the violence that ravished all of Mexico. Located only a few yards across the Rio Grande bridges from the vital Mexican town of Juarez, El Paso served as a safe haven for temporary politicians and warlords, a major shipping point for the supplies and weaponry of war, and a seething crucible in which countless intrigues came to a boil before spilling across the river. From 1910 until 1920, the surging currents of the revolution cascaded back and forth across that river, which naturally separated one metropolitan area sliced into two distinctly different nations after the Mexican War of 1846. When the first wild shots of the revolution went off in 1910, over 60 percent of the residents on the El Paso side of the Rio Grande still claimed to be of Hispanic descent.

In the course of the battles that frequently rattled through the streets of Juarez, stray shells and bullets flew across the river to strike buildings in El Paso's dangerously proximate downtown area. Some students of the revolutionary era suggest that at least some of the bullets were by no means stray at all but rather the direct result of rifles deliberately fired into the Texas city by Mexican shooters who apparently felt the need to express their long smoldering resentment toward the "Colossus of the North." Most of that ill will very likely stemmed from memories of the 1840s war that in the end caused Mexico to cede over a third of its territory to the victorious United States. Although that conflict came to its close some 60 years prior to the revolution, the Mexican nation as a whole would long remember its consequences and many would blame the United States for creating many of the factors that led directly to the revolution. Indeed, the very dictator whose 35-year heavy-handed reign crumbled in the face of an armed revolution had been keenly aware of the looming presence of his gigantic northern neighbor. "Poor Mexico," Porfirio Díaz once exclaimed, "so far from God but so near to the United States."

Further suspicion about the degree of US involvement in the Mexican Revolution arose when the first spark of the decade-long struggle took place in Texas. In 1909, Francisco Madero, the diminutive but successful instigator of the anti-Díaz movement, began his improbable journey to Mexico City's presidential palace from a small office in San Antonio. In 1911, Madero boldly established the seat of a provisional Mexican government in downtown El Paso. The headquarters of Madero's self-proclaimed new ruling entity was on the fifth floor of the Caples Building at 306 San Antonio Street. At the time, his offices were on the top floor of the building that has subsequently been enlarged to have seven floors. Once elegant, the Caples Building is now virtually derelict. From his Texas office, Madero was able to rally his followers to rise up against the forces of the hated dictator Díaz. Aided by such powerful lieutenants as Pancho Villa and Álvaro Obregón, Madero was personally but somewhat reluctantly victorious in the first true pitched battle of the revolution in the streets of Juarez.

It was this heated and bloody foray that proved to be so fascinating to onlookers on the El Paso side of the Rio Grande. The sounds of rifle fire and exploding grenades swept northward over the river as curious Americans crowded on El Paso rooftops to see firsthand the initial battle that would soon engulf all of Mexico. One of the favorite viewing points was the roof garden of the stately Hotel Paso del Norte, located at 115 South El Paso Street, only a half-mile from Juarez. Excited observers peered through the smoke and haze that drifted across the river to see uniformed soldiers dart from building to building, firing at other soldiers in strikingly similar uniforms as each side fought street by street to gain control of the city. When the hotel's roof became too crowded to permit unobstructed viewing of the fighting, spectators hurried a few blocks west to claim a spot in the tall turret of the city's Union Station. Although the red brick tower afforded less space for viewing, as well as requiring a strenuous climb up several flights of steep stairs, the range of vision proved much wider than that afforded onlookers at the hotel. Skirmishes could clearly be seen taking place throughout the Mexican city. Some of the more daring eyewitnesses to the struggle chose to stand on the immediate edge of the Rio Grande. Although this viewing point lacked the advantage of elevation afforded on the hotel roof or the Union Station tower, the sounds of firing were more distinct and the smell of cordite unmistakable. The shouted commands of officers could be easily heard, as could the screams of the wounded. Some who watched the fighting from ground level reported a palpable and thrilling sense of imminent danger and adventure not present at the more elevated sites. The occasional bullet or mortar shell that flew across the river surely added an even greater sense of danger to those brave or foolish enough to stand on the Texas shoreline. What are alleged to be holes created by errant bullets fired from Mexican riflemen can still be seen in some building facades near the Rio Grande. The most noted of these historic pockmarks are on the El Paso Laundry building at 901 Santa Fe. The authenticity of the bullet scars cannot be verified, although many descendents of witnesses to the Juarez battle claim they fully believe what their grandparents told them long ago about the time bullets crossed the Rio Grande to crash into the wall of the laundry.

Even before, and well after, the 1911 Battle of Juarez, strong ties to the revolution tightly bound El Paso to the struggle. Crossing from the Mexican city to its American counterpart across the river took mere minutes, yet the protection available to any political leader seeking short-term asylum was of the highest degree. As the official US policy on the Mexican Revolution was loose and flexible, agents known to be aligned with the various warring factions had only to cross the bridge to conduct their not-so-secret affairs without interference from US officials, either civilian or military.

During Madero's short one-year term as president, the political situation in Mexico stabilized enough, at least on its surface, for the United States to consider his new democratic government as a trustworthy international neighbor and partner. With the assassination of Madero in 1913, however, none of the other aspiring leaders could clearly be endorsed by the American government. In the place of relative stability came a violent rash of revolutions-within-the-revolution and a cast of ruthless leaders who greatly desired American support as they continued to flail away at one another in their quest for absolute power. It was during this decade that the traffic in intrigue reached epic proportions in El Paso. Agents and aides of such legendary cutthroats as Pancho Villa and Victoriano Huerta crossed the Rio Grande virtually around the clock, while the two leaders themselves had easy access to the American city they both clearly regarded as a friendly substation for their use and enjoyment.

Villa, likely far better known than Huerta, actually lived in El Paso on several occasions. He shared a home at 512 Prospect with one of his many wives in 1913, stayed in both the Linden and the Paso del Norte, and rented space in other downtown buildings to facilitate the smuggling of arms and other supplies past the not-so-keen eyes of US Customs officials stationed along the Rio Grande. Villa's brother, Hipolito, maintained a residence in the city in which he purportedly amassed a treasure trove to be used to finance Pancho's war machine in Mexico. When he was not in Mexico leading his band of revolutionaries, Villa could often be seen on the streets of El Paso. During a period of exile in 1913, he often met his cohorts in such places as the Dome Bar at the Hotel Paso del Norte and the Elite Confectionery at 201 Mesa. A teetotaler, Villa would nevertheless meet with American army officers and others at the hotel bar, but he seemed to prefer gathering at the confectionery, usually on a daily basis if the demands on an exiled revolutionary general so permitted. His affection for candy and ice cream was said to have been surpassed only by his legendary affection for women. Among the better-known images of Villa in El Paso is a photo of him standing with his later nemesis, Brig. Gen. John J. Pershing, on the International Bridge spanning the Rio Grande. During the time that various American officials favored Villa as the man to back during the Mexican Revolution, he was often seen in conference with Pershing, Gen. Hugh Scott, and other officers at various locations in El Paso.

Not quite as well known or anywhere nearly as popular as Villa, Gen. Victoriano Huerta was perhaps even more unscrupulous and downright evil. Although Pancho Villa reportedly shot a man who merely disturbed his nap, Huerta was capable of ordering assassinations without any clear-cut reason for doing so. He ordered the murderous elimination of his onetime comrade and sponsor, Pres. Francisco Madero, however, simply because Huerta wished to become the next president of Mexico. A full-blood Indian, Huerta rose to the top position in the Mexican Army under both Díaz and Madero before murdering his way into the presidential palace. He ruled Mexico with a hand every bit as ironclad as that of Díaz, the other Mexican dictator whom he had actually helped overthrow. When Huerta's Mexico engaged in a military confrontation with the United States, however, Woodrow Wilson, the previously pacifist American president, found the courage to demand his ouster and eventual exile. In a short time, Huerta returned from exile in Spain and soon defiantly made his way back to El Paso in hopes of crossing the Rio Grande and returning to power.

Arrested before he could make good on his threat, Huerta was escorted to El Paso by his American captors and received a hero's welcome by large throngs of supporters from both sides of the Rio Grande. The mayor of El Paso eagerly agreed to be his attorney as the deposed president vigorously challenged the right of the United States to arrest a Mexican citizen, let alone a former president of the nation. His

In early 1911, Francisco Madero used offices numbered 507–508 in the Caples Building in El Paso as his headquarters for planning what soon would be the Mexican Revolution. He became president of Mexico five months later in a nation torn by strife. *Courtesy of El Paso Public Library, Southwest Collection, El Paso, Texas.*

appearance on the streets of El Paso often touched off demonstrations by his many followers. Even though he curiously made no effort to slip across the border to again challenge and likely usurp the already unsteady Mexican government, he remained under observation by US Army authorities day and night. As the furor surrounding the possibility of his return to Mexico escalated, the former president was somewhat politely asked to leave El Paso, the gateway to the path that might well lead back to Mexico City. To get him as far away as possible, there were those who suggested he relocate permanently somewhere—indeed anywhere—in the northern reaches of the United States.

When events in Mexico strongly suggested the stage was being set for the immediate flight of Huerta across the Rio Grande, the United States finally ordered his rearrest and incarceration in the El Paso County Jail. This likely illegal act again triggered demonstrations in the city, and it soon became even more urgent that Huerta be physically removed from such immediate and dangerous proximity to his homeland. The general, however, refused to leave. He rejected any offers of immediate release that demanded his pledge to leave El Paso permanently. He declined an outright pardon and, acting on advice of his attorney, sneered at threats that he would be deported. A frustrated US government, fearing that the El Paso County Jail could not withstand the fury of a pro-Huerta mob, moved him under the cover of darkness to a far more secure cell on the army's well-guarded Fort Bliss military installation

Although two additional floors have been added since 1912, the Caples Building in El Paso was virtually derelict in 2009. Small shops occupied the street level, but the rest of the building remained vacant and in poor condition. *Thomas E. Alexander Collection.*

northeast of the city. No newspaper account told of the prisoner's involuntary transfer.

While in his cell at Fort Bliss, the general fell ill and was reportedly near death from jaundice, although rumors persisted he had been poisoned in a final effort to permanently discourage his return to Mexico. It is difficult to accept the poisoning thesis, because the army quickly released the suffering man to the care of his family and his doctor in El Paso. The care he received proved sufficient enough to cause him to rally. From his sickbed, the suddenly revitalized old revolutionary leader began to scheme once again about how to return to power in Mexico no matter how fervently the American president wished otherwise. Alarmed at his return to health and his potential for mischief, the Wilson administration once again ordered the army to arrest Huerta—for a third time—and whisk him back to his cell at Fort Bliss. Curiously, within days of his return, the prisoner developed the identical symptoms of the disease that had caused his release just weeks before. In what was becoming a routine, albeit a highly unusual one, the army once again had him transported back to his El Paso home. This time, however, whatever had caused him to fall so desperately ill as to be twice given up for dead proved truly lethal. The general died on January 14, 1916, at his home in El Paso within sight of the Mexico he had once so cruelly ruled. He is buried at Evergreen Cemetery in his involuntarily adopted town.

When the Wilson administration ultimately decided the revolutionary movement fronted by Venustiano Carranza was the most likely to satisfy the desires of the American government, Pancho Villa, the longtime hero of the Mexican Revolution and often a temporary El Pasoan, was forced into a desperate situation. Angry and frustrated by what he took to be a treacherous abandonment by the United States, he planned and led a raid against the American village of Columbus, New Mexico, located only 68 miles west of El Paso. That still inexplicable act triggered a full-scale invasion of Mexico by US armed forces. Villa's erstwhile acquaintance, Brig. Gen. John J. Pershing, assumed command of the so-called Punitive Expedition that futilely pursued the wily Mexican leader for over a year before its participants limped footsore but empty-handed back across the border. During the expedition, company after company of US soldiers rode the train from El Paso's Union Station to the yellow wooden depot at Columbus, and from there trekked through the hills of northern Mexico in search of the man who only a few years before had frequently enjoyed ice cream sodas at the Elite Confectionery.

The Mexican Revolution ended, more or less, in late 1920, but its effect endures. The exodus of the thousands of Mexican citizens who found themselves caught in the crossfire of that revolution caused the city of El Paso to double in population during the officially declared 1910–1920 revolutionary era. The descendents of those who fled the horrors generated by the likes of Huerta, Villa, and Carranza over a century ago still maintain a dominant Hispanic influence in El Paso. Today, across the Rio Grande, the turbulent city of Juarez writhes in a terror not unlike that which tore it asunder at an earlier time when Mexicans violently turned on one another in bloodied fury. Perhaps the seeds of revolution still exist in that troubled land.

Location: That part of downtown El Paso roughly extending north from the International Rio Grande Bridge at Santa Fe Street to the Union Station on the west, to Saint Vrain Street on the east, and Paisano Street on the north.
Access: Unlimited.

GLENN SPRING
(1916)

The site of the 1916 siege of Glenn Spring is without doubt among the more remote locations in Texas. It is situated some 20 miles south of Big Bend National Park headquarters on a rough road that challenges all but the most skillful and persistent off-road adventurers. Although the site's inaccessibility makes it an infrequent destination, its proximity to the Rio Grande made it an alluring target for an incursion into the United States on one historic occasion during the Mexican Revolution of 1910–1920. To reach the small village of Glenn Spring on the night of May 5, 1916, an invading Mexican force crossed the river at San Vicente and then traveled some seven miles in a northwesterly direction over a primitive track. The size of the raiding party was the subject of much speculation in the days immediately following the attack. According to those who found themselves surrounded by a horde of shouting riders at night, the number of men involved in the attack seemed to be at least 700. An article in the *Alpine Avalanche* reported that 400 raiders had been counted, while an official army report put the number at a more realistic 60 to 70 men.

In the confusion created by the sudden nighttime attack, it was difficult to determine the identity of the attackers. The raiders shouted cries of "Viva Villa" and "Viva Carranza" during the three-hour-long siege, but the absence of any even semi-uniformed soldiers suggested to some of the victims that their village was the object of organized banditry rather than a military target. Others, however, including army officers in the region, were convinced the attack had been carried out by former officers who had recently served under Pancho Villa. Among these officers identified during the attack was Rodriguez Ramirez, a onetime lieutenant colonel under Villa.

During the 10-year span of the Mexican Revolution, raids along the US-Mexico border were frequent occurrences. The raids were usually made by bandits who sought personal gain through looting and who had no particular interest in the national turmoil that plunged Mexico into an extended period of violence. However, when Pancho Villa mounted his vicious surprise raid across the border to strike Columbus, New Mexico, on March 19, 1916, the American government finally came to realize the Mexican Revolution posed a genuine threat to the security of the nation. The so-called Punitive Expedition commanded by Brig. Gen. John J. Pershing immediately received orders to march into northern Mexico in what proved to be a fruitless effort to find, let alone punish, the wily revolutionist.

The shocking news of the invasion at Columbus sent a keen sense of apprehension running the entire length of the border, but nowhere keener than in the remote Big Bend region of Texas. Bandit raids were nothing new along the part of the Rio Grande that flows though the desolate canyons of the Big Bend. That these Mexican raiders, be they revolutionary soldiers or civilian banditos with allegiance to no one except themselves, were now emboldened enough to strike with impunity raised Texans' concerns to a new level. Following the Columbus event and other alarming revolutionary actions in Mexico proper, the War Department, after considerable reluctance, agreed to station small detachments of soldiers throughout the Big Bend at locations deemed worthy of military protection. Glenn Spring, however, had already received its first very small platoon of soldiers much earlier because of the village's unique wax-making industry. Possessing a spring that produced a rare permanent flow of water, the site had at one time been the temporary home of Native Americans who tarried long enough to adorn large boulders with their distinctive rock art. Ranchers moved into the area once the Indians fled, but the grass and other forage crops proved too sparse to support profitable cattle ranching.

In 1911, just as the Mexican Revolution began escalating across the Rio Grande, C. D. Wood and W. K. Ellis established a wax factory at the spring. The raw material to be used in the factory process was the candelilla plant that grew in profusion in the area. Workers boiled the pencil-thin stems of the plant in large vats containing water augmented by sulfuric acid. When a waxy substance separated from the stems by the boiling, it rose to the surface where they skimmed it off and then boiled it again in other vats. The end product was a hard, durable wax used as a protective coating for tenting material as well as in household polishes of various kinds. The rendering of the wax proved to be difficult and very hot work, particularly given the extremely high temperatures common in the region nine months of the year. The workers, mainly Mexicans from both sides of the Rio Grande, usually received one dollar per day for their labor. The owners of the enterprise established a fairly large company store, which included a post office, to provide workers with a source for their necessities of life, albeit at a robust markup in price. The home of C. G. Compton, postmaster and manager of the store, stood next to the commercial property. At its peak in 1916, Glenn Spring had a civilian population estimated to have been from 80 to 100 people.

The army first constructed a so-called permanent camp south of the wax-making community in 1911. By 1916, members of the 14th Cavalry, formerly posted to Fort Bliss at El Paso, occupied the post. According to a sketch of the military encampment made two years after the raid, the army set up three orderly rows of presumably four-man tents a short distance from a large stable complex. A row of rocks placed across from the stables apparently served as a defensive bulwark against another raid by river-crossing bandits.

It is unclear why the raid against Glenn Spring was so carefully planned and executed, and historians disagree about exactly which Mexican forces participated in the action. At any rate, the raiders struck around 11:00 in the evening. Compton, the storekeeper, was awakened by several armed Mexicans who asked if there were any soldiers stationed nearby. Thinking for some obscure reason the men would go away, he declared there were no soldiers stationed anywhere near the factory, even though he knew at least nine cavalrymen were then asleep in their tents across the village's cleared area from his home.

After a short delay, the raid began without any further conversation. Hearing the gunshots and the shouts of the marauders, the US Army soldiers—most dressed only in their underwear and some without shoes—scrambled from their cots to find a stronger defensive position than that afforded by their flimsy canvas tents. Rushing to a nearby adobe building, the soldiers exchanged fire with the raiders for over three hours. When the Mexicans set fire to the roof of their shelter, the embattled and outnumbered soldiers ran out to seek better cover elsewhere. The Mexican riflemen then shot and killed three of them as they ran toward another building. In the commotion, raiders looted the store and all but destroyed the factory. A shot killed Compton's son, and four soldiers received serious wounds or burns. Their mission apparently accomplished, the raiders melted away into the dark vastness of the Big Bend.

While the raid was at its peak, another group of raiders split away from the main body to attack the Boquillas settlement, located some 10 miles east of Glenn Spring on the Rio Grande. There they took storekeeper Jessie Deemer and his assistant as prisoners. They looted the store and robbed a nearby mine office. By sunrise, all the raiders had crossed the Rio Grande to apparent safety.

Coming as they did so soon after Villa's Columbus raid, the two simultaneous Big Bend incidents produced a shockwave of fear along the border and a further hardening of resolve and purpose among the army's top commanders. Officials quickly determined that the murderers of the Glenn Spring soldiers had to be pursued into

A key US Army subpost in 1916, Glenn Spring was also the location of a civilian wax-making facility whose smokestacks can be seen in the left center. On May 5, 1916, this site was the scene of the second invasion of US territory by a Mexican military force. *Clifford B. Casey Collection. Archives of the Big Bend, Bryan Wildenthal Memorial Library, Sul Ross University, Alpine, Texas.*

Mexico despite the anticipated protests of the Mexican government. Acting upon the urgent order issued by Maj. Gen. Frederick Funston at Fort Sam Houston, troops from Fort Bliss and Fort Clark were on their way to the Big Bend within two days of the raids. After establishing the town of Marathon as their headquarters, elements of the 8th and 14th Cavalry units marched south over 80 miles through rough country to reach the Rio Grande. There, on the evening of May 10, the US Army crossed the river in force at the Boquillas ford, and in so doing launched the Second Punitive Expedition sent into Mexico in pursuit of raiders. Although short in duration, it proved to be far more successful than Pershing's punitive foray still groping its way deep into Chihuahua in search of Villa. Writing in the *Army and Navy Journal* in 1954, Col. William A. Raborn, a participant in the second expedition, made note that the army's crossing of the Rio Grande in May 1916 was the first invasion of Mexican territory from Texas since the opening of the Mexican War in 1846. While the colonel's statement was at least technically accurate, cavalry units stationed at Fort Clark in the late 1860s and into the 1870s had actually crossed the river on a number of occasions in pursuit of Indian marauders. At any rate, the 1916 river crossing event was unique in

This line of stones is all that remains of the army post and civilian industrial town that was once Glenn Spring. The site of the spring itself can still be found nearby. *Thomas E. Alexander Collection. Photograph by J. Travis Roberts Jr., October 9, 2010.*

one respect. Rather than riding horseback into Mexico, the army's field commander, Maj. George T. Langhorne, drove across in his open-top convertible.

As his troopers followed in trucks or on horseback, Langhorne pushed nearly 140 miles into Mexico before overtaking some of the suspected raiders and in the process killing a few of them without trial. The men recovered a small portion of the loot taken from both the company store at Glenn Spring and Jessie Deemer's store at Boquillas. Satisfied, the expedition turned back to the Rio Grande on May 21. In the meantime, the Mexican raiders released storekeeper Deemer and his assistant, who made their way back to Texas. Considerable speculation about Deemer's role in the Boquillas incident continued for years. Many thought the storekeeper arranged for Mexicans to raid his store and facilitate his kidnapping in hopes of gaining monetary compensation from the American government. Within days of his return, Deemer did in fact petition the army for a $10,000 reimbursement for trees he claimed had been damaged on his property by the troopers' horses. When the government repeatedly denied the claim, Deemer sold his store and moved to the safety of California.

Although the Mexican raids of May 5 were at least partly avenged by the success of the Second Punitive Expedition, rumors of other impending attacks fueled a constant fear that reached well inland from the river. Reports of Villa "spottings" occurred on a daily basis, even though history indicates he was not anywhere near the area at the time. Today, the name of Glenn Spring is all but forgotten even in the southwestern part of Texas. There is absolutely nothing to be seen standing where the tiny town and its factories once flourished. The spring itself still flows, but with no human demand for its water for nearly a century, a dense growth of trees and brush surrounds the site. While there are no clearly verifiable foundations, one concrete slab can be seen near the likely site of the home of one of the factory owners. Perhaps a proper investigation across the nearby Glenn Draw might uncover the remains of the adobe huts of the Mexican laborers who daily toiled in the sun. A rough sketch of the site drawn many years ago indicates the presence of a graveyard located not too distant from the laborers' homes, as well as the likely location of the tall smokestacks where the factories once stood.

As one of only three places in the United States to ever have been invaded by foreign military units since the War of 1812, Glenn Spring is deserving of more than a footnote in American history. Unfortunately, its inaccessibility continues to becloud its historical significance.

Location: Five miles southeast on State Highway 118 past Big Bend National Park headquarters, then another eight miles on narrow, four-wheel-vehicle route.

Access: Very difficult; road is deeply rutted and usually strewn with large rocks; impassable during wet weather. Check with the National Park Service office before making the trek.

CAMP RUIDOSA
(1916–1920)

The attacks by Mexican raiders at Glenn Spring and Boquillas, Texas, in 1916 brought an unprecedented burst of activity to the long-slumbering village of Ruidosa, as well as other tiny hamlets located along the Rio Grande. On May 10, 1916, just five days following the raids, US president Woodrow Wilson ordered into immediate federal service the National Guard units of every state in the union. The May attacks, however, were not the sole reason for Wilson's sweeping call to arms. Pancho Villa's raid on Columbus, New Mexico, in March 1916 combined with other quasimilitary incursions by various Mexican elements into the United States to create a growing public demand that the Mexican border be placed under constant military surveillance and protection. Further, mounting fears of an out-and-out war with Mexico also contributed to the pressure on the American government to assume a strong defensive military position along the 1,200-mile international border.

The sheer impunity of the Columbus raid increased what had been a steadily mounting demand for more effective border security since the beginning of the Mexican Revolution in 1910. Villa's deadly foray onto American soil not only emphasized how readily a successful invasion could be accomplished but also put into sharper focus the suspicion that there were certain other foreign intrigues likely at play in the border incidents. As the pitch of revolutionary warfare escalated deep within Mexico, as well as along the US border, it became increasingly apparent that Germany had taken a particular interest in the situation. There is ample evidence that Germany had a compelling motive in provoking a state of war between Mexico and the United States as soon as possible. With its attention and resources diverted by a war on its own threshold, leaders in Berlin reasoned, America would be far less likely to cross the Atlantic to join forces with Germany's foes in what was already being viewed as a world war.

Although a pacifist by nature as well as in policy, President Wilson could no longer ignore a second invasion of US territory, regardless of how relatively inconsequential the Glenn Spring and Boquillas raids had actually been. This further proof of the porosity of the border, the possibility of a German-orchestrated declaration of war against the United States by Mexico, and a deafening public clamor for immediate government action had prompted the president's decision to federalize the National Guard. The impact of that decision proved to be of immense importance not only to villages such as Ruidosa, but eventually to the entire United States as well. In response to the president's order, as many as 160,000 National Guard troops were in time mobilized into federal service. The immediate result of the mobilization was a widespread recognition that the National Guard was, for the most part, simply not capable of achieving even the basic standards mandated by regular US Army regulations. The successful intensive effort to overcome the many deficiencies in the level of training shown to prevail throughout the National Guard served to give the nation a far stronger military posture when it did enter the Great War in Europe in less than a year.

The immediate challenge given to the initially ill-prepared guard troopers was to prohibit forcibly any further crossings of the Rio Grande by either revolutionists or common bandits. To facilitate its mission, the army hurriedly established a series of small cavalry subposts along the river's shores, with the main headquarters located at Marfa's Fort D. A. Russell. There were 11 such subposts in a line that stretched from

Candelaria to Ruidosa and then on downriver to Presidio, Polvo, and Lajitas. Both Glenn Spring and Boquillas became home to National Guard detachments. From Fort Duncan at Eagle Pass down the Rio Grande to Fort Brown near the Gulf of Mexico, regular army soldiers held positions in an attempt to close the border to unwanted incursions.

The smaller guard posts were nearly identical in appearance. The one at Camp Ruidosa featured two adobe barracks built on thick concrete slabs, a mess hall with an unusually large kitchen, officers quarters, and a corral big enough to hold at least 40 cavalry horses and a few mules. The Ruidosa encampment also boasted a small but efficient power plant that provided enough energy to bring faint light to the interiors of the buildings. In the nearby village, however, the only sources of illumination were kerosene lanterns or candles. The post was on top of a fairly prominent hill immediately north of the village. From the elevated position, sentries had a clear view of the ragged little Mexican village of Barrancos de Guadalupe that hugged the shoreline directly across the river from Ruidosa. The outline of the distant mountains of the Sierra Grande loomed on the horizon beyond the village.

Ruidosa had suffered a violent past long before the American National Guard came to build the subpost. Founded as a penal colony by the Mexican government in 1824, the settlement was known as Vado Prieta in reference to the stony ford located in the river at the site. Comanche tribesmen frequently used the ford during their seasonal journeys in and out of Mexico. Apparently having no interest in dealing with a Mexican penal colony at their crossing point, the Indians eventually destroyed it, leaving no evidence of its existence. Later, the Indians raided agricultural establishments that dared to locate at the ford. In time, the Comanche and Apache threat diminished, and by 1916, the year the American cavalry built its post, the town had a population of nearly 250 people, mostly Mexicans and a few Indians occasionally in temporary residence.

The first military detachment to occupy the hilltop overlooking the river consisted of a lieutenant and 39 enlisted men. Their transportation consisted of 26 cavalry horses, two mules, and one wagon. Travel along the unpaved and rutted river road made the usage of automobiles and trucks uncomfortable at best and impossible at worst. According to orders dispatched from headquarters to every guard unit posted at the stations along the river, the mission of the citizen soldiers was "to patrol the border and to cooperate with county and state officers including the Texas Rangers." Small squads of six to eight troopers would ride out from the Ruidosa outpost every morning, usually just after daybreak. One squad rode upriver toward Candelaria while the other squad made its way down the river toward the Presidio subpost located some 35 miles away. When the Ruidosa troopers met riders from Candelaria going southeast and men from Presidio heading northwest, the squads would briefly rest before turning around to retrace their tracks and return to their respective sub-posts. The patrol pattern was consistent enough that anyone who wished to cross into Texas for whatever purpose could do so. According to one report, observers on the Mexican side frequently waited until the American squads departed from their midday rendezvous for the return trip to their post. Then, with no patrolling squad due from either direction for several hours, they easily forded the river without fear of any military detection.

When not riding the river patrol route, the troopers had little to do in the way of official duties. Drilling, rifle practice, and digging holes for new latrine locations occupied much of the guardsmen's time. Boredom created low morale, particularly as the months grew into years for some units. The almost total lack of any overt military action caused men from New York, Wisconsin, New Hampshire, and other far distant states to angrily question why they had been wrested from their homes to sit on a riverbank in hot—or cold—Texas and never see anyone who appeared to be an enemy. Further, troopers were under strict orders not to cross the river for any reason, including "the chasing of any Mexicans who managed to come across the boundary to raid and rob." It was not until the National Guard units were released from federal duty in early 1917 that any benefits of their recent border adventure began to become apparent. Officers had acquired field experience in troop move-ments, logistical techniques, and close staff coordination—experience they would never have attained during their usual weekend musters held once a month at home. Enlisted men acquired a new sense of discipline through the constant drilling they endured. They also learned to deal with such adversities as boredom, fatigue, and the frustration generated by being helpless to challenge the wisdom of obviously mindless rules of engagement.

When the United States entered into a real war in Europe in the spring of 1917, many of the guardsmen who had learned much about the army and probably even more about themselves were well served by their border experience. Senior US Army commanders seemed to have become aware of the lessons being learned on the bor-der. In late 1916, when it became apparent the guardsmen had benefited from their deployment along the river, the government federalized even more units. America's entry into the European war seemed likely by then, and the War Department wisely used its temporary authority to federalize as many guardsmen as possible in order to gain the military experience they might soon need across the Atlantic Ocean.

Today, the subpost at Ruidosa has all but disappeared, and the village it once loomed above is, by day at least, a ghost town. Its daytime population hovers around 15 to 20 souls, but on weekend nights, the last remaining cantina in town is kept busy by thirsty Mexican residents who cross the river to celebrate the end of an-other week of labor. Come Saturday noon the village sleeps again, but after sundown

With the Rio Grande in the middle distance and Mexico's Sierra Grande Mountains looming on the horizon, the American National Guard's 1916 Camp Ruidosa was the temporary
home of thousands of lonely soldiers during the decade-long Mexican Revolution. *Courtesy of
Archives of the Big Bend, Bryan Wildenthal Memorial Library, Sul Ross State University, Alpine, Texas.*

more lively revelry marked by frequent singing and occasional shooting fills the usually
humid nighttime air.

The cantina itself is more Mexican than American in appearance. Large posters
bearing the images of Emiliano Zapata and Francisco Villa adorn the stained and fis-
sured walls. The low ceiling of the small, usually smoke-filled room is made of old
wooden crate panels that bear the brand name "Arbuckle's Coffee." The panels are
not the atmosphere-generating false artifacts that are often found in themed chain
restaurants across America. These are genuine relics of a time long past. Arbuckle's
was the traditional chuck wagon brand of coffee favored by 19th-century cowboys.
According to the cantina's proprietor, over a half century ago someone found the
crate panels that comprise his establishment's ceiling in a shed on one of the huge
ranches in the region. Looming above the cantina is what some of the few longtime
residents still call Outpost Hill. Nearly all that remains of the military post that initially gave the hill its name are two long and curiously unblemished concrete slabs
spaced some 50 feet apart and parallel to each other. These are what remains of the
140-foot-long foundations of the post's enlisted men's barracks. Empty cartridge

The Rio Grande and the mountains of Mexico still remain, of course, but all that is left of Camp Ruidosa can only be found by venturing through the village dump, but the dramatic scene that unfolds is well worth the trip. *Thomas E. Alexander Collection. Photograph by Lyman Labry, Texas Historical Commission, Austin, Texas.*

casings can be found scattered about the slabs, and a few crumbling walls can also be seen.

To reach the site, it is necessary to make a torturous drive through what has clearly long been the village dumping ground. There is no order to this tangled jungle of rusted bedsprings, tilting refrigerators, and stacks of shredded tires, but the reward at the end of this challenging journey makes it worthwhile. The view across the river from the hilltop toward the dark and brooding mountains of Mexico is matchless. The setting is little changed from that experienced nearly a century ago by bored National Guardsmen from faraway states with nothing else to do but stare across the river at the land of their putative enemy.

Location: Forty-two miles northwest of Presidio on Farm-to-Market Road 170. Site of the camp is immediately to the north of the town of Ruidosa, off Pinto Canyon Road.

Access: Difficult; requires driving on an often blocked pathway through the local trash dump.

CAMP HOLLAND
(1916–1924)

Not all the US Cavalry subposts guarding the Mexican border during the 10 years of that country's revolution were situated directly on the Rio Grande. Camp Holland, for example, was some 20 miles east of the river in the northwest corner of the Big Bend region. The army built the camp at the eastern terminus of an ancient Indian trail that afforded a rare passageway over and through the 40-mile-long Sierra Vieja mountain range. At the end of the trail, at its western terminus, lay the Rio Grande and a violence-ridden Mexico in revolt. Although the trail through the mountain pass was precipitous and made up largely of dangerously shifting scree, it was the most direct route to the river through the mountains. As a result, Camp Holland's depot served as the principal source of supply for such river outposts as Candelaria and Ruidosa. Food, clothing, ammunition, and other military necessities came by rail or truck to the town of Valentine and were then shipped by wagon or mule train to Camp Holland 12 miles to the west.

The overall commander of the military district of which the camp and its supply depot were a part was George T. Langhorne, who as a major had pursued the Boquillas raiders into Mexico in the comfort of his Cadillac convertible. Promoted to lieutenant colonel following his bold and moderately successful 1916 foray across the border, Langhorne served as commander of the entire Big Bend Military District from October 1917 until early spring 1920. Under his command, the army designated Camp Holland as the base installation in the northwestern sector of the district, which had its headquarters at Camp Marfa 50 miles away. From Marfa, the colonel and his staff supervised all operations at Camp Holland as well as all the other river outposts.

Unlike the more rudimentary posts at Candelaria and Ruidosa, Camp Holland exhibited sturdy construction as though it might someday become a permanent installation. Its many buildings did in fact remain in excellent condition for many years, well into the 21st century. Situated in a narrow valley surrounded by towering mountains, the camp featured barracks for 400 men, a large commissary, relatively elegant officers quarters, a bakery, and a surprisingly spacious mess hall. Every structure had a white roof to reflect the heat of the sun. Sturdy walls fashioned of local stone remained stable through the use of an exceptionally durable white mortar. As a National Park Service researcher described it years later, the camp "[reflects] the persistent traditions and functions of the US Cavalry on the frontier. . . . The camp strongly evokes the atmosphere of an Indian Wars post." The supply depot located on the flat terrain immediately adjacent to the camp proved to be more utilitarian. There were sheds and warehouses of various sizes, loading docks, a small office building, and numerous corrals built sturdily enough to contain the notoriously cantankerous and willful pack mules and burros.

According to W. D. Smithers, who worked as a packer during much of the border patrol era, the regular army officers and men were usually on much friendlier terms with the mule-driving packers than they were with the National Guardsmen later assigned to the installation. The regulars relied on the mule trains and the dependable packers for their very subsistence, while they perceived the mostly ill-trained guardsmen as unreliable and untested. Most pack trains consisted of a number of individual units traveling at from 100- to 200-foot intervals over the Sierra Vieja trail in an effort to minimize the effect of dust. A pack master and the chuck wagon led the entire procession, followed by a unit consisting of 10 mules and two muleskinners. The skinners' curses were said to be even more biting than the sting of their whips. Following them 100 feet or so back was another unit of 10 mules urged onward by two more muleskinners. Depending on the amount of supplies needed at a cavalry outpost, some pack trains included more than 100 mules. On rain-free days, most of the trains averaged five miles an hour on the trail. To avoid the heat of a Texas summer, the caravans often moved out from Camp Holland as early as 3:00 A.M. If the needs of a particular outpost were less demanding, a single pack train of 60 mules might be used. Such a train required an average of 14 men to manage it, and according to packer Smithers, it could transport at least 9,600 pounds of supplies.

By October 1917, when Colonel Langhorne assumed full command of the Big Bend Military District, nearly all the National Guard units that comprised the vast majority of the troops stationed at the cavalry subposts had returned to their home states. Most were soon federalized to serve overseas in World War I. Some regular army cavalry units, however, remained on border patrol after the guardsmen departed, with their efforts now augmented by companies of the Texas Rangers. The rangers benefited from a widely known reputation throughout that part of Mexico that touched the Rio Grande. The army's rules of engagement discouraging soldiers from pursuing Mexican bandits deep into their homeland meant nothing to the rangers. Feared by potential cross-river raiders with more than ample reason, the Texas lawmen attained considerable success at reducing incursions through whatever method deemed necessary at the moment.

Through the combined efforts of the Texas Rangers and military units still on duty along the border, the number of significant raids across the river diminished during nearly all of 1917. Those that occurred usually involved the stealing of American horses and cattle from ranches, but with no loss of human life reported. On Christmas Day of that year, however, the first of two violent episodes clearly demonstrated that the border remained in turmoil. As a group of cavalrymen celebrated the holiday in Valentine, word came that a band of Mexicans had crossed the Rio Grande and engaged in looting the ranch store and stealing cattle on the Brite Ranch located 35 miles west of Marfa. In the course of their thievery, the raiders hanged and then cut the throat of Mickey Welsh, a hapless mail carrier whose daily delivery routine put him at the ranch just as the raiders struck.

The cavalrymen of Troop G were soon on the trail of the fleeing bandits, driving Hupmobiles and Oldsmobiles rather than riding horses. When the trail over the Sierra Vieja Mountains became impassable for their automobiles, however, the troopers continued the pursuit on horseback. The chase started at Camp Holland and ended 15 miles into Mexico when the soldiers recovered most of the stolen goods, along with some of the livestock. In the course of the pursuit, they shot and killed 18 of the robbers. As Robert Keil, one of the cavalrymen involved in the chase put it, "The Brite raid forced us to be more intensely alert." It was also the fatal incident at the ranch that moved Camp Holland into the forefront of the border action. Its proximity to the Sierra Vieja Trail leading to and from Mexico made it a key site in the defense of the border during the World War I years.

The next major Mexican raiding party crossed the river exactly three months after the Brite Ranch attack. Its target was the Nevill Ranch located on the western end of

Construction work on the US Army's subpost at Camp Holland, shown here ca. 1917, continued throughout the installation's eight-year existence. A large portion of the camp is obscured by the hill on the right of the photograph. *Clay Miller Collection. Archives of the Big Bend, Bryan Wildenthal Memorial Library, Sul Ross State University, Alpine, Texas.*

the pass that led to Camp Holland. In the raid of March 25, 1918, the rancher's son and a longtime employee died in a particularly gruesome manner. The cavalrymen ignored the stipulated rules of engagement to pursue the raiders across the river and killed an estimated 35 of them on Mexican soil. The Nevill Raid and the violent retribution it triggered were the last significant episodes in the undeclared war that enveloped the Rio Grande for over a decade. Although the border has never been without violence of some sort, that which was even remotely connected with the Mexican Revolution sputtered out in the early 1920s.

How long Camp Holland and its supply depot remained active military establishments is unclear. A curious absence of official records about the camp has left the telling of its story to local area ranchers, who themselves heard the story from their predecessors. Some say the installation operated until as late as 1924, while others contend that it was never fully garrisoned even during the peak years of the Mexican Revolution and cross-river banditry.

Hopefully, a factual recounting of its true role in the border wars will eventually be found, but in the meantime, Camp Holland remains much as it was in the early part of the 20th century. To visit the site, only after gaining the landowner's permission to do so, is to enter a ghost camp. The white roofs of the many fully intact buildings still

Camp Holland has looked much the same for over 90 years. The building shown in the foreground can easily be identified in the photograph taken in 1917. The Sierra Vieja Trail can be seen in the background, climbing steeply over the left shoulder of the hill. *Thomas E. Alexander Collection.*

support ventilators that spin about in the late afternoon breeze. Although the glass in the window frames remains in place, most of it has been cracked and shattered by strong Texas windstorms and hailstones. Even though the camp sits in a narrow valley, its elevation nevertheless provides a broad and breathtaking vista of the plains stretching eastward toward the now virtually deserted village of Valentine. In the flat land below the camp on the narrow roadway that once led to its main gate, small blocks of concrete remain, arranged in a large, uniform pattern. These were the footings for the many mule corrals that could hold hundreds of the animals before freighters harnessed them to make the dangerous trek over the Sierra Vieja Trail. The trail itself can clearly be seen on a tall bald mountain that is part of the Sierra Vieja range. Leading to the ancient pass that cuts through the mountains, the trail angles upward at about 15 degrees, creating a grade as challenging to the pack trains of the border patrols as it must have been to the Indians who struggled over it for centuries before the army came.

The remoteness of the camp has protected it from all elements of destruction except the weather. The owner of the ranch upon which the camp is located is both proud and very protective of this virtually unspoiled reminder of a turbulent time. In 1965, a National Park Service historian received permission to visit the site to undertake a study of its past. Though he was unable to draw any definitive conclusions about its history, he was impressed by what he found. "The [site] almost interprets itself," he wrote, "and is one of the most striking historic sites this writer has visited." Despite his admiration for what he termed the "splendid integrity of the site," the researcher wrote that the "raids in the Big Bend Country by Mexican renegades . . . are not of world-shaking importance." Further, invoking more recent political correctness, the writer stated that it "would be in bad taste to commemorate the political troubles that beset Mexico early in the [20th] century." His final recommendation to the National Park Service was that Camp Holland "not be classified as a site of exceptional value." Such appraisals are highly subjective, of course, but perhaps it is just as well that this old but still largely intact historic military site be allowed to stand at the foot of the Sierra Vieja Pass, untroubled by pressures of those who might flock to see and touch it were it open to the public. Without any such visitor pressure, Camp Holland will likely remain much as it was decades ago, a silent witness to a time of violence along the Rio Grande.

Location: Approximately 12 miles south of Valentine on private property.
Access: Restricted; very difficult traveling and requires owner's
   permission.

SOURCES

Ainsworth, Troy. "Boredom, Fatigue, Illness, and Death: The United States National Guard and the Texas-Mexico Border, 1916–1917." *Journal of Big Bend Studies* 19 (2007): 81–96.

Alpine Avalanche, May 11, 1916.

Army and Navy Journal, May 13, 1916; October 12, 1954.

Brown, William E. "Special Report on Fort Holland, Texas." Santa Fe: National Park Service Southwest Regional Office, 1966.

Casey, Clifford B. *Soldiers, Ranchers, and Miners in the Big Bend.* Lubbock: Texas Tech University Press, 1969.

Davenport, B. T. *Soldiering at Marfa, Texas, 1911–1915.* Kearney, NE: Morris Publishing Co., 1961.

Eisenhower, John S. D. *Intervention! The United States and the Mexican Revolution, 1913–1917.* New York: W. W. Norton, 1993.

Gomez, Arthur R. *A Most Singular Country: A History of Occupation in the Big Bend Country.* Salt Lake City: Brigham Young University Press, 1990.

Harris, Charles H. III, and Louis Sadler. *The Texas Rangers and the Mexican Revolution.* Albuquerque: University of New Mexico Press, 2004.

Herr, John Knowles, and Edward S. Wallace. *The Story of the US Cavalry, 1775–1942.* Boston: Little, Brown, 1953.

Katz, Friedrich. *The Secret War in Mexico: Europe, the United States and the Mexican Revolution.* Chicago: University of Chicago Press, 1981.

———. *The Life and Times of Pancho Villa.* Palo Alto, CA: Stanford University Press, 1988.

Keil, Robert. *Bosque Bonito: Violent Times along the Borderland.* Alpine, TX: Center for Big Bend Studies, 2002.

Knight, Alan. *The Mexican Revolution, 1910–1920.* Vols. 1 and 2. Cambridge: Cambridge University Press, 1986.

Osorio, Rubén. *The Secret Family of Pancho Villa: An Oral History.* Alpine, TX: Center for Big Bend Studies, 2000.

Raun, Gerald G. "The National Guard on the Border and One Soldier's Viewpoint." *Journal for Big Bend Studies* 6 (1994): 89–91.

Romo, David Dorado. *Ringside Seat to a Revolution: An Underground Cultural Journey of El Paso and Juarez, 1893–1923.* El Paso: Cinco Puntos Press, 2005.

Shorris, Earl. *The Life and Times of Mexico.* New York: W. W. Norton, 2004.

Smithers, W. D. Vertical file, Archives of the Big Bend, Bryan Wildenthal Memorial Library, Sul Ross State University, Alpine, Texas.

Stout, Joseph A. Jr. *Border Conflict: Villistas, Carrancistas, and the Punitive Expedition, 1915–1920.* Fort Worth: Texas Christian University Press, 1999.

Thompson, Cecilia. *History of Marfa and Presidio County, Texas, 1535–1946.* Vol. 2. Austin: Nortex Press, 1986.

Welcome, Eileen. *The General and the Jaguar: Pershing's Hunt for Pancho Villa: A True Story of Revolution and Revenge.* New York: Little, Brown, 2006.

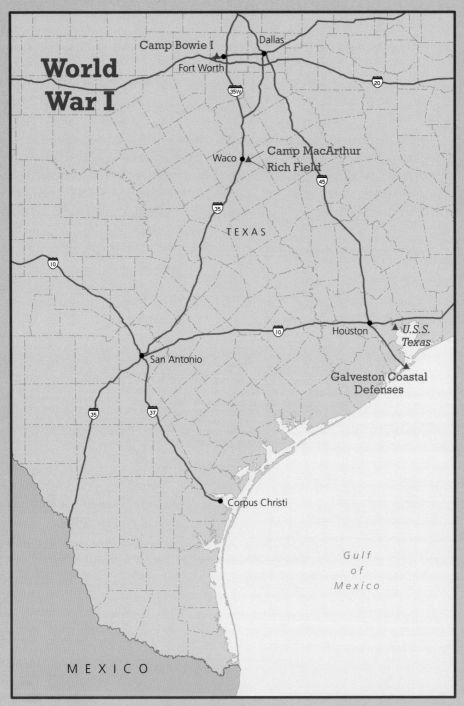

World War I

Camp Bowie I
Dallas
Fort Worth
35W
20

Camp MacArthur
Rich Field
Waco
45

TEXAS
35

10

Houston
10
U.S.S.
Texas
San Antonio
Galveston Coastal
Defenses

35
37

Corpus Christi

Gulf
of
Mexico

MEXICO

Map by Molly O'Halloran

WORLD WAR I
1917–1918

"I was in France as a soldier—where the flu was all around me, but had no effect on me whatsoever....Yet I was reported dead, on the roll call, so I called the sarjent, saying do I look like a dead man, he said you look alrite to me, go rite ahead & eat, & obey the rules until correction can be made."

*—Stephen Nolen,
Waco, Texas, 1963*

The causes of World War I are deep-seated, multilayered, and continually debated, but in general they stem from events that occurred in the late 19th century and remained unresolved until circumstances in the early 20th century made international conflict inevitable. In many respects, war was the result of a perfect storm of factors that largely centered on economics, power, and national identity. The growth of unprecedented nationalistic and cultural pride across Europe in the 19th century, coupled with intense rivalries for dominance in trade, colonial holdings, and military superiority, led to a breakdown of the traditional balance of power, which was in turn supplanted by a complex and intricately bound system of alliances. The intensity of international disputes drove diplomacy in those years, and short-term objectives often won out over the need for long-term solutions. Military strength, fueled by a global arms race, was increasingly seen as a viable solution to unresolved differences among nations. By 1914, all factors were in place for a war of unprecedented scope.

The spark came in the Balkans, a rugged and politically unstable peninsular region in southeastern Europe that had been the scene of considerable international fighting for decades. Ongoing disputes among emerging ethnic and political divisions within the Balkans could not be contained and so threatened to draw in larger powers through a series of entangling and often seemingly unrelated alliances. When a plot by Bosnian Serbs resulted in the assassination of Austria's Archduke Franz Ferdinand at Sarajevo in June 1914, the alliances, coupled with failed diplomacy, inadequate communication, and overarching nationalistic concerns, led quickly to a trans-Europe war. On one side was the Triple Entente of Russia, France, and Britain, and on the other was the Triple Alliance of Austria-Hungary, Germany, and at least initially, Italy.

Efforts by the United States to remain neutral in favor of an isolationist foreign policy proved difficult in the wake of relentless German submarine warfare that resulted in the loss of innocent American lives. As tensions mounted, the United States began enlarging its military and steadily preparing for the eventuality of war. Early in 1917, though, Germany made two significant moves that left the United States with few options. Occurring almost simultaneously were Germany's implementation of an unrestricted submarine offensive, which would again place American lives in harm's way, and its secret communiqué with Mexico calling for a military alliance between the two countries. The latter, sent by German foreign secretary Arthur Zimmermann, pledged assistance in reclaiming lost territory, including Texas, in return for Mexico's pledge to take up arms against the United States if it should enter the war. Although Mexico ignored the offer, news of the Zimmermann telegram leaked out through the media and infuriated Americans, spurring increased calls for action. Despite his campaign pledge to avoid the conflict, Pres. Woodrow Wilson reluctantly bowed to the inevitable and petitioned Congress for a formal declaration of war, which it approved on April 6, 1917.

Texans were quick to respond, and the fervor with which they responded to the call matched or even surpassed that shown in the Spanish-American War only a few years before. Military action along the Rio Grande in the years leading up to the war had prepared troops as well as citizens for the sacrifices ahead, and it had also provided invaluable field and command experience for those involved in the action—Texans and non-Texans alike. From the ranks of those who served along the border would come some of the earliest leaders in the European fighting. Residents of the Lone Star State registered for the draft or signed up voluntarily for service in impressive numbers, while others bought war bonds, worked to secure and maximize the effectiveness of the home front, converted industries to wartime production, supported communitywide efforts to attract new military bases and camps, and otherwise exhibited selfless patriotic support for the war effort.

Climatic and environmental conditions in Texas proved favorable to extended training operations, allowing large numbers of personnel from across the nation to cycle through the various programs in preparation for war. Mobilization was at a high level, with expediency a key factor, and the state figured prominently in that continuing effort. Entering the war late, as it did, the United States could not afford undue delays. Vast military camps opened quickly at Waco, Fort Worth, Houston, and San Antonio. Appropriately, given the integral role Texas played in the development of military aviation, there were also aviation training centers such as Hicks Field (Fort Worth), Rich Field (Waco), Call Field (Wichita Falls), and Kelly Field (San Antonio). There were complications, to be sure, most notably with the development of infrastructure, the devastation of an influenza pandemic, social injustices committed against German Texans, and racial inequality within the military and in military towns, but there was also a collective resolve to make a difference in Europe, and that brought significant and far-reaching change to the state. The "war to end all wars" had a dramatic impact on the state and helped establish Texas as a key player in US military preparedness, but in the process it also left behind a mixed legacy of related sites that all too soon vanished from the cultural landscape.

USS *TEXAS*
(1914–PRESENT)

The story of the battleship *Texas* may at first seem strangely out of place in a book about forgotten military sites. It is, after all, not forgotten at all. Instead, it is proudly on display at its berth near the San Jacinto Monument, east of Houston, and has welcomed thousands of visitors each year since shortly after World War II. It has also served as a backdrop for countless public events and gatherings, including the elaborate commemoration of the Texas Sesquicentennial in 1986. Only two years later it left its berth for what would prove to be one of the largest nautical restorations in the history of the United States. The *Texas* is not forgotten in the general sense we associate with abandoned vestiges of the past.

Nor is she technically a Texas military site. She was born in another state and saw military action in foreign waters from Mexico and Europe to the South Pacific, only briefly stopping by the Lone Star State on occasion through the years. But throughout the ship's history, she has represented her namesake with distinction, and many Texans have been included among her leadership and crew. In the early years it was the name that made the primary connection, but for decades now the ship has made her home in Texas waters.

Hence, this is the story not of a forgotten military site or artifact, but rather forgotten elements of the associated history. It is also, in memoriam, the story of an earlier battleship *Texas*. Central to an understanding of this story is the concept of historical interpretation—the process by which historical information is conveyed to the general public and then in turn how the public chooses to remember and commemorate. For a military site with a complex history such as the *Texas* has, and with an evolutionary presence borne of modernization and continual rehabilitation, interpretation can be complicated and involve looking beyond the present façade. For those who can successfully manage to make that paradigm shift, the rewards are broader perspectives and a greater appreciation for the expanded historical context. The bottom line is there is more to the *Texas* than meets the eye.

Although several ships have carried the name Texas throughout the years, only two would be considered battleships in the modern use of the word. The first, built in the Norfolk Navy Yard in Virginia and commissioned in 1895, was only 309 feet in length, small in comparison to the vessels in service only decades later. It was the first of two steel-hulled battleships that ushered in a new era in US naval power and strategy at the close of the 19th century. The other was the ill-fated USS *Maine*. Both would see service in the Spanish-American War, where an explosion aboard the latter in Havana Harbor in 1898 triggered formal US military action against Spain. The resulting conflict proved to be short-lived, in large part due to the overwhelming superiority of the US Navy. The most decisive action occurred at the Battle of Santiago in July 1898, when the Spanish Navy tried unsuccessfully to break through a blockade that had effectively bottled them up in Santiago Bay. The *Texas* was among the battleships that set the blockade and also bombarded and pursued the enemy fleet as it attempted in vain to escape.

Following the war, the *Texas* saw limited service as a training vessel, as her armaments were by then considered outdated. New vessels coming online in the US Navy in the early 20th century sported much larger guns arranged in more effective patterns. Utilized as a station ship in Charleston, South Carolina, only a decade after its greatest glory in battle, the vessel gave up its name three years later, becoming the USS *San Marcos*. The name change paved the way for development of a new USS *Texas*, one that would prove more integral to the nation's evolving naval strategy. In 1920, seven miles south of Tangier Island in Chesapeake Bay, the early *Texas*/*San Marcos* ended her brief existence by serving as a target for gunnery practice, finally succumbing to rounds from the USS *New Hampshire*. In later years, she remained an aerial bombing landmark, and eventually the navy had the remains demolished so they would no longer interfere with shipping lanes in the area.

Planning for the new USS *Texas* began in 1910 with congressional authorization for funding of a battleship on the general scale of the British ship whose name came to define an era of increased naval might: the HMS *Dreadnought*. Increased speed, heavier armor, and enhanced firepower, including dramatically larger central batteries, marked the new class of warships. The Newport News Shipbuilding and Dry Dock

Company of Virginia received the contract for the new *Texas,* and in April 1911, workers laid the keel. Christening came on May 18, 1912, with young Claudia Lyon, daughter of prominent Texas Republican leader, Cecil A. Lyon, breaking the traditional champagne bottle against the bow. With her at the event was Mary Colquitt, daughter of Texas governor Oscar Colquitt. A movie camera recorded the event, providing what is believed to be the first filmed launching of a US naval vessel.

The christening ceremony marked the beginning of more intensive construction on the unfinished battleship that would continue at a steady pace for almost two years. Following completion of the vessel and a successful series of trial runs, the battleship *Texas* received her formal commission in March 1914 under the captaincy of Albert Weston Grant, a graduate of the US Naval Academy and, interestingly, a veteran of the Battle of Santiago, then serving aboard the USS *Massachusetts.* Not long after his service with the *Texas,* he would become a vice admiral.

In profile and overall design, the original version of the second *Texas* differed markedly from the ship that served with distinction in World War II and is now so familiar to heritage tourists. Powered by coal, it measured slightly more than 573 feet in length and 95 feet in width, with twin open-mesh cage masts that at the highest point reached 140 feet above waterline. The impressive main battery consisted of 14-inch guns, paired on turrets, with two sets forward and three aft. The .45-caliber breech-loaded rifles were the largest models available in any navy in the world. They used both armor piercing and high-capacity shells propelled by separate smokeless powder charges in large silk bags that required a separate ignition charge. The payload and range of the shells, however, more than made up for the involved loading system. The secondary battery featured 5-inch, .51-caliber rapid firing guns—21 in number—with additional support provided by other ordnance, including a 3-inch field gun and two .30-caliber machine guns, as well as a number of field, boat, and saluting guns. The ship also had four torpedo tubes, two on each side. Absent from the arsenal were any antiaircraft guns, as military aviation had not by then advanced to the point of being a threat to naval operations. The *Texas* first carried a crew of around 950, including enlisted men, officers, and a number of marines.

The normal procedure for a new ship at sea was to spend time in a shakedown cruise, where the personnel could get to know the vessel, learn how it handled under various conditions, and train extensively for optimum teamwork and efficiency. The *Texas,* though, launched under different circumstances; revolution raged in Mexico, and the federal government worried the unchecked fighting could potentially threaten US national security and business interests. With tensions already high, the federal government under Pres. Woodrow Wilson chose not to recognize the newly imposed regime of Mexican general Victoriano Huerta that had risen in violent opposition to Pres. Francisco Madero. The US military monitored the situation in Mexico carefully, making its presence known by utilizing naval forces to shadow key coastal areas. In April 1914, the temporary arrest of several US servicemen triggered an international incident known as the Tampico affair, and it brought immediate action from the Wilson government, which moved more forces in place and occupied the port city of Veracruz. The *Texas* moved swiftly to support the effort but saw no action. Instead, the crew used the time off the Mexican coast to complete its shakedown testing.

The *Texas* moved back and forth in the Atlantic from the United States to Mexico throughout much of 1914. On one trip back to home waters in November, she sailed to Galveston, where in a formal ceremony recognizing its namesake association with the state of Texas, Captain Grant accepted an elaborate silver service set presented by Governor Colquitt. By that time, war in Europe between the Central Powers and Allied Powers continued to escalate, threatening to widen to other nations, even those pledged to neutrality. Although hoping to avoid involvement, the United States nonetheless methodically prepared for the eventuality of war by a number of means, including the upgrading and modernization of outdated weapons. As part of that effort, in 1916 the *Texas* received two 3-inch, .50-caliber antiaircraft guns, the first battleship in the navy to be so equipped.

The following year, Germany's relentless submarine campaign against Great Britain took its toll on neutral nations as well, eventually drawing the United States into the Great War. With the formal declaration in April 1917, military training escalated quickly. Aboard the *Texas,* then in Chesapeake Bay, the crew intensified its battle preparedness while also providing gunnery instruction for units that would be assigned to US merchant ships. While American destroyers made their way to Great Britain to assist with submarine hunting, the *Texas* sailed to New York for scheduled maintenance. In late September, it left the Navy Yard for Port Jefferson along the Long Island Sound. Her readiness for battle proved to be short-lived, however. Running dark and moving cautiously to avoid antisubmarine mines in the area, the *Texas* ran aground hard off Block Island, south of Kingston, Rhode Island. Three days later, as tugboats strained to break her free, the crew of the nearby *New York* and other onlookers exhorted her with cries of "Come on, *Texas,*" a phrase that afterward served as the ship's motto. Damages to the hull required her to remain behind for repairs as other ships in its division sailed for Great Britain.

Once again ready for action, the *Texas* sailed from New York without incident in January 1918, joining up with other US ships that comprised the Sixth Battle Squadron of the British Grand Fleet at Scapa Flow in the Orkney Islands off the Scottish north coast. Within days of its arrival in February, orders came for an expedited response to reports that Germany's High Seas Fleet was on the move, most probably in an attempt to break out to the North Sea from where it had otherwise been bottled up.

Historian John C. Ferguson described what happened next in his book *Historic Battleship* Texas: *The Last Dreadnought:*

> After the sun came up over the storm-tossed North Sea, the *Texas* sailed along with the other battlewagons. When the ships ahead of her suddenly swung out of line, lookouts on the *Texas* spotted a submarine periscope one thousand yards away on the port bow. The crew of the number twenty 5-inch gun fired one shot at the periscope, after which destroyers raced to the spot and immediately began dropping depth charges. The submarine disappeared, no more to be seen. Although the number twenty 5-inch gun did not hit the U-boat, it did have the distinction of firing the first combat shot from the *Texas*. (46)

The anticipated naval battle never occurred, though, as the High Seas Fleet, learning of the countermove to intercept, judiciously returned to Germany.

The close encounter with a submarine would not be the last for the crew during the war, but the *Texas* managed to avoid any torpedoes. Throughout the remaining months of the war, the ship remained battle ready, although one never occurred. Instead, the *Texas* moved between bases at Scapa Flow and the Firth of Forth, near Edinburgh, participating in a variety of escort sorties, from merchant vessel convoys to mine-laying operations, and also serving with the fleet in response to rumors of German naval movements. When the war ended on November 11, 1918, the crews of the Grand Fleet celebrated their role in bringing about victory. They had successfully held the High Seas Fleet at bay, keeping it bottled up and therefore of little strategic value to the Central Powers. On November 20, the *Texas* and other US ships joined with their British counterparts to affect the surrender of the German Navy. Meeting the High Seas Fleet in the North Sea, they escorted the captive vessels to Scapa Flow. Its role in the war complete, the 6th Battle Squadron returned to New York City on December 26 to jubilant and thankful crowds.

If the formative years of the USS *Texas* were from 1914 to 1918, its maturity came in the decade that followed the Great War. Amid an atmosphere of emerging naval strategies and talk of global peace and arms limitations, it gained in stature and strength with more diverse armaments, an expanded profile, and renewed purpose. In 1919, only a few months after armistice, it helped usher in a new era of naval aviation when Lt. Cmdr. Edward O. McDonnell successfully flew a British Sopwith Camel from a *Texas* turret platform—the first such launch from an American ship. Soon, other battleships included similar "flying-off platforms" for artillery spotter planes, but over time, as planes grew heavier, catapult systems became the standard for launch-

This 1919 photo of the USS *Texas* shows lines markedly different from the more familiar ones of the ship today. Note the distinctive basket-weave masts. Lacking the increased armament added later, as well as the addition of side blisters and sponsons, the *Texas* presented a much leaner appearance during its formative years. *Photo from the Library of Congress, LOC 3b05912r.*

ing planes. Since onboard landings were not an option, the seaplanes landed near the ship, where cranes hoisted them back aboard. Also in 1919, the *Texas* made its way through the locks of the Panama Canal to join the Pacific Fleet, the first of several similar transfers over the years.

Significant changes for the *Texas*—and indeed the entire US Navy—began in 1922 with the signing of a multinational naval arms limitation agreement known as the Washington Treaty. Under the provisions of the treaty, the nation's leading naval powers—the United States, Great Britain, Japan, France, and Italy—agreed to a moratorium on new vessels, instead opting for modernization measures, as well as limits on tonnage and firepower. In the rotation that followed, the Texas returned to Norfolk for a major overhaul in 1925. What followed was the second incarnation of the second USS *Texas*. The most significant changes were conversion from coal power to oil; removal of the cage masts in favor of larger tripod structures that supported more sophisticated fire-control operations; a redesigned forward superstructure; construction of sponsons, or side projections, that provided for gun emplacements

The USS *Texas*, restored to its World War II appearance, is berthed adjacent to the San Jacinto Battleground State Historic Site. Restoration of the vessel is an ongoing effort made possible through the Texas Parks and Wildlife Department, the USS *Texas* Foundation, and extensive volunteer assistance. *Photo by John B. Chandler. Courtesy of Texas Parks and Wildlife Department.*

extending beyond the hull line; new antiaircraft guns; an airplane catapult; removal of the torpedo tubes; and the addition of side blisters, or expanded panels outside the lower hull, to provide extra protection against torpedoes. With the extensive changes complete by 1927, the *Texas* became the flagship of what was then known as the United States Fleet, and it made its way once again via the Panama Canal to the West Coast.

The 1925–27 changes to the *Texas* were extensive, dramatic, and for their time, state of the art. It was, in effect, a new ship on an old hull, and it barely resembled its 1914 design, a reality not missed by those who had served aboard the ship in its formative years. Paul Schubert, in his 1930 book *Come On, Texas,* uses the voice of a fictionalized and unnamed petty officer on the opening page to describe the new vessel:

> She's Flagship of the *Fleet* now, modernized until her old hands feel like
> strangers in her. Stark tripods, supporting box-like armored battle-tops, have

replaced her graceful basket masts. Amidships she's built up into a bulky citadel, abristle with broadside and anti-aircraft guns. One of her old smoke pipes is gone, like a missing tooth. Her hull is "blistered." She carries airplanes squatting on flat catapults. Her very cranes have changed their shape.

The old *Texas*.

With the advent of another world war in Europe in 1939, the *Texas* returned to the waters of the North Atlantic as part of Pres. Franklin Roosevelt's Neutrality Patrol, designed to ensure the protection of national interests. In that capacity, the ship—and the United States—narrowly missed being brought into the war much earlier than it was when it became a potential target for a German U-boat off the coast of Greenland in June 1941. Ultimately, second guessing by German military leaders and evasive measures taken by the battleship crew meant that it lived to fight another day.

When Japanese forces attacked Pearl Harbor in December, drawing the United States into the war, the *Texas* was in Casco Bay, near Portland, Maine. From there, it intensified its patrols in the North Atlantic and provided invaluable escort service as well to various points. Outfitted with radar and additional guns, including more anti-aircraft firepower, in 1942 the ship was ready to answer the call for the tough assignments ahead. It served with distinction in North Africa as flagship of an attack group in Morocco; at Normandy, where it provided invaluable cover for the intense fighting at Pointe du Hoc; off Cherbourg, France, where it took two enemy shells, one of which exploded at the conning tower, killing the helmsman, and the other that never detonated, providing a special "battle souvenir" for the crew; and at post D-day landings in southern France. Arguably, though, its greatest period of service occurred near the end of the war when, once again in the Pacific, the old battleship proved instrumental in intense fighting at Iwo Jima and Okinawa. Scheduled to participate in the anticipated invasion of the Japanese home islands, the *Texas* instead made its way to Pearl Harbor following the Japanese surrender and completed numerous personnel transport runs back to the United States.

Crossing through the Panama Canal one final time in 1946, the grand old battleship, which by war's end had outlived its position in an ever-evolving modern navy, made its way back to Norfolk for mothballing. There, ironically only a few miles south of the submerged ruins of the first USS *Texas,* it awaited its fate. Given the opportunity to, in effect, bring the ship "home," the people of Texas approved a plan—enthusiastically supported by descendants of Gen. Sam Houston—to berth the battleship adjacent to the San Jacinto Battleground near La Porte. There, on San Jacinto Day, April 21, 1948, it was transferred from the federal government to the State of Texas. Appropriately, Fleet Admiral Chester W. Nimitz, a native of Fredericksburg, Texas, and a hero of World War II, provided the keynote address that day.

Location: 3523 Highway 134, La Porte, Texas.

Accessible: Operated as a state historic site by the Texas Parks and Wildlife Department.

GALVESTON COASTAL DEFENSES:
FORT CROCKETT
(1897–1953)
FORT TRAVIS
(1898–1949)
AND FORT SAN JACINTO
(1898–1959)

Galveston Bay has played an integral role in the development of Texas, from the sustenance of prehistoric cultures to its growth as a center of immigration and incubator of modern commerce. As the critical gateway to the vast resources of the bay and beyond, to the Houston area and the interior of Texas, the city of Galveston thus continually evolved in importance as a strategic military point, first regionally and then nationally. As a result, it became a center of defensive military installations early on, with artillery positions situated along the shore, on opposite sides of the entryway, and in the back bay. The coastal defenses there came into play during the Civil War, as noted in an earlier chapter, and later expanded to meet broader strategic concerns by the end of the 19th century as the United States began emerging as an international power.

Defensive installations around Galveston changed over the years to accommodate larger and more sophisticated weaponry, but within that perimeter and mission, three key points remained essential to military planning: the coastal approach to the city, the easternmost end of the island, and immediately across the bay channel at a place called Point Bolivar. In time, three federal installations marked those points, respectively: Fort Crockett, Fort San Jacinto, and Fort Travis. From the era of the Spanish-American War until the end of World War II, the three forts at Galveston provided not only protection for the vital shipping channel, but also training opportunities for coastal artillery units as well.

Named for famed Alamo defender David Crockett, Fort Crockett began in 1897 as the nation prepared for war with Spain. It consisted initially of 125 acres bounded by 45th Street on the east, 53rd Street to the west, Avenue U to the north, and the Gulf of Mexico beach to the south. There was no seawall at the time and thus no Seawall Boulevard, which cuts across the southern line of the old fort site today. Construction at Fort Crockett continued after the Spanish-American War, but the devastating hurricane of 1900 that wrecked much of the city, resulting in an estimated

12,000 casualties on the island, took its toll on the fort as well. The government suspended work for a few years as the city rebuilt, but rehabilitation of the fort began in earnest in 1903. The county conveyed additional land to the federal government to facilitate completion of the new elevated seawall in the vicinity of Fort Crockett, expanding the boundaries slightly to the east. In keeping with the seawall design elsewhere in the town, countless tons of sand fill pumped onto the property permanently lifted the horizon of the installation more than 10 feet (17 feet in some places) and secured newly constructed batteries.

Although the guns remained operational in the ensuing years, the fort was not garrisoned until 1911, when it became a mobilization and training center as a result of the mounting tension related to the Mexican Revolution. Under the command of Brig. Gen. A. L. Mills, Fort Crockett expanded rapidly to accommodate units from Louisiana, South Carolina, Alabama, Georgia, and other coastal states, forming three provisional regiments. In 1911, more than 4,000 troops were stationed there. Among the facilities constructed at the time were an administrative building, hospital, post exchange, stables and wagon shop, ordnance facilities, fire station, guardhouse, and living quarters. According to a 1911 souvenir booklet for Fort Crockett, "The buildings have all been constructed to meet the requirements of the climate. Wide galleries have been provided and to a large extent the mission style of architecture has been carried out. . . . The view of the great expanse of water from this vantage point is inspiring, and there is not to be found in any part of the country a more pleasant spot for the location of Uncle Sam's fighters." The distinctive white stuccoed buildings with red tile roofs were evocative of a Mediterranean setting, appropriate for their location adjacent to the Gulf waters.

Throughout the conflict in Mexico, Fort Crockett continued to provide artillery training. It also for a time served as a training and deployment center for the 12th Infantry Brigade. Following service at Veracruz, the brigade returned to the fort in time to ride out the 1915 hurricane. Although the storm laid waste to their tent city, the soldiers found safe haven in the fort's concrete buildings, designed to withstand such severe weather. In the years that followed, Fort Crockett, like the military command it served, slowly made the transition from service in Mexico to preparedness for war in Europe. US involvement came in 1917, and the Galveston installation began focusing on two primary missions: training and coastal defense. While the Coast Artillery Corps proved to be the central focus, other units, including the 3rd Texas Infantry, the 8th and 9th Marine Regiments, and batteries of both the 1st and 3rd Trench Mortar Battalions also stationed there prior to shipping out to European battlefields. As the United States entered the fighting late in the war, military leaders understandably emphasized rapid deployment, so troops were in constant movement through Fort Crockett. At times, though, there were as many as 3,000 personnel at the site.

In addition to training, Fort Crockett also served as an active defensive installation, with troops always vigilant for enemy activity in the Gulf of Mexico. Of particular concern were German submarines, whose actions in the Atlantic had been a prime factor in bringing the United States into the war. Installations consisting of siege guns and searchlights at Sabine Pass and near Freeport complemented the fixed batteries at the fort and fell under the base command. There were, as noted earlier, the Coast Artillery Corps installations at Fort San Jacinto and Fort Travis.

Fort San Jacinto, named for the nearby decisive battle of the Texas Revolution, shared a Spanish-American War pedigree with Crockett. Construction at the site on the eastern extremity of Galveston Island began in 1898 and continued into 1901, providing strategic channel cover with three batteries through World Wars I and II. Equally essential to the defense of the bay was Fort Travis, named for William B. Travis, commander of Texas forces at the Alamo. Situated east of the channel on sizeable acreage of the Bolivar Peninsula it too dated from 1898. Two batteries with 12-inch guns were in place by the time of World War I, with two other batteries added later. Also on the site were a number of barracks and associated structures for personnel serving there.

Despite vital service during the war and continued operations in the years afterward, it appeared the Galveston defenses may have outlived their effectiveness by the early 1920s. Amid planning by the War Department that favored increased use of aviation and naval cover in harbor areas rather than fixed installations, Fort Crockett became nonessential. The resulting uproar by the Galveston citizenry led to political intervention by local Congressman Clay Stone Briggs, who used his political influence to reverse the federal decision. Consequently, the fort inherited a new mission as home to the 3rd Attack Group, transferred from San Antonio's Kelly Field in 1926 under the command of Maj. Frank D. Lackland. With the change came the development of an airfield on leased land. Tragically, a subsequent commander, Lt. Col. Horace Meek Hickam, died in a crash while on night approach to the field in 1934. The following year, a new airfield in Hawaii was named in his honor, and six years later Hickam Field gained national attention during the Japanese invasion of Pearl Harbor.

The mission of Fort Crockett changed again in 1935 when the 69th Coast Artillery Anti-Aircraft Regiment—one of only four in the nation—took over the site. Searchlights and battery firing associated with nighttime target practice thus became a regular occurrence for local residents. Increased military activity in the area during the years that followed, as war in Europe again threatened to involve the United States, not only bolstered Galveston's economy but provided a sense of security as well. The latter proved particularly important, given the rapid expansion of the local petrochemical industry, a vital concern for national security, and the port city's increased vulnerability as the regional transportation gateway. Construction of new facilities at

As this 1911 photo of the Fort Crockett parade ground shows, early facilities at the installation included both tents and permanent buildings. Additional structures, including an extensive system of casemated bunkers, contributed to the continued viability of the site through World War II. *Library of Congress. Entitled* Parade, 3rd Prov. Regt., Fort Crockett, Galveston, Texas.

In 2010, the fate of remaining structures at the site of Fort Crockett remained in doubt, but planning discussions continued between the owners and the Texas Historical Commission. *Courtesy of Texas Historical Commission. Photo by William A. McWhorter.*

the fort began in the 1930s and intensified following the advent of US involvement in the war during the 1940s. Changes included the casemating, or greatly enhanced protective covering, of Battery Hopkins, and the development of a prisoner-of-war compound for the internment of captured Germans. The compound extended west beyond the post boundary to 57th Street and reached from Avenue Q south to the shoreline, crossing Seawall Boulevard, which remained closed during the war and the years immediately following. The prisoner-of-war facility, which housed 650 prisoners, closed in May 1946.

Following the end of World War II, the military installations at Galveston again faced an uncertain future. This time, though, there was no political reprieve, and the federal government formally moved to deactivate them for sale as surplus properties. Fort Travis closed in 1949, and the site of Fort San Jacinto remained in use for military purposes for several years by both the Coast Guard and the US Army Corps of Engineers. Despite some speculation on a new life for Fort Crockett, the US Army formally transferred ownership in the 1950s.

While many of the former structures and emplacements associated with the Galveston forts have been demolished to make way for a variety of commercial and public service projects, evidence of the three Galveston fortifications that remained active from the time of the Spanish-American War through World War II can still be found in the area. Perhaps the most noteworthy and accessible vestiges are the remains of the Battery Hopkins casement, now incorporated into the landscape of the San Luis Resort Hotel, and a number of base buildings, some of which have been extensively remodeled over the years to such an extent that they no longer reflect their prior military association. Some, such as the small collection of buildings located along Sarna Court (east of 45th Street and north of Seawall Boulevard), retain their distinctive and historic stuccoed exteriors and red tile roofs. They are not, however, at the time of this writing, in a good state of repair, and their future preservation remains a source of ongoing negotiations between the federal government and the Texas Historical Commission, which holds protective covenants on the site. Some of the structures date from 1910 and therefore provide a visually interpretive sense of the built environment during the World War I years. Others date from 1939 and the period of increased development leading up to US involvement in World War II. At this point, preservation remains uncertain.

Location of Fort Crockett: Seawall Boulevard at 45th Street, Galveston.
Access: Buildings can be observed from nearby streets; battery acces-
**   sible at San Luis Resort Hotel.**
Location of Fort Travis: Fort Travis Park, US Highway 87, Point Bolivar
Access: Open.
Location of Fort San Jacinto: Extreme eastern end of Galveston Island
Access: Not accessible to the public due to health and safety concerns.

CAMP BOWIE I
(1917–1919)

When completed three miles west of downtown Fort Worth on August 24, 1917, Camp Bowie held the potential to serve as the eighth largest population center in Texas. Home of the soon-to-be-famous 36th "T-Patch" Infantry Division, the installation spanned nearly 2,300 acres, most of which became the Arlington Heights residential and commercial district after World War I. The camp's population usually exceeded 35,000 men. The army built the camp in 32 days, utilizing 4,500 workers, at what was then the astronomical cost of $2 million. The City of Fort Worth gave to the 1,410-acre encampment area a 750-acre rifle range, a 125-acre trench warfare training area, a three-lane paved highway, a railroad spur, and a complete utility package to the federal government free of any charge.

The 36th Division was a unit of the National Guard comprised of citizen soldiers living in Texas and Oklahoma. Its first commanding officer was Maj. Gen. Edwin St. John Greble, a veteran of the Mexican Revolution border crisis of 1910–1920.

General Greble's assignment was to oversee the intensive training of the National Guard units to make them quickly ready for combat in France. Although Greble accomplished his difficult task efficiently, the popular general was not able to lead the men he had trained into battle in Europe. When he failed to pass the new stringent physical examination demanded of all senior officers by army commander John J. Pershing, Greble had to surrender command of the division and be reduced in rank to brigadier general. He was, however, allowed to remain at Camp Bowie to supervise the training of new recruits and to continue his highly successful relationship with the camp's host city.

The original construction plans for the camp called for at least 250 buildings to accommodate the needs of the thousands of soldiers expected to arrive when the facility opened. The first group to be processed included 27,000 men from Texas and Oklahoma. By the time the war ended just over a year later, nearly 100,000 troops had been trained at the camp and sent overseas. The patriotic rush to enlist in the nation's armed services after the United States generated more new soldiers than anticipated. Even though enlistment in the 36th Division was temporarily suspended for a time, large numbers of recruits created a backlog in processing and put a strain on the newly built facilities. While crews erected wooden barracks, most of the men lived in unusually tall pyramid-shaped canvas tents. Although each tent could comfortably accommodate eight soldiers, the unexpected influx of troopers made it necessary for 12 to share the limited space.

The tents were arranged in long rows called "company streets" by the army's old-timers. At the end of each row stood a wooden mess hall large enough to feed from 70 to 80 men at a time. Although the siding and the roof of each eating facility was sturdy enough to withstand the frequently strong winds of North Texas, the floors remained packed earth. The floors of the tents were also nothing but dirt, pounded down and lightly sprinkled with water every morning and night. When the camp opened in the traditionally torrid month of August, the natural flooring proved at least endurable, but when the cold north winds began to blow in January, frequently accompanied by sleet and icy rain, living conditions deteriorated dramatically. The absence of heating stoves in the tents until late in the first winter season only made matters worse.

The War Department's praiseworthy efficiency in building such a large facility so swiftly was all but nullified by its inability to promptly supply the resources necessary to operate it. As a result, the 10 commodious warehouses built in a matter of days remained empty for months. There were no uniforms or equipment for the soldiers, who found it necessary to make do with the well-worn uniforms they brought to the camp. During the unusually severe month of November 1917, there were only 8,000 overcoats on hand to be issued to a lucky few among the 27,000 guardsmen.

After the direct intercession of Texas governor William Hobby, an adequate number of the warm coats finally arrived at the camp just a few days before Christmas.

Further supply problems continued into the first months of operation. As a combat-ready divisional command training center, the camp had many facets, including artillery, signal corps, supply functions, and an engineering brigade in addition to its basic infantry training program. Because of the failure of higher command headquarters to bring adequate resources to the camp, the artillery brigade had no guns, the signal battalion had no apparatus with which to transmit messages, and the engineers had no tools. The National Guard troops that came directly to Fort Worth from duty along the Mexican border were the only ones who had modern weapons and other essential gear. Particularly cold weather and disease greatly exacerbated the supply problems at the camp. Men living in the crowded, unheated dirt-floored tents proved to be highly susceptible to measles, mumps, and pneumonia. At one time, the unusually large camp hospital reportedly housed 600 soldiers. One guardsman who saw duty there believed the hospital had a 1,000-bed capacity, while another account added that an additional 600 beds could be accommodated by crowding four to five patients into a space intended for use by only two.

In early January 1918, the still infamous Spanish influenza epidemic began sweeping across America. Congested living conditions on military bases made them particularly vulnerable to the disease. General Pershing's headquarters announced much later in the year that over a half-million soldiers had died in the epidemic. The general himself declared, "More soldiers died of influenza than were killed in the war." When a reluctant War Department belatedly announced that 107,204 men died in action in France, Pershing's comment proved to be 500 percent accurate. Reportedly, more than 2,000 soldiers of the 36th Division died at Camp Bowie. Additional fatalities occurred in May 1918 when the 144th Infantry Regiment participated in a field demonstration being observed by 10,000 other trainees. The exercise involved the setting up and firing of trench mortars, a key tactical weapon on the battlefields of France. Apparently, soldiers inserted a shell into a mortar that already held a missile in its chamber, and the resulting explosion killed the entire 15-man gun crew and seriously wounded 20 others. Despite the accident, training in trench warfare continued. The 125-acre trench war simulator area was located near present-day Benbrook south of Fort Worth. Barbed wire entanglements like those being used by both sides in France snaked their way across and through deep and often water-filled trenches. The instructors in this crucial phase of the combat training were British and French officers who had survived the real trench warfare experience in battle and earned what was likely a very welcome posting to North Texas.

The Oklahoma National Guard units that came to Camp Bowie included one that contained more Native Americans than any other infantry company in the entire army. Company E of the 142nd Infantry Regiment consisted of members of such tribes as the Apache, Creek, Sioux, Mohawk, Iroquois, and Choctaw, along with other lesser-known tribes. Upon completion of their training, the men accompanied their division to France, where an enterprising colonel took advantage of their native language to confuse the enemy. When German soldiers abandoned a frontline position in the Meuse-Argonne sector in France, for example, they deliberately left radio telephone communication lines connected to their receivers open, hoping to eavesdrop on American transmissions. Discovering the scheme, the colonel asked his Choctaw soldiers to relay tactical messages to American headquarters from the front in their native tongue. A Choctaw on the receiving end at headquarters then translated the information back into English and passed it on to senior commanders. Germans listening in on the message were incapable of understanding what was being transmitted. This practice proved to be successful in keeping German field officers unaware of American tactical plans. It was also the forerunner of the Navajo Codetalker Project used a quarter of a century later in World War II.

The arrival of the Oklahoma and Texas National Guard units at the camp essentially increased the population of Fort Worth, the host city, by 33 percent in short order. The prospect of such population growth was apparently a much discussed issue. An article that appeared in the *Fort Worth Star-Telegram* on August 11, 1917 reflects the concerns being addressed two weeks before the camp opened. "They [the citizens of Fort Worth] are determined that the correct environment shall be thrown around them [the soldiers]," the article declared, "and that every opportunity for pure, wholesome amusement shall be theirs." After assuring its readers that "the moral welfare of the soldiers will be safe," the paper went on to note that "all restrictive measures will be in full force and effect." The article took further pains to point out that "the people of Fort Worth have realized that red-blooded young men are coming here and they have realized that 'sissy' amusements will not appeal to them." In the same issue, the paper advised its readers that houses of "ill fame" were then under constant surveillance by local law officers and that stringent rules forbidding the sale of intoxicating beverages to soldiers in uniform would be rigorously enforced.

The "wholesome amusement" to be offered to the soldiers included free reading and writing rooms, church picnics, and invitations to "mingle in the best homes in the city." A service board organized by the chamber of commerce coordinated the benign activities. Further, the Knights of Columbus built a $30,000 Service Club to accommodate off-duty soldiers, and the YMCA erected a similar facility close to the camp. Despite such well-intentioned efforts, there were a dozen streetcar stops on the camp where soldiers could catch a ride down newly laid tracks directly to Fort Worth's infamous "Hell's Half Acre." Within that district located immediately next to

Fort Worth's Rivercrest Country Club, shown here soon after it was built in 1911, was nearby Camp Bowie's unofficial officers' club during World War I. *Courtesy of Southwestern Mechanical Company Collection, University of Texas at Arlington Library, Arlington.*

the Tarrant County Courthouse, gambling houses, saloons, and bordellos continued to flourish much as they had since the days of the cattle drives of the late 1800s.

On April 11, 1918, the 36th Division left Fort Worth to go to war in France. Training elements remained behind to process replacement troops, but nearly 30,000 of the men participated in a "Farewell to Fort Worth" parade that a 1987 newspaper article still referred to as "one of the greatest parades ever staged" in the city. An estimated 225,000 onlookers cheered wildly as "the iron-handed yet kind-hearted" General Greble led his troops down Main Street passing Hell's Half Acre on their right. Gov. William Hobby stood proudly on the reviewing stand. As the men marched by, someone asked the 40-year-old governor if he would like to be going with the boys to France. "Good Lord, yes," Hobby cried, reportedly with great passion.

Six months after the parade, the 36th Division had been tested in battle in the Meuse-Argonne offensive. Before being relieved on October 28, 1918, they had fought the Germans for 20 days only to advance 13 miles in the effort. They had also suffered a 10 percent casualty rate, with 2,601 men killed or wounded in action. Although what was then called the "Great War" ended exactly two weeks following their first major

Today's elegant Rivercrest Country Club is a far cry from the earlier structure frequented by officers stationed at Camp Bowie during World War I. *Thomas E. Alexander Collection.*

engagement, the men of the 36th Division did not leave France until May 19, 1919. Most received their discharge papers immediately upon returning to Camp Bowie, but those still suffering from battle wounds received medical treatment at the base hospital. The camp served as a large demobilization center from late May until mid-August 1919. As soon as the installation deactivated, the demolition of the hundreds of buildings immediately began. The destruction was total. Except for one stone wall of an ammunition dump discovered by a local historian in 1983, nothing else is known to remain.

The Camp Bowie story is somewhat unique and in many ways a testimony to the foresight and business acumen of Fort Worth's city leaders at the time. First, they saw a golden opportunity to gain a large military base and then cobbled together a real estate, transportation, and utility package that, because it was offered at no cost, the army could not refuse. The city enjoyed the financial benefits provided by the payrolls of construction workers and then later the military personnel, all the while basking in the well-earned glow of patriotic duty.

When the war came to a close, the army returned the camp land to the City of Fort Worth with all of its utility, communication, and transportation infrastructure still intact. The city then platted the vast acreage and sold parcels of the site at a profit to eager developers, who quickly converted an abandoned army camp into the attractive and still prestigious community known as Arlington Heights. The impressive thoroughfare that slices through the bustling district still bears the name Camp Bowie Boulevard. It is the sole remaining visible indication that a massive army post once flourished at the end of the boulevard.

Location: The site of the 1917 army camp is now Arlington Heights, located in West Fort Worth. Camp Bowie Boulevard more or less bisects the original military post.
Access: Unlimited.

CAMP MacARTHUR
(1917–1919)
AND RICH FIELD
(1917–1921)

West-northwest of downtown Waco is a sizeable expanse of mixed-use properties—largely residential but interspersed with commercial developments—that primarily reflect the city's suburban growth in the mid- to late 20th century. The relatively close-in neighborhoods of bungalows, ranch-style homes, and more modest housing stock, along with churches, schools, and strip commercial centers, effectively mask the area's earlier history as an important military site. One possible clue can be found in the name of a local route, MacArthur Road, but those who might make a historical connection are likely to speculate about an association with the celebrated Gen. Douglas MacArthur of World War II and Korean Conflict fame. Instead, the road and the World War I military camp it once crossed are named for his father, Gen. Arthur MacArthur, a noted military leader in his own right and a distinguished veteran of the Civil War, Indian Wars, and Spanish-American War.

In 1916, with war escalating in Europe but not altogether certain for the United States, army officials visited a number of towns in anticipation of the need for new training installations should the nation be drawn into the fighting. Waco seemed a logical choice for several reasons: it had sufficient size—approximately 30,000 in population—to support such an establishment; there was sufficient open farmland nearby that could be converted quickly for military purposes; the city was also a rail hub, located along the Brazos River, with several lines serving the area; and the weather in Central Texas provided year-round training capabilities. Additionally, military units that had recently served along the Texas border relative to the Mexican Revolution could be easily redeployed through a new regional center. Equally vital to the mission was community support, and prominent Waco business leaders worked in conjunction with the chamber of commerce to secure necessary land rights and pledges of support, primarily in terms of infrastructure and materials.

The United States formally entered the Great War in April 1917, and on June 11 came the official word that Waco had been selected as the site for a major infantry training facility. As the newspaper staff readied the copy and banner headline for the afternoon edition, word spread quickly through less formal channels, and soon sirens, church bells, and factory whistles sounded across the town as the patriotic citizenry celebrated what many termed "the big prize." Waco was now a major player in the military effort to follow, and with that commitment also came the promise of economic prosperity, at least for the short term. That evening, residents of the city gathered in the Cotton Palace Coliseum to learn more about the camp and the continued support that would be required of them.

The US Army moved quickly to develop the 8,000 (later 10,000) acres of land the federal government leased through Waco's business leaders. As work on railroad spurs, roads, and utility lines ensued, the Fred A. Jones Construction Company of Dallas staffed up to meet its contract for hundreds of structures that would eventually serve an estimated 30,000 to 40,000 troops, a contingent larger than the city's existing population.

In July came word the new camp would be named for Lt. Gen. Arthur MacArthur. The name proved to be important historically, not because of ties to Waco or even Texas, but because of the general's association with those who would first train at the camp. Born in Massachusetts to Scottish parents, Arthur McArthur (the spelling of his last name would change when he entered military service) migrated westward with his family to Wisconsin. Although a teenager at the time the Civil War broke out, he managed to sign up with the 24th Wisconsin Volunteer Infantry, which saw service in such key battles as Perryville, Chickamauga, Stones River, Chattanooga, Kennesaw Mountain, Franklin, and Missionary Ridge. It was during the latter engagement in the Chattanooga Campaign, when he was but 18, that he gained lasting fame for gallantly spurring his unit forward with shouts of "On, Wisconsin." For his bravery, he received the Medal of Honor, albeit many years later. Sadly, he died in 1912 while attending a Milwaukee reunion of his former Civil War unit. MacArthur's valorous allegiance to his home state and his country in times of war, his bravery under fire, and his stellar military career made his name an appropriate one to honor with a military installation, but especially one associated with the Wisconsin troops who would be among the first stationed there.

As work at the site during the summer of 1917 continued at a remarkable pace—core facilities would be ready in 25 days—other pieces of the puzzle that was Camp MacArthur began to fall into place. Soon after the formal federalization of National Guard units came word that guardsmen from Wisconsin and Michigan would transfer to Waco for infantry training. The city also received welcome news of federal approval for an airfield and aviation school on a site near the camp. Work began in September on Rich Field, named for Lt. Col. Perry Rich, an army pilot killed in a plane crash in the Philippines only a few years before. The new field became the home of the 374th Aero Squadron, which saw service in England and France.

Progress on the installations did not proceed without a measure of controversy, however. Expressions of concern came from congressional leaders representing Wisconsin and Michigan who feared environmental conditions at Waco might prove as harsh and inhospitable as those their guard units had recently experienced along the Rio Grande during defensive actions relative to the Mexican Revolution. There were also unfounded rumors of a malarial outbreak in Texas. Congressman Tom Connally, who represented the Waco area in Washington, countered that Waco was different—a land of clear streams, abundant shade, extensive parks, and countless opportunities for enjoyable recreation. He backed up his claims with assurances that the boys from up north would find the people of McLennan County welcoming, warm, patriotic, and supportive. Acting in anticipation of unwelcomed community support by a select group of local residents, though, Brig. Gen. James A. Parker called on the City of Waco to close its well-known and publicly tolerated red-light district, known as "the reservation," for the duration of the war. The action, as the local newspaper reported, was in keeping with similar concerns at other army installations. "Some weeks ago notice was given to the demi mondes of San Antonio to vacate, and similar orders were given to each city where public houses of prostitution have been maintained." The article further noted, "All of this week is to be given the women in the reservation district here to make arrangements for leaving Waco, but their presence in the city is not to be tolerated after next Saturday morning, August 11."

Also controversial and potentially incendiary in the racially charged climate of Waco at the time was the army's decision to bring in the 24th Infantry, an African American unit, to guard the camp construction site. Cautious to avoid any outward reticence or aversion to the decision that might unduly affect either the continued development of the camp or chances for a more permanent military installation later, city leaders reiterated their support of the army, especially when they secured assurances the unit's presence would be temporary. Regardless, an incident involving a confrontation between soldiers and white citizens on the evening of July 29 resulted in gunfire—but no casualties—and momentarily threatened to derail army operations in the city. Cooler heads prevailed, however, and the men of the 24th Infantry diligently resumed their duties, albeit with tighter controls and increased security measures.

With the initial construction largely completed and moral safeguards addressed, troops began arriving at Camp MacArthur by late August and early September. There, the Michigan and Wisconsin units merged to form the 32nd US Infantry Division for deployment to France. Later, they would be joined by other soldiers from Texas, Arkansas, Missouri, and New Mexico. The camp commander, General Parker, a New Jersey native and West Point graduate, initially established his staff headquarters in the Tom J. Primm home (since razed) near the intersection of 19th Street and Bewley Lane (now Park Lake Drive). Nearby, an illuminated boardwalk area of several blocks in length accommodated local businesses. Farther from town, in an area now partly under the waters of Lake Waco, was an extensive training area that replicated a typical European battlefield, complete with bunkers and pillboxes, barbed wire defenses, and lines of trenches. The soldiers lived in a vast but tightly arranged city of canvas Sibley tents; woodstoves provided warmth in the winter, and slit trench latrines served as sewage facilities. Although the living conditions were far from harsh, they later proved detrimental to public health concerns at the camp.

In the spring of 1918, medical officials at Camp MacArthur began to notice a steady and alarming number of Spanish influenza patients, and soon the site was embroiled in the pandemic then sweeping the country and other nations as well. Within months, the initial wave of the deadly virus gave way to a larger and more costly onslaught, and efforts to curtail its effect by isolating patients and opening up the tents to fresh air proved futile. As Wacoan Ann Martin later recalled, "There was a Funeral Home across the street from Toby's on South Fourth Street, and almost daily—sometimes two or three times a day—we would look out and see a group of nurses, trim in their red-lined navy dresses, or a group of khaki-clad boys, marching by or standing at attention while taps were being blown for a Buddy who had fallen victim to the killer." Frank Locke, who contracted the flu while stationed at Waco, remembered, "Camp Headquarters had ordered every fourth mess hall converted into a field hospital. . . . We were on cots, almost side by side, with head and feet alternating in opposite directions. . . . Once or twice daily, ambulances took several patients to the general hospital. But as crude as the facilities were in the field hospital," he noted, "none of us wanted to go to the general hospital for we soon learned that only the most critically ill were being admitted there. The thought 'in by ambulance, out by hearse,' prevailed." Regardless, he added, "There was no panic." Ultimately, the influenza epidemic of 1918, as previously noted, would prove many times more devastating in terms of casualties than the war itself.

Despite the difficulties associated with camp life in 1917–18, trained units left Waco on a regular basis, headed for the front lines in Europe. The 32nd Division, in particular, served with distinction as a key unit in the battles of Marne and Oise, as well as the Meuse-Argonne offensive. The first Allied division to break through the Hindenburg Line, the 32nd Division later recognized the feat in a special red arrow patch symbolizing its ability to pierce any defenses. The French referred to the unit as *Les Terribles,* a term of enduring respect for its ability to fight against overwhelming odds in inhos-

Headquarters of Camp MacArthur in 1918, Waco. *Photo courtesy of the Texas Collection, Baylor University, Waco, Texas.*

pitable terrain. In what is perhaps a fitting tribute to Arthur MacArthur—and his son, Douglas—the 32nd served admirably in the Philippines during World War II.

Late in 1918, Camp MacArthur became headquarters for the Central Infantry Officers Training School under the command of Col. John J. Boniface. Three schools of cadets underwent training at Waco before news of the war's end arrived in November 1918. The camp remained in operation for a few months, serving as a processing center for returning units and equipment, but its final function ended by January 1919, and reportedly salvaged structures were either sold to local farmers for agricultural purposes or dismantled and used in the construction of border crossing stations along the Rio Grande. Rich Field remained in limited operation following the war, but in August 1921 a newspaper report noted the last plane, piloted by base commander Lt. R. H. Magee, would be transferred to Kelly Field in San Antonio within days. The site later became the home of a new Rich Field, the city's municipal airport, which served until a new airport opened following World War II.

Today, any extant remains of the two World War I installations are largely archeological in nature. Waco High School (formerly Richfield High) and the Heart of Texas Coliseum are later landmarks on the site of Rich Field. Within the much larger

The former site of Rich Field, in operation during World War I and later, is now marked by a mix of structures, including the Heart of Texas Coliseum. *Photo by Dan K. Utley.*

Commercial development at the site of the Camp MacArthur headquarters shows the extent of urban change that has taken place on the former installation property since World War I. *Photo by Dan K. Utley.*

footprint of what was Camp MacArthur—which stretched in an irregular pattern from Herring Avenue on the southeast side to Park Lake Drive on the north, and from south of Hillcrest Drive on the southwest to 17th Street on the northeast, with the western limits extending to the general vicinity of Lake Waco—are numerous residential neighborhoods, small commercial centers, and the Waco Center for Youth (formerly the Waco State Home), established in 1922. And through the site of the former camp runs MacArthur Road.

Location of Camp MacArthur: An Official Texas Historical Marker commemorating the site of the World War I training headquarters is located at 3716 North 19th Street in Waco. Currently, no marker exists for Rich Field, but the Waco High School campus and the grounds of the Heart of Texas Coliseum provide visual reference for the air training base.

Access: Unlimited to both sites via public roads, although much of the land is now privately owned.

SOURCES

The Army Almanac. Harrisburg, PA: Stackpole Publishing, 1959.

"Army's Camp MacArthur Boomed for Two Years," *Waco Tribune-Herald,* October 26, 1975.

Bailey, Brad. "War Reminder: Little Remains of Short-Lived Troop Camp," *Waco Tribune-Herald,* March 22, 1980.

Baker, Eugene W. "The Camp MacArthur Story," *Waco Heritage and History,* Winter 2001, 1–19.

Baylor University. Influenza Epidemic of 1918 file and Camp MacArthur file. Texas Collection. Waco.

Caulfield, Tom. "In Days of Camp MacArthur, Waco Had More Soldiers Than Residents." *Waco Tribune-Herald,* October 2, 1960.

Christian, Garna. "The Ordeal and the Prize: The 24th Infantry and Camp MacArthur." *Military Affairs,* April 1986, 65–70.

Dallas Morning News, August 11, 1917, and August 8, 1921.

England, Mark. "When Waco Went to War." *Waco Tribune-Herald,* November 11, 1993.

Ferguson, John C. *Historic Battleship* Texas: *The Last Dreadnought.* Abilene, TX: State House Press, 2007.

Fort Worth News-Tribune, February 18, 1983.

Fort Worth Public Library vertical files on Camp Bowie.

Fort Worth Record. October 1917 and July 1918.

Fort Worth Star-Telegram. August 11, 1917; April 7, 1937; October 26, 1937; October 30, 1949; and August 15, 2001.

Freeman, Martha Doty, and Sandra L. Hannum. *A History of Fortifications at Fort San Jacinto, Galveston Island, Texas.* Reports of Investigations, Number 80. Prewitt and Associates, March 1991.

Garcia, Margaret. "The Three Forts in Galveston County." *Junior Historian of Texas* 28, no. 4 (January 1968): 29–30.

Henson, Rose Mary, and Golda Ruth Phillips. *The Fort Worth Story, Yesterday and Today.* Fort Worth: Fort Worth Public Schools, 1967.

Keegan, John. *The First World War.* New York: Alfred A. Knopf, 1999.

Maurer, J. M., photographer. *Souvenir of the Encampment of First Separate Brigade US Troops at Fort Crockett, Texas.* Published by J. M. Maurer, 1911.

Maxfield, Bernice Blanche Miller, and William E. Jary Jr. *Camp Bowie, Fort Worth, 1917–1918.* Fort Worth: B. B. Maxfield Foundation, 1975.

McComb, David G. *Galveston: A History.* Austin: University of Texas Press, 1986.

Peterson, Dorothy Burns. *Military Presence in 19th and 20th Century Galveston County, Texas.* Bloomington, IN: Xlibris Corporation, 2003.

Power, Hugh. *Battleship Texas.* College Station: Texas A&M University Press, 1993.

Schubert, Paul. *Come On, Texas.* New York: Jonathan Cape & Harrison Smith, 1930.

Selcer, Richard F. *Hell's Half Acre: The Life and Legend of a Red-Light District.* Fort Worth: Texas Christian University Press, 1991.

Texas Historical Commission. Camp MacArthur marker file. Fort Crockett files, Division of Architecture. Austin.

Texas State Library and Archives Commission. Camp Bowie vertical file. Austin.

Young, Kenneth Ray. *The General's General: The Life and Times of Arthur MacArthur.* Boulder: Westview Press, 1994.

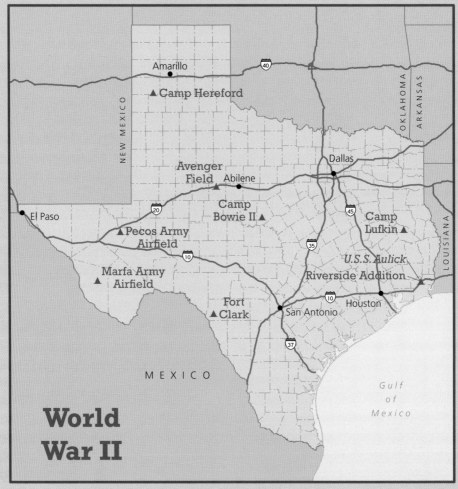

Amarillo

▲ Camp Hereford

NEW MEXICO

Dallas

Avenger
Field   Abilene

El Paso

Camp
Bowie II ▲

Camp
Lufkin ▲

▲ Pecos Army
   Airfield

U.S.S. Aulick

Riverside Addition

Marfa Army
▲ Airfield

Fort
▲ Clark

Houston

San Antonio

OKLAHOMA

ARKANSAS

LOUISIANA

M E X I C O

Gulf
of
Mexico

World
War II

7

WORLD WAR II
1941–1945

*The news of Pearl Harbor
fell even colder than the
Panhandle Rain.*
—Elmer Kelton

I have no idea when I will return.
—Dwight D. Eisenhower to his
wife, Mamie, Fort Sam Houston,
Texas, December 12, 1941

*The war made such an
enormous impact on our Texas
culture it's almost like talking
about two different planets
separated by only four years!*
—Col. Knox Bishop, USAF (Ret.)

The author Studs Terkel once declared that World War II was "the last good war." At first glance, such an observation might seem grossly inappropriate for an international catastrophe that claimed the lives of approximately 32 million people worldwide, including both military and civilian deaths. Another 7 million on the Allied side alone still remain unaccounted for but must obviously now be presumed dead. The United States suffered the loss of 292,000 military personnel and an additional 670,000 wounded in combat. In the grim shadow of such overpowering statistics, it is difficult to accept that there was anything at all good about World War II. In the now archaic conventional sense of warfare, however, and in view of its nearly unanimous public support, it perhaps should be considered as having been at least unique if not exactly good. The war was fought in accordance with time-honored rules of engagement, unlike the so-called little wars of the last 60 years. The adversaries in World War II battles were readily identifiable, fighting as they did in uniforms and under the easily recognized flags of their respective nations. Also unlike latter conflicts, it was a war that pitted one group of nations battling to attain clearly stated goals against another alliance of nations just as fervently fighting in order to attain totally different objectives.

From the American perspective, World War II had a now rare, well-defined beginning at Pearl Harbor on December 7, 1941, and a distinct ceremonial conclusion onboard the USS *Missouri* in Tokyo Bay on September 2, 1945. The nature of the Japanese attack on Pearl Harbor launched America's involvement in the war on a tidal wave of patriotism and resolve that continued relatively unabated throughout the three and a half years of conflict. The nation remained united in support of the war effort despite early setbacks in the fighting, personal sacrifices, and civilian hardship, as well as a steadily mounting death toll at the front. Unfortunately, the conflicts that followed World War II have failed to mirror that extraordinary level of unquestioning patriotism and national unity.

If World War II were truly a "good war," or rather the last understandable one, is perhaps an open question, but there can be no doubt that it was the seminal event of the 20th century. Its powerful impact upon the state of Texas was particularly instantaneous, limitless, and everlasting. When the war began, much of Texas languished in 19th-century attitudes and social conditions, even though the 20th century was almost half over. Nearly 60 percent of all Texans lived on farms, ranches, or in small isolated rural communities. Few people lived far from their place of birth in the countryside. Six out of 10 did not complete high school. Women were mostly limited to being housewives or, if they were a minority race, servants, and minority males had few employment opportunities beyond field hand or common laborer. Only one in five residents in the state owned an automobile, and even fewer living in the rural areas had access to a telephone. Further, the entire state was mired in the Great Depression in the late 1930s. Eastern demands for Texas agricultural products had dwindled because of the severe downturn in the nation's economy. Unemployment remained high in the larger cities.

By 1939, it had become apparent that America would soon be involved in the fighting already taking place in Europe and Asia. Taking advantage of the vast amounts of inexpensive land and almost ideal flying conditions to be found in Texas, the War Department began constructing large army airfields throughout the state, particularly in its more remote western part. When the war began in late 1941, further construction of military installations took place around the clock. By the time the war neared its conclusion, Texas was home to 175 major training and operational military facilities. There were 65 airfields, 35 army forts and camps, along with seven naval installations. In addition, the state also supported 60 prisoner-of-war camps.

As the war came to Texas, so did Texans go to war. Over 750,000 men and women from the state saw service during the conflict. Although the population of the state represented only 5 percent of the national total at the time, 7 percent of the country's military personnel came from Texas. Nearly 22,000 of those did not survive the war—over 8 percent of all American combat casualties. Those Texans who did not serve in uniform helped win the war by working in defense plants in cities or by staying on the farms and in the oilfields producing vital products and goods for military use. Housewives helped by planting victory gardens, while children got involved by collecting scrap iron and rubber for conversion to necessary war-related products. By all accounts, the winning of the war was clearly a statewide priority.

Two of the senior commanders of the three major theaters of war were native Texans. General of the Army Dwight D. Eisenhower, who oversaw the European theater, was born in Denison, while Fleet Admiral Chester W. Nimitz, who shared supreme command in the vast Pacific theater, was a native of Fredericksburg. General of the Army Douglas MacArthur, the top commander of the Southwest Pacific region, was a graduate of San Antonio's Texas Military Institute, and Killeen's Col. Oveta Culp Hobby commanded the Women's Army Corps throughout the war.

As the Texans were leaving home in large numbers to serve their country, over 1.5 million other servicemen and -women came into the state to learn the skills of war at the many airfields and army installations recently built. They brought with them different attitudes and behavioral traits that often put them in conflict with the usually more conservative and long-established social standards of their civilian hosts. Though problems were not uncommon, even the most isolated and tradition-bound communities offered warm hospitality to their military guests and usually turned a collective blind eye toward all but the most egregious transgressions. As one small-town sage put it, "Them boys could get away with murder as long as nobody got hurt."

By the time MacArthur and Nimitz stood on the deck of the USS *Missouri* to receive Japan's formal surrender, Texas had been literally transformed. It had been socially awakened by the very war it had so significantly helped to win. Texas was no longer primarily an agrarian state, and its women and minorities had been set firmly on the path toward civil equality. The bonds of the Great Depression had been shattered by the needs of military families, while educational improvements reflected modern trends. A large number of veterans who served in Texas during the war liked what they saw and experienced during their tour of duty in the state. Many married local girls and brought them back home to live in Texas towns when the war ended. The state's population increased by some 20 percent in the years immediately following the conflict, while two specific locations increased even more: San Antonio, a particularly important military city during the war, saw an increase of nearly 50 percent when the war came to a close, as did the subtropical Harlingen area, the wartime site of a large aerial gunnery school.

Relatively little physical evidence of its World War II experience can be found in Texas today. Of the 65 airfields that were operational during the war years, only seven remain. The number of major army installations has shrunk from a wartime level of 35 down to three. Some remnants of the prisoner-of-war camps can be found, mostly in East Texas, but also at Hereford and Marfa. Many small towns and villages that once proudly hosted bases and camps have never fully recovered from the shock of military closures at war's end. The impact on such small communities when the installation was in operation was immense, and the changes brought about by the war were especially profound. So, too, is the palpable sense of economic loss that still prevails more than six decades after the last airplane took to the sky or a nearby military installation staged its final pass in review. Now, only fading memories remain of what just might have been a pretty good war after all, at least when compared to the conflicts that were to follow.

FORT CLARK
(1852–1946)

The future site of Fort Clark was briefly occupied by American soldiers en route to Mexico during the 1846–48 war between the two nations. Troops of the US 1st Infantry marching west from San Antonio stopped at the location on Las Moras Creek before swinging south to enter Mexico some 40 miles away at Eagle Pass. Maj. John B. Clark, the regiment's commander, made a detailed report of the artesian springs that provided what some early-day plainsmen claimed to be a year-round source of excellent water on an otherwise arid and chaparral-infested prairie. Although Clark died in combat at the Battle of Churubusco in Mexico not long after he and his troops marched away from this rare Texas oasis, his report about the ever-flowing springs made its way to the War Department.

After the war with Mexico, the army began choosing sites along the Military Road between San Antonio and El Paso for a chain of outposts to protect travelers—the steady stream of settlers and gold seekers heading west to the newly acquired lands of California—from Indian attack. Major Clark's report, along with another equally enthusiastic one submitted by Lt. W. H. C. Whiting, served to convince the War Department that further investigation of the Las Moras site would be appropriate. Additional studies proved that the reliable supply of water adjacent to the Military Road, coupled with the site's strategic proximity to the Rio Grande border with the still-nettlesome Mexico, made Las Moras an ideal place for an outpost. In recognition of his posthumous role in identifying the site's viability, the major's onetime camping grounds eventually became officially known as Fort Clark. To provide legal claim to the site, the army consummated a deal with landowner Samuel A. Maverick for a lease term not to exceed 20 years.

The first detail of soldiers to occupy the new military site lived in tents scattered alongside the creek during the construction of more substantial buildings, which were initially *jacals,* vernacular structures made of pickets and mud or stone. By 1855, three years after the signing of the Maverick lease, what had been a steady stream of westward-bound settlers in 1850 increased to become a daily surge. As a result, the Native American tribes that had long viewed all of West Texas as their natural domain launched an all-out but belated attempt to halt, if not actually reverse, the western flow of white settlers. The marked increase in warlike activities of Lipan Apache, Comanche, and Kickapoo tribesmen triggered a concomitant increase in the size of the garrison at Fort Clark, which seemed to always be in some degree of expansion. The region's usually harsh weather conditions, which ranged from unbearably hot in the summer to cold and raw during the blue "northers" of winter, also made it necessary to construct even sturdier and more weather-resistant buildings.

At the beginning of the Civil War in 1861, Confederate forces took control of the fort, but they abandoned it by mid-1862. When the war ended, the US Army returned to find the installation in need of costly repairs, so a significant rehabilitation program soon began. The War Department deemed the revitalized and expanded Fort Clark necessary because of the recent resurgence in Indian violence that began during the Civil War and then continued for another decade. It was during this time that American cavalrymen received clear instructions, if not actual official orders, to cross the international boundary at the Rio Grande to pursue Indian raiders who frequently sought refuge on the Mexican side of the river. The Seminole Negro Scouts serving under Lt. John L. Bullis played a pivotal role in tracking the Indian raiders into Mexico and contributing to their eventual subjugation.

When the United States entered World War I, some three decades after the end of the Indian Wars in Texas, Fort Clark had grown to be one of the army's most impressive facilities in the West. It spread over nearly 4,000 acres of mostly cactus and brush. In contrast, however, the inhabited part of the fort remained attractively landscaped. Still relying on the never-failing waters of Las Moras Creek, the onetime barren outpost on the Military Road had evolved into something of a cavalry showplace, at least in comparison to many other mid-19th-century Texas military installations. Most of its buildings were of stone construction, including an imposing residence for the commanding officer, handsome quarters for married and bachelor officers, and a well-stocked commissary. Vast corrals, ample barns, and a massive feed storage granary all served as evidence of the fort's primary mission as a major cavalry station.

Despite occasional threats by the War Department to close the remote fort because of the expense involved in maintaining it, the facility managed to stay open for almost 100 years. Among those who argued in favor of decommissioning the post was none other than Gen. William T. Sherman, who declared it to be "the largest and most expensive military post in Texas if not in the United States." The fact that the Southern Pacific Railway had for some unknown reason chosen to build its main line

10 miles south of Fort Clark at Spofford, instead of constructing it immediately parallel to the Military Road, apparently influenced Sherman's reasoning. But even though
he was the army's highest-ranking officer at the time, civilians in the War Department
overrode his direct order to abandon the installation.

The little village of Brackettville that developed on the northern edge of the fort
played a key role in keeping the post active. Its very existence depended on the many
dollars spent by military personnel in the saloons, gambling halls, and bordellos that
lined the town's dusty main street. At the slightest hint of the fort's closure, Brackettville's leaders joined wealthy local area ranchers in petitioning their elected officials to
spare the post, and until 1945 those efforts proved successful. Life on the installation
was apparently pleasant enough, considering its remote location and, save for a night
on the town in Brackettville, the absence of any off-post social recreation. When not
on duty, the men hunted in the arroyos and on the hills of the military reservation and
beyond, while their wives enjoyed sewing circles, afternoon teas, and book clubs. The
Officers' Club held weekly dances and provided access to a well-utilized bar every
day and night of the week.

After the threat of all Indian-related danger had been removed and the Military
Road eventually transformed into US Highway 90 mainly for civilian use, Fort Clark
became less important in the eyes of the War Department. With the outbreak of the
Mexican Revolution in 1910, however, constant raiding activity along the Rio Grande
kept cavalry patrols in their saddles on a regular basis until the early 1920s. During
World War I the army enlarged the fort, and it continued to be a principal station for
the training of mounted cavalry. Toward the end of the conflict in 1918, it became
increasingly apparent that the days of the horse-mounted cavalry would soon disappear. During the Indian Wars, the Civil War, and the patrolling duties of the Mexican
Revolution, assignment to the United States Cavalry had been one of the most highly
coveted posting for any young career-oriented officer. Dashing in combat and colorful in
their dress uniforms, cavalry officers were considered to be the elite of the army. Heirs
to such cavalry legends as Jeb Stuart, Phil Sheridan, and even the flamboyant George
Armstrong Custer, the cavalrymen of the late 19th and early 20th centuries saw themselves wrapped in the same glorious folklore as their historic heroes. "They rode hard
by day," as an army saying had it, "and drank even harder when the sun went down."

With this colorful legendary theme as its backdrop, an assignment to the cavalry
at historic Fort Clark in the years between the two world wars appealed to many
officers, although their wives seldom favored moving to the desolate and remote
Texas post. According to the biographer of one of the army's last but still widely
remembered horse soldiers, "Fort Clark was considered a good duty station for cavalry officers." That famous horse soldier was a general, holder of the Medal of Hon-
or, and one of the more tragic figures of World War II. His name was Jonathan M.

Wainwright, and many in the War Department considered the general's command assignment to Fort Clark in 1938 to be his last posting. He reportedly shared that same thought, but as a cavalryman for more than 30 years, he seemed determined to revel in the glory of the traditions of the US Cavalry until his retirement became mandatory.

If hard drinking was considered to be a necessary aspect of those cavalry traditions, General Wainwright would be among its foremost apostles. People in Brackettville who still remember his tour of duty at the fort can point to "the General's Room," an alcove just off the former main bar in the post's Officers' Club. There, they say, Wainwright held court, each afternoon and well into the night, to tell and retell the legends of the horse cavalry. He actually began his active duty at Fort Clark in 1906, immediately following his graduation from West Point. He served in the Philippines, fought at St. Mihiel and the Meuse-Argonne during World War I, and then progressed through the army's various high command schools to become commander of the 3rd Cavalry at prestigious Fort Myer, Virginia, in 1935. It was at Fort Myer that his career nearly came to its close. The sociable and heavy-drinking Wainwright got deeply in debt and was just barely able to avoid bankruptcy. Because of the proximity of Fort Myer to War Department offices located just across the Potomac, his plight became well known in official circles. Rather than force the retirement of the popular 55-year-old colonel who had once shown such promise, the army promoted him to brigadier general and then exiled him, likely forever, to Fort Clark, far from the prying eyes of the War Department.

By all accounts, Wainwright proved to be popular at his new duty station. He often led his fellow officers in such off-duty activities as hunting, fishing, and crossing the Rio Grande on long horseback adventures. He apparently was a good commander who allowed his junior officers a fairly free hand in conducting their official duties. Of particular interest to him were extended cavalry maneuvers that took his entire 1st Cavalry Brigade out onto the great brush country that stretched for hundreds of miles west of Fort Clark. After enduring up to 10 hours in the saddle each day, the men spent their evenings in much the same way that they did back at the fort. The officers would drink and sing old cavalry songs around the campfires, pausing from time to time to hear the tall tales told by their general. He clearly enjoyed being in the wilds with his men. Once, after orderlies set up his special tent and his portable washstand and privy, Wainwright remarked, "If I knew generals were taken care of like this, I would have been a general a long time ago." No matter how much he enjoyed his rank, according to one of his biographers, Wainwright, like others, sensed Fort Clark would be his last command. Perhaps as a result, he again spent profligately, more than even a general's salary warranted. He also began to drink more heavily and even earlier in the day, once falling from his horse in a stupor during a midday review.

Built in 1857, Fort Clark's commanding officer's quarters has been home to such army notables as Ranald S. Mackenzie, William R. (Pecos Bill) Shafter, and at the time of this 1940 photograph, Brig. Gen. Jonathan M. Wainwright, later of World War II fame and misfortune. *Courtesy of Fort Clark Historical Society Collection.*

The commanding officer's quarters at Fort Clark has a superb view of the full length of what was until the early 1950s the post's parade ground. Each morning, General Wainwright would step down from his porch to mount one of his excellent horses and ride the short distance around the parade ground to his headquarters. In doing so, he cantered directly in front of the house that had just been vacated by a colonel assigned to Fort Myers to replace him. That colonel was a 1909 graduate of West Point named George S. Patton Jr. It had been Patton's exemplary, if very short, tour of duty as the commander of Fort Clark's 1st Cavalry Division that propelled him directly into the same position that Wainwright had just been forced to leave. One of Patton's biographers notes that the emotional colonel exhibited distress upon receiving orders to leave Fort Clark. A true cavalryman, much like Wainwright, Patton reveled in the rugged outdoor life and convivial camaraderie to be found at the legendary Texas post.

It is somewhat ironic that the careers of these two cavalrymen whose names were soon to become so well known in every American household should have had such

With the exception of the now towering Italian cypress trees, the Fort Clark commanding officer's quarters has changed very little over the years. It did somehow survive the reportedly boisterous parties staged there by onetime resident John Wayne when he filmed his Alamo movie nearby in the 1960s. *Thomas E. Alexander Collection.*

a curious confluence just before World War II began. Wainwright, spared a forced early retirement, received a reprieve when America entered the war in 1941. His orders sent him to the Philippines, where circumstances eventually compelled him to surrender the largest American military force in history to a victorious enemy. Broken by over three years of harsh imprisonment by the Japanese, Wainwright was freed in time to be present at the formal surrender of the same enemy that had overwhelmed his forces in 1942. Much to his surprise, Wainwright received the Medal of Honor soon after the surrender ceremony and as a four-star general returned to Texas as commanding officer of the US Fourth Army at San Antonio's Fort Sam Houston. He died in 1953. George Patton had a much more successful experience in World War II than did the long-imprisoned and humiliated Wainwright. He led his famous Third Army to victory in Europe and finally received his coveted fourth star despite some occasional public relations setbacks. An unquestioned hero of the war, Patton died in a freak automobile accident in 1945.

Fort Clark itself played an important role in the war. The army's last horse cavalry unit trained there until deployment to Europe in early 1944. With no reason to maintain its clearly obsolete horse cavalry operations after the war, the army declared the fort to be surplus in 1945 and closed it in 1946. In time, it became a private resort facility featuring the still-flowing Las Moras Creek as a special attraction. A large swimming pool General Wainwright ordered built for his men remains in operation virtually year-round. Many of the buildings constructed at the fort as early as the mid-1800s continue to be used. Barracks eventually housed motel rooms, and one-time officers' quarters alongside the parade ground became private residences. The commanding officer's house, where General Wainwright frequently entertained, is every bit as imposing as it was when first built well over a century ago. During a brief period in the fall of 1959, the actor John Wayne lived and reportedly also frequently entertained in the house while filming his epic movie about the Alamo on location at a nearby ranch. The house briefly occupied by George Patton is also still standing just a half block away from the commander's quarters.

Before the army deactivated the fort in the mid-1940s, it utilized a large part of it as a German prisoner-of-war camp. Following repatriation of the prisoners after the war, the government had their vacant barrackslike buildings flattened by bulldozers, with walls and corrugated roofs falling in piles of rubble onto the slab foundations. Until the early 1990s, it was possible to walk past these numerous and curious reminders of the war. Streets and sidewalks remained clearly delineated. Debris piles contained broken china and shards of glass once used by the men of Erwin Rommel's elite Afrika Korps, who as prisoners had to sit out at least some of the war in the hot Texas sun.

There is an almost palpable aura of history that hovers around old Fort Clark, more than what might be perceived at any other similar military site in Texas. Perhaps this is because so many famous general officers at one time or another rode through its still imposing gateway. Over the years, Sherman, Sheridan, Mackenzie, Bullis, and, of course, Wainwright and Patton each watched as soldiers raised the large flag on the tall mast at the parade ground. Some historians contend that both Robert E. Lee and Ulysses S. Grant rode through that same gate, but that cannot be confirmed. What is undeniable, however, is that this grand old cavalry post remains fairly intact and worthy of the time of anyone wishing to study its now faded days of glory.

Location: Now known as Fort Clark Springs Resort, the old post is located immediately across US Highway 90 from Brackettville. Access: Requires easily obtained visitor's pass at entry gatehouse.

CAMP BOWIE II
(1940–1946)

The US Army began building the World War II version of Camp Bowie four miles south of Brownwood in September 1940, well over a year before the nation actually entered the war. It was not only the first of many major military installations to be constructed in Texas during the early 1940s, but it also became one of the larger ones when the government expanded the original 2,000-acre site to encompass 123,000 acres. Soon after the new camp opened, it accommodated 33,000 soldiers, but as the war progressed it is estimated that at least twice that number saw assignment to the Brownwood base at any one time. The soldiers at the camp served in the same 36th Infantry Division that occupied the World War I Camp Bowie at Fort Worth some 20 years earlier. Although the camps used in both wars were ostensibly named for James Bowie of Alamo fame, a Brownwood newspaper article suggested that the camp then being built south of town actually honored the previous war's Fort Worth site. No official records could be found to substantiate this claim, however.

The building of the second Camp Bowie provides an interesting glimpse of wartime construction efficiency. Motivated by the rapidly escalating probability of war and fueled by unlimited federal funding, workers transformed a mesquite-choked rangeland into a sprawling modern military installation in a matter of months. Brownwood, with its total population of 13,323, clearly could not provide the labor force required to accomplish what the War Department mandated. As a result, the Robert E. McKee Company of El Paso, general contractor to the government, in a short time assembled an initial construction crew of 16,000 workers from across the state. To determine how quickly a structure could be erected, the company randomly selected a 365-man team consisting of carpenters, electricians, plumbers, and painters to construct and finish out a single test building in the least amount of time. The men began the project at 9:00 on a Tuesday morning and by 3:00 that afternoon, a completed 90-foot by 25-foot administration building stood ready for immediate occupancy. Encouraged by the results of the test, the construction company set about building the other 1,099 structures planned for the huge camp. Protected from any labor disputes by government regulations, the workers overcame the effects of an unusually severe winter to complete the initial phase of the project ahead of schedule. Barracks, theaters, service clubs, post exchanges, chapels, warehouses, gymnasiums, a bakery, and a hospital soon rose from the prairie thanks to crews working around the clock.

To feed the anticipated number of soldiers, the installation included 200 mess halls with seating available in each for up to 250 men. There were 219 recreation halls constructed ranging in size from company "day rooms" to regimental centers that accommodated hundreds at a time.

Demands on the initial post exchange were such that 27 smaller stores had to be erected throughout the camp. In addition to a 2,000-bed hospital, three dental clinics provided care for the men. In their off-duty hours, soldiers could play on the camp's golf course or read at one of three well-stocked libraries. On Sundays, 14 chapels held services from dawn to late evening. Most of the materials used in the construction came to the site from all parts of Texas, as well as other states. The army kept a precise accounting of all materials used, and as a result, the records indicate there were 37,700 linear feet of water lines and 34,000 feet of natural gas pipes, along with 627,000 feet of electric lines and 210,000 feet of sewer pipes. The cost of the greatly expedited construction schedule, the immense payroll with its overtime surcharges, and the expense of the materials quickly exceeded the initial budget estimate. What the general contractor had pledged to be a $4 million undertaking eventually exceeded $18 million.

In addition to the host 36th Infantry Division, the camp also served the 113th Cavalry Brigade, the Iowa National Guard, the Eighth Army Corps, and eventually the entire Third Army under Lt. Gen. Walter Krueger. There was a vast variety of army operational training conducted on the camp simultaneously. A field artillery brigade shared the remote 88,000-acre practice range with an armored division and a tank destroyer company. Infantrymen trained at the numerous pistol and rifle ranges, and Signal Corps battalions maintained communications between the various units on duty across the bustling site later in the war. A detachment of the Women's Army Corps arrived to be assigned, for some unrecorded reason, to the Tank Destroyer Company. In all, some 250,000 troops passed through the camp in six years.

The commanding general of the 36th Regiment when the camp first became operational was Claude V. Birkhead, a Texas lawyer-turned-general. He had enlisted as a private during the Spanish-American War of 1898, advanced to the rank of colonel in World War I, and made brigadier general in 1923. Succeeding to the command of the 36th in 1936 as a major general, Birkhead retired as a lieutenant general in 1948. According to contemporary newspaper accounts, Birkhead was as popular among the citizens of Brownwood as he was with his troops. In May 1941, Lt. Gen. Walter Krueger assumed command of the Third Army stationed in San Antonio before moving to Camp Bowie. The Prussian-born onetime private had participated in Pershing's Punitive Expedition into Mexico before serving in France during World War I. Later, after being at Camp Bowie, Krueger commanded the Sixth Army as it fought its way across the Pacific during World War II. A prominent hill that overlooks the site of Camp Bowie was the location of General Krueger's home. The promontory bears his name and the house is still standing.

World War II brought great change to Brownwood. The sudden arrival of the construction workers in late 1940 more than doubled its population. When the soldiers arrived to occupy the completed camp a few months later, the population increased fourfold. Before this flood of workers and military men surged into the community, Brownwood was in the grips of the Great Depression. The building of the camp and its eventual occupation by the army brought an abrupt end to the extended economic decline. According to one report, the payroll for the construction workers averaged over $500,000 per week. As a result, new stores opened to attract customers who had a great deal of disposable income for the first time in years, and the entire downtown business district benefited from the rejuvenation of old buildings as well as the new construction. When the camp became fully operational, even more new businesses came to Brownwood.

Many officers preferred to live quietly in the city rather than at the bustling camp. A reported 900 new homes were under construction in the town during the camp's first year of operation. Those officers who chose to rent housing in Brownwood seemed willing to pay inflated rental fees. One local couple vacated their house and moved in with the wife's parents when an officer offered to pay them a rent that was double the amount of their monthly mortgage payment. The demand for houses greatly outstripped the supply. A movie house became a dormitory after the last picture played each night. Garages outfitted with haphazard heating devices served military families, and an out-of-business skating rink filled with cots provided quarters for those who spent their waking hours seeking more permanent facilities. A hotel that stood on Baker Street in downtown Brownwood catered more to the needs of soldiers on weekend nights than to long-term residents. Jack Gordon, the local newspaper's regular columnist, made sly reference to the hotel and its shady romantic wartime reputation in his article of May 8, 1950. After listing all the long-gone familiar businesses that had flourished downtown just five years earlier, the writer concluded by noting, "This isn't the Brownwood [of] 1941 to 1945. Even that hot little hotel on Baker Street is shuttered."

Based on oral histories recorded in the town years after the war, not all citizens of Brownwood believe the economic benefits derived from the camp fully compensated for the social problems that soon arose. Thousands of young men exploring the streets of the city on any given Saturday night often created social stress. There were two USO Service Clubs in town that provided off-duty soldiers with an opportunity for recreation, and frequent dances also allowed the men to meet local area girls, but on a strictly chaperoned basis. Despite the best efforts of the chaperones, however, rules forbidding after-hours fraternization between the USO patrons and their dancing partners were frequently disregarded.

A number of race-related issues came to life through the oral histories. In 1940,

This oversize athletic field house was one of hundreds of "permanent" buildings constructed on sprawling Camp Bowie near Brownwood during World War II. Others included a 2,000-bed hospital, seven theaters, 14 chapels, and housing to accommodate thousands of soldiers. *Courtesy of Brown County History Museum, Brownwood, Texas.*

only 571 African Americans lived in all of Brown County, of which Brownwood is the county seat. Army reports, however, indicate there were three times as many African American troops stationed at the camp than there were living in the rest of the county during the war years. In recognition of the recreational needs of the minority segment of the army's contingent, a separate USO opened for their exclusive use in downtown Brownwood. Problems soon arose, though, when far too few local African American girls could be found to attend dances at the USO or to serve as hostesses. Efforts to recruit girls from other nearby communities proved only partly successful. Friction occurred when the African American soldiers who came from northern and eastern states encountered southern racial attitudes and conventions. One oral history interviewee recalled an incident involving a black sergeant driving a tank into town to aim its cannon at the jailhouse door in an effort to have a fellow African American soldier set free. However, no official accounts of this adventure have been found. There are also no known newspaper reports that tell of any violent clashes between the races such as those that occurred in other cities in Texas and other states.

In February 1942, the 36th Infantry Regiment completed its battlefield training and departed for Camp Blanding, Florida. Following additional training, the division shipped out of New York City in early April 1943, bound ultimately for North Africa.

With different siding but with the original roofline, the former Camp Bowie field house is now the headquarters of Diamond Enterprises. Still located at its World War II address, it is one of very few wartime buildings still to be found at the camp. *Photograph courtesy of Clay Riley, Brownwood, Texas.*

On September 9, 1943, the division went ashore at Salerno, Italy, to begin a long and costly march through Italy. Despite its commanding general's protests to higher command, the division participated in the still-controversial crossing of the Rapido River on January 20, 1944, and in the process, the unit suffered nearly 1,700 casualties. The division nevertheless remained active in battles in Italy, France, Germany, and Austria, but at a continuing heavy cost. At the end of the war in Europe, the 36th had sustained 19,466 casualties, including 3,717 killed in action, 12,685 wounded, and an additional 3,064 missing in action. Despite these losses, the unit captured 175,806 enemy troops while earning 12 Medal of Honor citations and six presidential unit citations. In all, the 36th spent an unparalleled 400 days in combat in Europe.

On Christmas Day 1945, the army demobilized the unit. Ten months later, on October 1, 1946, the camp at which they had trained for those 400 days in combat permanently closed. Demolition of most of the buildings on the camp began immediately. Some, such as the service club, were spared, but most were either reduced to scrap or moved away intact. Unlike what took place at many other World War II sites in Texas, however, Brownwood put the largely vacant area to good use. Part of the land went for construction of a major medical center, including a hospital complex and various supporting facilities. Major manufacturing companies built plants on the site, while other parts of it became parkland. One of the park areas is dedicated to the memory of Camp Bowie and to the thousands of men who trained there to fight in a war from which many did not return.

Location: The World War II army camp site is located on the southwest edge of Brownwood off US Highway 377.
Access: Unlimited.

AVENGER FIELD
(1941–1969)

Sweetwater's Avenger Field was the site of several unique military aviation missions during World War II. Before being converted into an army flight training facility in 1941, however, it had served as the town's municipal airport for nearly 13 years. Among the more famous early-day aviators who landed at the field were Jimmy Doolittle, Wiley Post, Claire Chennault, and the fiery advocate of military airpower, Brig. Gen. Billy Mitchell. When it first became operational in 1929, the municipal airport had one runway and one hangar, as well as one directional beacon. The town's convenient location roughly halfway between El Paso and Dallas on the trans-Texas air route made the primitive but functional Sweetwater Airport a regular refueling stop as commercial air travel increased in popularity during the 1930s. Further, a scheme featuring a combination of air and rail transportation made it possible to fly directly from the hub city of St. Louis to Sweetwater and then to board a Texas and Pacific passenger train for a pleasant trip on to Los Angeles.

In the late 1930s, well in advance of the anticipated World War II, teams of army air officers traveled across Texas to explore the military potential of the state's many civilian airports. Sweetwater's favorable reputation as a reliable air facility won it quick recommendation for military use by some of the early-day aviators who had then become officers in the rapidly expanding US Army Air Corps. As a result of their enthusiastic endorsement, Sweetwater's city officials proceeded to acquire additional acreage surrounding their airport that would be required for the conversion to military use. By January 1941, almost a year before the United States entered the war, all necessary land had been purchased for less than $100 per acre. In November of that year, the 600-acre field became fully operational. During the course of the war that began three weeks later, the army airfield grew to encompass almost 1,000 acres, with two additional runways and two new hangars. The army also built dormitories, dining halls, and recreational facilities. By the end of the war, what had been a $15,000 municipal airport in 1929 had been transformed into a $2 million major military air training facility. Seeking a new and more warlike name for Sweetwater's totally re-vamped airfield, the local newspaper sponsored a contest among its readership. By suggesting Avenger Field, Mrs. Grace Favor received a $50 war bond along with the privilege of actually christening the newly named field at its main gate on May 14, 1942.

By the end of May, the first class of flight cadets arrived at Avenger Field to begin training. To the surprise of many local residents who had expected young American men to arrive, 50 English would-be pilots were the first to occupy the newly built dormitories. As if to prove that they were more surprised than disappointed, the townspeople made great efforts to welcome the newcomers. When they were not on duty at the field, the young Britons attended rodeos as honored guests, visited ranches to ride horses, and ate Texas barbeque, likely for the first time in their lives. When the Royal Air Force cadets completed their training in August 1942, American cadets arrived to take their place. In addition to these newcomers, the army also introduced an experimental project known as the Air Transport Command Training Program. The plan called for 150 enlisted men and civil service employees who had learned basic aviation skills to undergo 50 hours of multi-engine flight training. Those who completed the course would be used as pilots flying transport planes to free more skilled officers for combat flights. The plan was a failure, though when only one enlisted man proved to be adequately qualified to enter the program. When 40 of the next round of 68 candidates failed to make the grade, the army cancelled the entire project. Meanwhile, the regular flight instruction program continued on the field from August 1942 through early April 1943. During that time, 820 aviation cadets success-fully completed their training.

Having watched the RAF cadets take to the sky before welcoming any American trainees, the local residents had also looked on in dismay at the failed air transport experiment. Likely expecting another class of young Americans to continue training at Avenger Field for the duration of the war, those same local observers were once again surprised, even shocked by some accounts, when the next wave of aviators reported for duty at Sweetwater. Rather than another warmly anticipated group of male aviation cadets, it was instead a social and cultural tidal wave of female pilots that next washed onto the barren earth at Avenger Field. In March 1943, on the heels of the recently graduated male cadets of Class 04–43, the first of the Women Airforce Service Pilots (WASP) arrived in Sweetwater.

The WASP had begun their training two months earlier in Houston despite the serious misgivings of army air force chief, Lt. Gen. Henry H. "Hap" Arnold. In July 1942, the general issued a statement he later came to regret. "The use of women pi-lots serves no military purpose," he proclaimed, but the fortunes of war soon forced him to completely reverse his thinking. As losses mounted in air battles over Europe and in the Pacific, it grew alarmingly apparent that every pilot currently flying cargo planes, towing sleeve targets at gunnery schools, or transporting generals around the United States was urgently needed in the war zones. Persuaded by the world-famous aviator Jacqueline Cochran, Arnold approved the formation of an organization of women pilots to assume what he referred to as "domestic flying assignments" so the men could go directly to the shooting war. Calls for applicants to join the new organization resulted in an almost overwhelming positive response. Over 25,000 women applied for the 1,800 authorized appointments, despite the fact that the standards for qualifying were very high and the compensation and benefits were absurdly low in comparison to what male pilots received. To qualify for admission, each woman had to have a private pilot's license, which cost over $700 in 1940. Each pilot also needed to prove she had logged 35 hours of flying time and be willing to provide her own transportation to her duty station at her own expense. Further, the WASP received no uniform allowance, nor did they qualify for government-provided life insurance should they die while on active duty. From the March 1943 inception of the program until the war's end more than two years later, 38 of the WASP did die while serving in uniform, without any insurance or even the right to a government-funded funeral. Despite the drawbacks, and while also having to endure the initial scorn of the army's male pilots, the WASP proved to be resourceful and highly beneficial in bringing the war to a successful conclusion.

The reception of the WASP in the small West Texas town of Sweetwater had been far less cordial than that extended to the English and American men who preceded them. In the first place, many local citizens initially resented the concept of an all-female air base. The official history of Nolan County makes note of the fact that "the advent of the girls to Avenger Field was received with mixed emotions by the citizens and field personnel alike." In the second place, these newcomers smoked and drank hard liquor, which were acts seriously frowned upon by the straight-laced residents of the legally bone-dry Nolan County. More than that, and apparently of even greater discomfiture to many of the local women, the ladies of the WASP wore pants instead of proper skirts.

The almost palpable attitude of civil displeasure did not go unnoticed by the women pilots. One wrote an article in the base newspaper that stated "they [the towns-people] didn't understand us and so misjudged us." "In the first place," she continued, "we came here with two strikes against us. We were supposed to be rough and uncouth and not quite right in the head." In closing, the writer lamented, "We acquired the titles of drunks and roughnecks." Later accounts indicate there might well have been at least some validity to the "drunk" part of the public's perceptions. The worldly-wise WASP located a kindly gray-haired proprietor of an apparently respectable gift shop who also operated a successful bootlegging operation in the otherwise dry community. For two dollars a pint, she provided the ladies of Avenger Field with what even the most sophisticated of them declared to be a "fairly good bourbon." Perhaps as a result of that illicit beverage being imbibed too freely, one WASP found herself in a city jail cell on a charge of "sleeping on a park bench after 9:00 P.M." She was soon set free only to receive 10 demerits for arriving back at the field after curfew.

During two years at Avenger Field, the WASP managed to capture the admiration of many of those who initially made them feel unwelcome. The impression they made on the young girls of the city was particularly noticeable. One 16-year-old girl wrote much later that "I'll never forget them. They were so independent and so self-assured. To me, they symbolized what I had suspected for some time. There truly could be a bright future for us girls beyond the city limits of Sweetwater if we had the courage to seek it."

During the short time the WASP program was at Avenger Field, 1,074 candidates successfully completed the flight training and received their wings. Having learned to fly the army way, the graduates received assignments to large airfields across the country. No aircraft was too large for them to handle and no assignment too difficult. They towed targets for relatively inaccurate aerial gunnery students, ferried aircraft across the Atlantic, and flew as test pilots when no else would assume the risk. By early 1944, even the initially skeptical General Arnold came to accept the proficiency of the women pilots. "I am looking forward to the day," declared the general, "when Women Airforce Service Pilots take the place of practically all AAF [Army Air Force] pilots in the United States for the duration."

In July 1944, the War Department determined there were more than enough male pilots in the training pipeline to warrant the cancellation of the WASP training program at Avenger Field. Despite a strong defense mounted by General Arnold, Texas congressmen, and even the citizens of Sweetwater, the program terminated at the end of that year. By January 24, 1945, however, Avenger Field was back in the flight training business. An all-male advanced fighter pilot school was in full operation. When the war ended eight months later, 150 officers still flew daily training missions at the field.

Following the war, Avenger Field continued to be relatively active. Even though the army declared the base surplus and the four hangars and other buildings conveyed back to the city in July 1947, the coming of the Cold War in 1952 brought the field back into Air Force service. It remained operational, first as a practice field for the jets at nearby Webb Air Force Base and then as a radar surveillance station. The site featured lengthened runways, as well as new buildings constructed to replace those that had only recently been demolished when World War II ended. In 1969, military leaders again marked the base for closure, despite the millions of dollars expended

A proud graduating class of the Women Airforce Service Pilots (WASP) marches past the reviewing stand in June 1944 with Avenger Field's main hangar serving as a backdrop. *Thomas E. Alexander Collection.*

by the government to keep it active since 1952. Fortunately, a master plan put into place soon after the thawing of the Cold War brought new vitality to the fading airfield. Through its implementation, several closed military airfields across Texas faced conversion into civilian educational facilities. Known collectively as the Texas State Technical College System, the institutions offered trade and technical training at old bases in Waco, Harlingen, and Amarillo, as well as at Avenger Field. In addition to the educational facility, the Sweetwater airport, once again a general aviation facility, is now home to the National WASP World War II Museum, housed in an original wartime hangar. The veterans of the now legendary organization are arguably among the more highly motivated World War II groups dedicated to keeping their legacy alive, and the pride they show in their preservation efforts is clearly evident to all who learn of their story.

Location: The former WASP training field is located three miles west of Sweetwater on Business Interstate 20.

Access: Unlimited as to general area, but the National WASP World War II Museum at Avenger Field is open Thursday through Monday only, 9:00 A.M. to 5:00 P.M.

The only physical reminder of the WASP presence at Sweetwater's Avenger Field during World War II, the field's old hangar now fittingly houses the National WASP WWII Museum. *Thomas E. Alexander Collection.*

PECOS ARMY AIRFIELD
(1942–1945)

Like many other towns in West Texas, Pecos was a direct by-product of the Texas and Pacific Railway Company. By 1881, workers drove the last spike to hold fast the rails of steel, and the first of countless cars filled with cattle departed the little town on its journey to the big livestock markets back east. At the time, the economic future of Pecos appeared to be both bright and enduring. Unfortunately, while Pecos did prosper as a ranch supply center and cattle shipping point for nearly 50 years, its booming economy enhanced by promising oilfield explorations and thriving cotton production came to an abrupt halt in 1936. The Great Depression that began in the eastern United States in late 1929 had slowly but inexorably rolled westward into Texas. The seemingly limitless previous demand for beef, cotton, and even the famous Pecos cantaloupes fell sharply, first in eastern markets and then all across the nation. By the mid-1930s, the often-repeated cycle of boom-and-bust experienced by many cities had made its unwelcome debut in Pecos. Although the town's population had become swollen by suddenly unemployed cowboys and farm workers streaming into town seeking jobs, the number of local businesses began to shrink. According to one account, nearly one of every four firms doing business in Pecos in 1934 had closed its doors by 1937. Very soon, however, World War II would provide Pecos with at least a temporary solution to its economic problems.

By 1939, the town's leaders, well aware of the wars already raging in Europe and Asia, realized that amidst the horrors of war there might be a glimmer of economic salvation for their stricken community. It was clear to many observers that if the United States were to become directly involved in the rapidly expanding conflict, American airpower, which won its laurels in the skies over France in World War I, was certain to play a major role in this latest 20th-century war. When President Roosevelt convinced Congress to provide $300 million for a vast increase in the size of the Army Air Corps, state and civic leaders across Texas put in motion aggressive plans to obtain more than a lion's share of the federal funds.

On September 14, 1940, the citizens of Pecos approved a $10,000 bond issue to provide funds to expand the city's municipal airport. With admirable foresight, given the region's hard-pressed economy at the time, the city council earmarked a portion of the bond money to buy 400 acres of vacant mesquite-filled prairie that adjoined the soon-to-be-refurbished 22-year-old airport. Workers quickly cleared, graded, and then securely fenced the newly acquired city property. For over a year, the city sent its representatives to Washington, as well as to various army headquarters elsewhere, in an effort to convince federal officers, both military and civilian, that Pecos would be an excellent location for an army airfield. Such lobbying activities were not publicized, but according to one source, many townsfolk knew of the campaign. "I had an uncle who worked for the chamber [of commerce] in 1939 and on into 1940," recalled Marie Thurmond many years later, "and he told our whole family that the Air Corps was fixin' to come to Pecos."

During the first 11 months of 1941, it became increasingly apparent to anyone who watched the newsreels at the movie theater or listened to such radio commentators as H. V. Kaltenborn that America would soon be in the war. Immediately after the Japanese attack on Pearl Harbor, which proved the commentators' predictions to be accurate, the army, responding to both an enemy action and a long-running lobbying effort by the city, sent an inspection team to Pecos. There they discovered the city's enthusiastic claims about its refurbished airport proved to be true. Long runways were in place, although they would eventually need to be made even longer, and enough acreage now surrounded the municipal field to provide adequate space for the army to set up its preliminary operations. The inspection trip was among the worst-kept secrets in the history of Pecos. The plan called for only the city's top officials and the chamber to be involved in the visit, but word of the army's presence soon spread rapidly throughout the town's populace of 4,800. The thought that Pecos might play a role in striking back against those who had attacked US interests at

Pearl Harbor created a groundswell of public pride coupled with national patriotism. According to one source, however, such altruistic sentiments had as their foundation a strong touch of practicality. "What we wanted from the government," read an internal chamber communication, "was just anything to provide a payroll."

Those few townspeople who missed out on the promising news about the army's visit and what it might mean for Pecos could share with their neighbors the excitement generated by the front-page story that appeared in the *Pecos Enterprise* on December 19, 1941. The gist of the story was communicated in the large banner headline that boldly proclaimed "Pecos Is Considered for a Flying School." What the citizens of the town did not know at the time was that the army was also considering at least 50 other Texas cities as possible sites for flying schools of various types. Pecos, it later developed, had been but one stop on a statewide junket of site investigations made in the immediate aftermath of the Pearl Harbor attack. A month passed with no further exhilarating headlines about either big air bases or big payrolls. On January 23, 1942, however, two more army officers arrived in Pecos to take a second look at the airport and its surrounding fenced acreage. This visit produced instantaneous results that were very hopeful but not yet final. After considerable negotiations with the city council, the army officers obtained a lease on the airport and its acreage, with a binding condition that Pecos must acquire an additional 320 acres adjacent to the main runway as part of the lease agreement.

Believing the stage set for an official announcement by the army, the city council was stunned when yet another delegation of army officers arrived in town on January 30, just one week after the signing of the lease. Following their visit to the airport, the officers met with the council to advise them that now an additional 1,800 acres would be needed for approval. For three weeks, no word came from Washington, even though the city had complied with the demand for additional acreage. On February 27, 1942, the War Department made the cryptic announcement that funding had been approved for "a major West Texas project." With no official word from Washington, the city could only hope that the project referred to was in fact the long-sought army air training facility at Pecos. Fearing its hopes might be dashed by some contractual misconception, the city council set about ensuring all necessary funds would be readily available at the time of the final agreement. Through a highly successful $50,000 bond issue, all aspects of the funding for the additional acreage were in place, and in early April, the War Department confirmed plans for a pilot training facility at Pecos. While that was heady news for the town, the best news of all was the further announcement by the War Department that construction costs on the new installation would be in excess of $5 million. As one longtime resident of the region put it, "You'd have to admit that the army came to our rescue . . . just like the cavalry used to back in the Indian days." Another Pecos native put the coming of

The large post theater at the Pecos Army Airfield was the favorite place for military personnel to escape both the extremes in weather and the boredom frequently encountered at the remote West Texas installation. *Courtesy of West of the Pecos Museum, Pecos, Texas.*

the military airfield in a broader perspective. "The establishment of this Army Flying School at Pecos," said Bill Davenport, "was probably the most exciting segment of Pecos history."

The excitement generated by the army airfield had several facets. The vast sums of cash that flowed into the community reversed the downward economic spiral that plagued the city and the Reeves County region for nearly a decade. Although many of the subcontracting firms engaged in building the field brought their own crews to the construction site, other workers, both skilled and unskilled, rushed to Pecos to find employment. Reports indicate as many as 2,000 workers were on the base each day, as the demand for trained pilots rapidly escalated during the early days of the war.

For a small town with only a hundred or so businesses in 1942, the influx of so many outsiders put a tremendous strain on the entire infrastructure. Housing became the first challenge. There were no adequate apartment facilities in town, and demand quickly outdistanced the supply of rooms "to let" in private houses. It soon became necessary for the federal government to impose rent-ceiling restrictions on the few quarters that were available. Vehicular traffic that had not been a problem in prewar Pecos was such that military police had to be stationed at key intersections at shift

After the government deactivated the Pecos airfield in 1945, the post theater was moved into the city of Pecos on B-29 aircraft tires to become the town's fire station. It was still serving that same purpose in 2010. *Thomas E. Alexander Collection.*

changes. Crime increased as off-duty workers, often from large out-of-state cities, sought opportunities to prey upon their trusting small-town hosts. On balance, however, the euphoria created by the building of the airfield more than offset the tribulations that stemmed from a changing social structure. Poor Pecos, long suffering from an economic drought, had finally snared the golden ring of a military base. The boom was on.

In short order, an air base began to take shape. Top priority went to the building of the long runways essential to training fields. In time, the 1,933 acres finally cobbled together by the eager and accommodating Pecos city council contained three asphalt-covered runways, the longest one running east–west a length of 7,200 feet and 150 feet in width. The other two, oriented on north–south compass points, each measured 6,200 feet in length. In addition, there were soon three hangars standing where only mesquite trees had flourished just months before. One was 200 feet long and 162 feet in width, making it easily the largest building in volume in Reeves County at the time.

Housing for the airmen soon to arrive seemed to take a low priority as opposed to the construction of operational facilities. As the completion of the field neared, the army erected a tent city to serve as quarters until barracks and officer housing could be built. The situation in general was dire enough to compel the manager of the Pecos chamber of commerce to lend his own home to the newly arrived base commander and his family. Despite construction complications due to dust storms, in time the base included 200 houses, a hospital, an officers' club, and perhaps most important of all from the creature-comfort standpoint in West Texas, two swimming pools. For the most part, however, the construction of the "nonoperational" buildings was of the tar-paper shack level of acceptability at best. Regardless, the construction cost for the field exceeded the initial $5 million estimate by an additional $3 million. In terms of 2008 dollar equivalency, the Pecos Army Airfield would cost $105 million to build today.

The air base officially opened in six months' time, and training classes began almost immediately with new classes averaging 125 cadets arriving every month to enter the nine-week regimen. More than 4,000 new pilots completed the training by the time of the base's deactivation in April 1945. At the peak of its activity, in mid-1944, the airfield served as home for more than 4,000 military personnel, roughly equivalent to the prewar population of Pecos. As the training at the field continued at a brisk around-the-clock pace for nearly three years, with noisy airplanes continually shattering the town's traditional silence, there were some longtime residents who increasingly came to believe the price of economic well-being produced by the airfield far outweighed its worth. When the base commander implemented a plan to remove trash, wrecked automobiles, and discarded appliances from front yards in the town, the locals voiced loud opposition to what they viewed as martial law. A few weeks later, the same commander declared that all of the milk being sold and consumed both in the city and on his airfield was unfit for human consumption. The outraged citizens, with some justification, protested to higher army authorities. Their complaints were strident enough to cause the transfer of the overreaching colonel to another airfield.

As the war drew to its successful conclusion in mid-1945, the US Army calculated it had more than enough pilots to finish the job. As a result, it deactivated Pecos Army Airfield on April 30, before the war officially ended on September 2, 1945. Having worked for so long to get the army base for their town to reap the vital harvest of a military-fueled cash flow, the city's leaders worked tirelessly to keep the field open despite the odds, but visits to various army headquarters to plead their case proved futile, and by the end of the year little remained of the once bustling installation. As one resident put it, "things just seemed to stop" when the army left. To be sure, the skies over Reeves County grew silent again, but then so did the service stations, the cafes, and the stores in downtown Pecos. Another local man who served in the navy during the war came home to discover a Pecos rapidly returning to its prewar level of hard times. He also noticed another change that to him seemed even more unsettling.

"I guess the army boys liked our Texas gals," he lamented many years later, "because when I got back home, almost all the good ones had married soldiers and moved away."

In many respects, the boom had clearly disappeared once again. Even decades after the wartime airfield closed, vacant buildings in downtown Pecos stood as evidence of the town's wartime heyday. At the site of the former air base on the southwest side of town, however, no structures from the glory years remained by the year 2000. At that time, the original airfield's rotating beacon continued to sweep the night sky over what had again become the city's municipal airport. Its beams no longer touched endless rows of silvery US Army planes and towering hangars but only concrete slabs where barracks once stood and overgrown sidewalks that led nowhere. Except for such archeological evidence, Pecos Army Airfield has literally disappeared. Only a handful of older citizens can recall the time not that long ago when the roar of aircraft engines echoed over their city's streets night and day.

Location: The army airfield was located two miles south of Pecos at the current site of Pecos Airpark.

Access: Unlimited, but only the former officers' club golf course remains intact.

NAVAL OPERATIONS IN WARTIME ORANGE: CONSTRUCTION OF THE USS *AULICK*
(1941–1942)

RIVERSIDE ADDITION FEDERAL HOUSING
(1942–1980S)

A settlement called Green's Bluff developed along the Sabine River near Louisiana in the years before the Texas Revolution. Later known as Madison, it became Orange—named for a local cultivated grove of orange trees—in 1858. Its riverine location and access to the Gulf, albeit by means of a channel with a somewhat limiting sandy bar, afforded the settlement great promise as a shipping point for regional agriculture, primarily cotton and cattle. Later, with the advent of local sawmills that exploited the vast natural tree stands of the East Texas Piney Woods, Orange became a center for both shipping and production during the bonanza era of Texas timber, which reached from roughly the 1880s to the 1930s. Construction of a rail line to the community greatly aided its growth and commercial viability in the early years. During the Gilded

Age, Orange was the home of timber barons, and their collective visions and entrepreneurship fueled an era of unprecedented growth for the seat of Orange County.

The economic base of Orange changed significantly over the years, but local business leaders proved adept at diversification and adaptability. The town continued to develop as an industrial center through the period of economic restructuring, thanks in large part to the discovery of oil nearby and the development of deepwater port and shipyard facilities. During World War I, supplied by timber and steel from local mills, it emerged as a significant shipbuilding center. When the timber industry later waned, due to unchecked harvests and the absence of conservation measures in an era of "cut out and get out," the citizens of Orange found themselves unable to stem the tide of an economic depression. Business slowed significantly, and for a brief time the long-held promise of prosperity seemed only a part of the distant past.

As in other areas of the state, though, the weak economic outlook began to change as the nation prepared for the eventuality of another global war. In 1940, as the conflict raged in Europe and elsewhere, the federal government systematically began funding production of military supplies and armaments. In the wake of the new activity, the government awarded an $82 million contract to the Consolidated Steel Company in Orange for the construction of a dozen naval destroyers of the Fletcher class. News of the endeavor spread quickly, and soon large numbers of laborers—many unskilled in shipbuilding but willing to take advantage of training opportunities that sprang up—moved to Orange. The city's population boomed as a result, increasing from less than 10,000 to more than 60,000 in only a few years. Work on the first two destroyers—the USS *Aulick* and the USS *Charles Ausborne*—progressed quickly, and in May 1941, workers laid the keels for the two vessels. That event signaled not only the successful revitalization of the shipbuilding industry in Orange but also the first stage of many related construction projects that would far exceed the initial contract. The nation was not yet at war, but that would occur only a few short months later. In the meantime, Orange assumed a leadership role in wartime preparedness on a grand scale.

Appropriately, the 1942 launch of the USS *Aulick,* the first destroyer built in Texas, occurred on March 2—Texas Independence Day—amid much fanfare and celebration, but also apprehension. Since this was the first launch of its kind in the Orange shipyards, some people speculated it might not go as planned, and some even worried the great steel ship could sink or break apart. Nonetheless, the ceremonies proceeded as planned and without incident. Lillian Thomson, the wife of Capt. Thaddeus Austin Thomson Jr., a native Texan and then the acting commander of the Eighth Naval District in New Orleans, christened the vessel, followed by patriotic music from the Orange Bengal Guards. A crowd estimated at 6,000 was on hand to view the momentous occasion. The USS *Aulick,* the second ship named for the distinguished

US naval officer John H. Aulick, whose service included the War of 1812, successfully completed its shakedown training in the Gulf of Mexico and Casco Bay, Maine, by the end of the year and in early 1943 sailed from Philadelphia to the South Pacific via the Panama Canal.

While the *Aulick* was the first major naval vessel constructed at Orange during World War II, it marked only the beginning of what would prove to be an impressive wartime industrial contribution by local business, labor, and government in the port city. The three major maritime construction operations—Consolidated Western Steel Corporation, Weaver Shipyards, and Levingston Shipbuilding Company—each contributed to the unprecedented effort that produced more than 500 new ships by war's end. So too did scores of related industries and suppliers in the area. Given the magnitude and urgency of the projects, and the need for large numbers of laborers, it is no wonder the city's population skyrocketed seemingly overnight, placing incredible demands on the public infrastructure. Not only was there an immediate need for greatly expanded transportation, communication, and utility lines, but there were also concomitant concerns for new schools, commercial operations, and housing. The latter, in particular, drove the planning for the others and so presented an immediate call for action. Workers poured into the city from local rural areas but also from urban areas farther distant. Their presence quickly overwhelmed the available residential stock, and soon it was not uncommon to see individuals living in garages, tents, or even without adequate cover in vacant lots. By 1942, the housing problem in Orange was at a critical stage, and local business and political leaders personally petitioned the federal government for assistance. Their persistence paid off, and the promise of relief came quickly with an announcement in May 1942 of funding for the immediate construction of 2,000 homes—representing the first phase of a much larger residential complex—on a tract of land along the west bank of the Sabine River. The new residential area bore the name Riverside, and the second phase would be formally designated Riverside Addition.

Like much of the area in the lowlands along the lower Sabine, the Riverside tract proved to be marshy and uneven. As a result, extensive dredging operations got underway first, starting in August. With an emphasis on speed, crews laid water lines as quickly as spoil from the riverbed settled across the site, and soon after, others added concrete streets that went in without reinforcement from steel, which was needed elsewhere in wartime. While such methods later proved problematic, they were an integral part of the planning for the Riverside complex, which was considered temporary, designed only to be occupied through the duration of the war. Adding to the temporary nature of the housing was the reliance on prefabricated or demountable duplexes that offered floor plans for up to three bedrooms, with furnishings compliments of the government. The site's close proximity to the shipyards

Ongoing construction of the USS *Aulick* at Orange, Texas, in 1941. *Courtesy of Howard C. Williams, MD.*

proved advantageous to the residents, given wartime rationing of gasoline and tires. Within the fan-shaped housing complex were basic commercial operations, as well as a community center. There were also three schools, appropriately named for the first local men killed in action during the early war years. As was the custom of the time, both the housing units and the schools remained segregated. A much smaller federal complex, known as the Booker T. Washington Addition, provided housing for African American workers. In addition, there were dormitory-style facilities for single men and women.

The various federal housing units at Orange served their intended purpose, greatly aiding the construction of various kinds of naval vessels for the war effort. As the war came to a close, however, it appeared that the end of defense contracts might presage a period of economic decline for Orange and thus an end for Riverside. As it turned out, though, the US Navy was not ready to end its association with the city, and the promise of continued prosperity prevailed. At the core of the government's decision was the matter of what to do with the remnants of what by then was the

This wartime aerial photograph shows the magnitude of the Riverside housing complex that was a vital component of the unprecedented shipbuilding efforts at Orange, Texas. *Courtesy of Howard C. Williams, MD.*

Visible reminders of the abandoned Riverside complex include roadways, sidewalks, and building foundations. *Courtesy of Texas Historical Commission. Photo by William A. McWhorter.*

largest navy in the world. There were, after all, no assurances the period of peace following World War II would last any longer than that following the previous world war. International relations on many fronts remained tenuous at best, and the United States had to plan for an uneasy future, which might include reactivating its naval arsenal. As a result, planning began for a program of "mothballing" many of the vessels, while at the same time providing regular maintenance to keep them in a reserve status. Orange thus became the location for a US naval station charged with maintaining the inactive ships.

Construction of the new naval base and a series of piers kept many workers employed, but about 250 of the federal housing units had to be sold and moved to provide the necessary space. The inactivation process began in November with the arrival of the first ship, the USS *Matagorda,* and others soon arrived from all over the world. Eventually, more than 150 inactive vessels would make their temporary home along the Sabine. Within just a few years from the end of World War II, the wisdom of the navy's decision became apparent when the government recalled more than 30 ships from the mothball fleet back into service during the Korean Conflict. Some of those would eventually return to Orange for another round of inactivation following their wartime service. By the 1960s, the US Navy began phasing down its program of mothballing ships from the World War II era. While some work continued at Orange under a limited command, and much of that with reliance on civilian personnel, the facility closed in 1975. The government scrapped the remaining ships, transferred them to other facilities, or sold them on the international market. All were gone by 1980.

Riverside in many ways mirrored the eventual decline of naval operations at Orange. As employment opportunities waned, many of the former shipbuilding workers left for other jobs or returned to their prewar hometowns. Most, however, stayed on as city residents, finding new jobs in another phase of industrial development, one centered on petrochemicals. The temporary housing at Riverside, hastily built during wartime and designed for a maximum life of 20 years, failed to make the transition. The original tract was conveyed to private ownership in 1948 and, despite another sale in the 1970s, it could not survive as a viable complex. The last units, like the last ships in the mothball fleet, were gone by the 1980s.

The USS *Aulick,* whose construction marked the beginning of wartime naval operations in Orange, had a longer life, albeit in part under a new name and nation. While in the South Pacific during the war she provided valuable escort service, troop support, and patrol capabilities before damage caused by a collision with a reef off New Caledonia required extensive repairs that put her out of commission for months. Following temporary stateside service as a training ship, the *Aulick* returned to action in the Pacific. In September 1944, while in the Philippines, she took direct hits that caused limited damage but killed one crewman. The following month, she participated in the massive Battle for Leyte Gulf, the largest naval engagement in history. Then in late November, while on submarine patrol, she came under attack by Japanese planes that, while not completely crippling her, nevertheless killed 31 crewmen and left another 65 wounded or missing in action.

Following still another round of extensive repairs, the *Aulick* eventually made her way back to Leyte Gulf in the Philippines and later provided troop transport for the invasion of Mindanao Island. At war's end, she was off the coast of Okinawa. Returning to New York soon after, the *Aulick* crew prepared for the ship's decommissioning in 1946. Thirteen years later the United States loaned her to Greece, where she sailed under the name *Sfendoni* (slingshot). Formally purchased by Greece in the 1970s, she remained in service to that country until the 1990s. The end came in 1997, when salvage crews scrapped the Texas-born vessel at Turkey.

The stories of the *Aulick* and Riverside reflect the depth of history associated with military efforts during wartime Texas. They are evocative of the dramatic economic and social changes that took place during the war years and immediately afterward. It was an era that marked the growth and evolving identity of cities such as Orange, as well as the related outmigration from rural areas. What happened along the Sabine River shipyards in the 1940s was, in microcosm, central to the broader story of the US home front and to an understanding of how communities sought prosperity in a time of war and then tenaciously held on for the transition that followed.

Location: An Official Texas Historical Marker for Riverside is located at Green Avenue and Simmons Drive in Orange. A marker for the USS Aulick is in Ochiltree Park at Third and Front Streets. Both markers are in the general vicinity of the topics they commemorate.
Access: Limited; private property.

PRISONERS OF WAR IN TEXAS: HEREFORD MILITARY RESERVATION AND RECEPTION CENTER
(1942–1946)

CAMP LUFKIN
(1944–1946)

While the US government had contingency plans for dealing with prisoners prior to its involvement in World War II, the planning intensified following the attack on

Pearl Harbor in December 1941. Work on the first prisoner-of-war (POW) camps in the United States began early in 1942 under the supervision of the army. Following guidelines of the 1929 Geneva Convention, the government had to balance the need for housing prisoners along with concerns for public safety. To those ends, the states of the South and Southwest provided ideal locales, with available open land, relatively few defense industries, and landscapes and climates thought to be compatible with those from which the prisoners came. So, went the conventional wisdom, Nazi prisoners might be more at home in Texas, for example, where the surroundings were apparently evocative of their native Germany. While there is room for debate on such thinking, the Lone Star State nonetheless had more POW camps—more than 70—than any other state.

In general, the POW facilities were of two different types: base camps and branch, or spike, camps. The former, at major military installations such as Camp Maxey in Lamar County, Fort Bliss in El Paso County, Camp Fannin in Smith County, and Camp Hood (later Fort Hood) in Bell County, afforded maximum security by utilizing large numbers of trained military personnel. There were also a number of base camps set up specifically to deal with POWs, and those included Camp Hearne in Robertson County, Camp Hereford in Deaf Smith and Castro Counties, and, at least temporarily, Camp Huntsville in Walker County. The typical base camps, whether associated with existing military training installations or not, followed a standard pattern that consisted of ordered rows of minimally constructed frame barracks secured by wire perimeter fencing, floodlights, guard towers, and other security measures. The branch camps, on the other hand, might appear more temporary in construction and were usually associated with work projects, primarily agricultural in nature. As the war progressed, especially after the Allies gained footholds in North Africa and Europe, the numbers of Axis prisoners increased dramatically, with estimates of nearly 50,000 serving time in Texas alone. That represented more than 10 percent of the total number of POWs held by the United States.

The two sites presented here demonstrate the wide range of POW camps in the state. The first is the Hereford Military Reservation and Reception Center, also known as Camp Hereford, located on the High Plains of the Panhandle. Situated on 800 acres astride two counties, it was one of the largest POW camps in the United States—built to house approximately 5,000 prisoners. Planning and construction began in 1942, with troops deployed to the site early the following year. The first internees—Italians captured during action in North Africa—arrived in April. In a scene played out countless times in the next few years, they came by train to nearby Summerfield, from where US soldiers escorted them on an eight-mile march through the countryside to the Hereford camp. The vast majority of the prisoners there were Italians, save a small group of Germans temporarily located at the camp while they awaited transfer to another facility.

Although designed as a maximum security base camp, the Hereford center also allowed for outside work details on local farms and ranches. Given the shortage of manpower during the war years, prisoners represented an important labor source that could be legally tapped, and the army often approved contracts with farmers and ranchers, who in turn provided transportation, meals, and some wage compensation. As anticipated, such contracts, although limited in scope, proved crucial to maintaining wartime agricultural production levels, but they had a secondary beneficial effect as well. Through the interaction between prisoners and local residents, and even the US soldiers on base, lasting friendships formed. While there were no doubt tensions and fears at times, numerous personal accounts of that era indicate that, at least at Hereford, there was a semblance of rapprochement. It played itself out in numerous ways, even after the war years, but two stories in particular point to the unique situation in the camp, and both reflect strong religious and artistic ties.

At the request of Father John Krukkert, who headed St. Mary's Catholic Church in the predominantly German community of Umbarger, in nearby Randall County, Italian prisoners agreed to paint the building's interior. Themselves Catholics, they created ornate works of art—paintings and murals—to adorn the walls. In 1955, a decade after the close of war, the members of that small painting detail returned to the church to present a special commemorative plaque bearing an inscription of peace, as well as their names. Thirty-three years later, one of the crew, Franco DiBello, returned to the Hereford camp and recalled, "We believe in your battle for freedom all over the world, and to this purpose we will always be at your side. . . . We are glad to have returned as friends and as free men to this marvelous state. We were your enemy to the first degree, but today we are your friend to the highest degree." The church building now serves as a community center in Umbarger, and the artwork of the Italian prisoners still adorns the interior.

On the grounds of Camp Hereford, Italian prisoners who were skilled craftsmen and artisans constructed a small memorial chapel to honor five of their own who died during incarceration. The five individuals were initially buried in the vicinity of the chapel, but their bodies were exhumed and returned to their homeland at the end of the war. Completed in 1945, the chapel reflects Art Moderne styling in its simple lines and interior altar with bas relief detailing. Because of its architectural and historical significance, the Texas Historical Commission declared it a Recorded Texas Historic Landmark following restoration work in the 1990s.

Although the government of Italy surrendered to Allied forces in 1943, Italian prisoners of war continued to be held at Hereford until the close of the conflict. In the course of its brief existence, the camp held a total of 7,000 internees. Approximately 3,100 remained by early 1946, when special troop trains began carrying them to Los Angeles for debarkation. As DiBello remembered from his POW days, "We used to hear a train come by at night. It always whistled for a crossing near the camp.

Chapel constructed by Italian prisoners at Camp Hereford during World War II. The graves of several prisoners who died at the camp were originally located nearby, but their bodies were later repatriated to their homeland. *Courtesy of Texas Historical Commission.*

We used to tell each other we would be on that train someday." And, he added, the time finally came when "we got on the train and went to the West Coast, through the Panama Canal and Home." With the last prisoners gone, the government soon sold the camp location as surplus property, and it reverted to agricultural purposes. Today, the historic chapel is the only remaining building at the site, and in seasons of bounteous crops it virtually fades into the surrounding landscape.

Across the state in Lufkin, in the Piney Woods, a much different POW story unfolded during the war. The timber industry, like agriculture, suffered severe wartime manpower shortages, and in 1943 the US government formally declared the nation's pulp and paper industry essential to the war effort. That cleared the way for the establishment of POW camps in several timber-producing states, including Texas, to utilize prisoner labor in the harvesting of trees. In all, Texas had 12 branch camp locations to oversee German prisoners assigned to that task, including one at Lufkin that operated at two separate sites.

Work on Camp Lufkin Number 1 began north of the city in November 1943, at a recently vacated Civilian Conservation Corps camp leased from the US Forest Service. The intent was for the branch camp to provide pulpwood for the nearby Southland Paper Mills, established only a few years before as the nation's first producer of newsprint from Southern yellow pines. Utilizing German prisoners from Camp Huntsville in the construction, the Lufkin site officially opened in February 1944, housing up to 300

The Camp Hereford chapel, October 2009. Relatively isolated and surrounded by agricultural fields, the chapel has been subject to vandalism over the years, but local preservationists have worked diligently to keep it restored and accessible as a unique memorial to those who served on both sides of the war. *Photo by Dan K. Utley.*

As part of its Texas in World War II initiative, the Texas Historical Commission funded a special marker at the site of Camp Lufkin in 2007. The marker is located at the former entryway to the camp. *Courtesy of Texas Historical Commission. Photo by William A. McWhorter.*

workers. The timing for completion of the camp proved particularly fortuitous, as an unusually severe and devastating ice storm hit the East Texas Piney Woods on January 13–14, laying waste to an estimated 400,000 acres of timberland. The situation called for a rapid response in order to salvage stock for pulpwood; downed trees not harvested within six months would no longer be viable for the mills. When the scope of the operation proved too critical and too daunting for one camp, approval came for a second one, which opened on the site of the county fairgrounds southeast of town. In mid-1944, oversight of both camps formally transferred to Camp Fannin, an infantry training installation near Tyler. Camp Lufkin Number 2 closed in September 1944, but the earlier facility remained operational until the final transfer of internees in 1946. While short-lived, the timber salvage efforts at Lufkin and similar spike camps proved successful, utilizing enemy soldiers captured in war to sustain a critical wartime industry in the United States.

The POW camps at Hereford and Lufkin are emblematic of the much broader context of the personal side of war. It was apparent in the complexities of wartime management of battlefield survivors how the home front was directly affected by overseas military actions, government decisions at the highest levels, and pressing business concerns.

Locations: The POW Chapel, designated a Recorded Texas Historic Landmark, and the remains of a water tower are the only visible reminders of the Hereford Military Reservation and Reception Center. To reach the chapel, take US 385 south to FM 1055 and continue south on it until reaching Deaf Smith County Road 1. Turn west to County Road H and then turn south. The chapel is set back from the unpaved road on the right, just inside the Castro County line. Some signage is present along the route. An Official Texas Historical Marker for the site of Camp Lufkin Number 1 is located at 2221 North Raguet Street in Lufkin.

Access: The Camp Hereford POW chapel is located within a designated commemorative area accessible by the public. Surrounding property, however, is privately owned farmland. The site of Camp Lufkin is on US Forest Service property and not accessible to the public without permission. The state marker situated along the camp's stone gates, however, is accessible, although parking in the general area along a busy street is limited.

MARFA ARMY AIRFIELD
(1943–1945)

The far West Texas town of Marfa had a military history that predated its World War II experience by over 30 years. In 1911, elements of the US Cavalry established Camp Marfa on the south edge of the village that was at the time home to fewer than a thousand hearty souls. The camp's site was partly chosen because of its location on the main east–west line of the Southern Pacific Railway but mainly because of its strategic proximity to the Rio Grande, the contentious international boundary between the United States and Mexico. At the time of the camp's establishment, some of the violence associated with the Mexican Revolution was already beginning to spill across the river and onto US territory. Ever-increasing revolutionary military activities and outright banditry on both sides of the Rio Grande caused Camp Marfa to grow in importance. By 1913, it had become the headquarters of an American army district that included 14 observation posts scattered along the Texas side of the river. It also became the center of flight operations for the army's fledgling air reconnaissance squadrons, a fact that would prove fortuitous for Marfa a few years later.

By 1918, Camp Marfa had become a major army installation. The warm relationship between the townspeople and their military neighbors reportedly made assignment to the camp a pleasant experience despite its isolated location. Memories of that hospitality, as well as an appreciation for the generally excellent flying conditions in the Marfa area, eventually persuaded Air Corps officials to look favorably toward the region when another and more urgent national emergency arose less than a quarter century later. Marfa remained a relatively important military site during the years between the two world wars. Its original cavalry and aerial reconnaissance center, renamed Fort D. A. Russell in 1930, temporarily closed in 1933 but reopened in 1935 as an officer training facility. In the meantime, the region's population increased nearly fourfold largely because of the expanded military presence. Its overall economy accordingly flourished even during the dark days of the Great Depression.

Soon after America entered World War II in December 1941, Marfa's warm 30-year-long embrace of the army yielded an immediate and positive benefit. An official record of fine flying weather, the availability of vast expanses of inexpensive land, a location on the Southern Pacific railway line, and the advent of a new coast-to-coast highway prompted government authorities to place the town high on the army's priority list of potential airfields. As a result, inspecting officers arrived in Marfa in late March 1942 to locate a suitable site for one of the many new airfields urgently needed for the war effort. Within two months, the local newspaper announced that a nearly 3,000-acre parcel of ranchland had been acquired by the army for what would soon become Marfa Army Airfield, a multi-engine pilot training facility. The newspaper's claim that it would require only 90 days to clear the land and construct the huge base proved to be optimistic. Although work began in May 1942, the first training aircraft did not arrive until the last week of November, nearly 270 days after construction commenced. The first cadet class of 180 pilot candidates began training in AT-17 aircraft on December 7, 1942, the first anniversary of the Japanese attack at Pearl Harbor. The new facility was among the larger flight training schools that the army operated in the United States. It had four hangars, the largest of which was 32,000 square feet in size. At its operational peak, nearly 500 aircraft were assigned to the field, taking off and landing around the clock on five runways that each stretched nearly a mile and a half across the Texas landscape. The initial cost estimate to build the gigantic installation was $3 million, but the actual cost proved to be more than twice that amount mainly because of overtime labor expenses and unforeseen costs incurred in transporting construction material to the remote site. According to some sources, work on the airfield appeared to be continuous and ceased only when the army deactivated the base nearly three years later.

As was always the case during the war years, there was an immense social and economic impact on the community created by the construction and eventual opera-tion of the airfield. During the initial building stage, workers flooded the area only to find limited opportunities for housing. The Marfa chamber of commerce began what eventually became a three-year advertising campaign that implored local citizens to open their spare bedrooms and even their garages to the thousands of men who labored at the construction site. When the bulk of the work neared completion, a wave of military newcomers quickly occupied whatever meager living space had been vacated by the construction crews. Many officers rented houses in Alpine, 25 miles to the east, when every square foot of suitable space in Marfa had long waiting lists. Other officers and some enlisted men commuted to the field from Presidio, located 60 miles to the south, or from Fort Davis, some 20 miles away over mountain passes. The estimated population figures for Marfa increased by more than 50 percent from 1943 to 1945. The volume of mail processed through the local post office nearly doubled during that same period even though the airfield had its own postal facility that handled on average 3,000 pieces of mail each day.

Although Marfa had been the sporadic host city to Fort D. A. Russell since the early 1900s, it found itself unprepared for the influx of nearly 5,000 permanent per-sonnel assigned to the base by mid-1943. Not only were housing resources com-pletely inadequate, there were at first no entertainment diversions to be found in the community except for the town's sole motion-picture theater. As time went by, the army attempted to provide its off-duty officers and men with suitable social and athletic activity. The airfield eventually had an officers' club, a similar facility for noncommissioned officers, several theaters, a large gymnasium, numerous athletic fields, and stores where personnel could purchase clothing as well as an array of foodstuffs never before to be found in the Marfa area. Although the beleaguered but economically prospering town did have a number of churches clustered around its magnificent courthouse square, the large chapel on the field offered a special reason to attend its services. Army chaplain Capt. H. H. D. Landeck discovered an immensely gifted singer to lead his choir, and word of the talented tenor quickly spread throughout the region. His name was Alfred Arnold Cocozza, and according to onetime Marfa mayor Fritz Kahl, Cocozza offered to lend his talents to nearly any group in town that asked him to sing. "He was a military policeman when he was on duty," remembered Mayor Kahl many years later, "but if any church or civic organization asked him to perform he took off his MP armband and hurried into town." Kahl served as a flight instructor at the field and returned to Marfa after the war to marry a local rancher's daughter. Sitting in the movie theater in nearby Alpine with his new bride, he was surprised to hear the voice and see the image of Cocozza on the theater screen. The former sergeant's new name, Kahl soon learned, was Mario Lanza.

Civilians throughout the Marfa area made their new military neighbors feel welcome. Perhaps the late Fritz Kahl summed it best when he declared, "They took us in and assimilated us into their society. We were foreigners in a vague sense and they accepted us fully." Private citizens opened their doors to the cadets and young officers in training at the field. Mr. and Mrs. V. E. Smith, for example, placed an ad in the December 12, 1943, issue of the *Big Bend Sentinel* inviting any four soldiers to come to their home for Christmas dinner on a first-come, first-served basis. The response from the airfield's soldiers proved great enough to necessitate moving the feast to the Marfa High School cafeteria. Both Marfa and Alpine sponsored year-round social events for base personnel. Area businessmen donated gift parcels to USO patrons, the contents ranging from one dollar bills to certificates for free long distance calls to homes across the nation. For those soldiers who found the card games and apple-bobbing activities offered at the USO to be too mild, the many enticements to be found in nearby Mexico were difficult to ignore. According to some accounts, military officials did not condone three-day passes for soldiers intent on going to the border, but neither was it forbidden to do so. Venereal disease prevention was the topic of an ongoing campaign on every military installation during the war, but there is evidence that the efforts to combat such diseases were particularly intensive at army posts located within a hundred miles of the border.

The flight training regimen at the field remained strenuous. The A-17 trainer aircraft and eventually B-25 bombers stayed in the air all day and well into the night. As a result, flying mishaps and ground accidents were common. Despite the fact that Marfa Airfield suffered three fatal crashes in a 90-day period in the summer of 1943, the field somehow managed to have the second-lowest accident-to-hours-flown ratio in the entire Air Training Command. The records do show, however, that eight airmen perished in airplane crashes during the three and a half years that the base continued in operation.

Even though the demand for highly trained pilots began to lessen by late 1944, government contracts provided for continued expansion and improvement of the Marfa field. New quarters for the cadets replaced the barrackslike buildings hurriedly built in early 1942. Construction on new service clubs continued, even though the flow of officers and enlisted men coming to the field clearly underwent reductions. Some of the personnel assigned to Marfa late in the war came from foreign lands. A group of Chinese officers arrived in September 1944 to begin their flight training. Because their knowledge of the English language was limited, the use of special instructions ensured both in-flight and ground safety. In addition to the Chinese, pilot trainees from various Latin American nations learned to fly at Marfa. In total, 8,000 officers received their silver wings at the field.

Fort D. A. Russell, the army's original installation at Marfa, continued to receive new officers until late in the war. It eventually became something of a substation for the airfield, with a primary mission of housing German prisoners of war. Most of the Germans served in Field Marshal Erwin Rommel's Afrika Korps. They had been sent to Texas because some supposedly well-meaning government authority determined that the state's climate and terrain were most likely much the same as the men had encountered while fighting in Africa. Considering the vast differences in the climate experienced by prisoners at East Texas camps compared to the harsh environs of West Texas, the logic behind the placement of POW camps is obscure at best. Many of the Germans housed at Fort D. A. Russell were trucked through town and then on east along the highway to work on the continuing expansion of the airfield. Myrtle Shepherd recalled that her YWCA and Baptist Church women's group frequently baked cookies for the prisoners. She and her associates seemed genuinely pleased to have the captives in Marfa. "They were such good-looking blond boys," she recalled years later.

While most of the prisoners seemed content to stay among the cookie-baking ladies of Marfa, three Germans made an escape in April 1944. According to Raymond Moler, the leader of the group, the plan was to head due south from Marfa to cross the Rio Grande into the perhaps friendlier political climate of Mexico. Once in that country, Moler later related, the trio planned to continue moving southward to reach South America. Given the known sympathy of certain South American countries toward Nazi Germany, the men assumed it would then be easy to catch a submarine ride back to the fatherland. The many assumptions of Moler's plan remained untested. In their eagerness to get back into the war, the three prisoners ran away in the exact opposite direction they had intended to take. By the time officials apprehended them at Sierra Blanca, Texas, the weary trio had travelled 130 miles north instead of south. Had their course been as planned, they would have made it some 70 miles south of the Rio Grande in the same number of days with at least a faint ghost of a chance of going home to fight the Soviet army.

Returned to captivity at Fort D. A. Russell, the men rejoined their comrades in working on the ever-expanding airfield east of town. By April 1945, however, rumors began to circulate that both the airfield and the POW installation at the old fort were soon to be deactivated. The fact that the war still raged in the Pacific theater prompted army officials to vehemently deny any such allegations. Col. Harry R. Baxter refuted the deactivation rumors in a speech to the Marfa Rotary Club on May 1, 1945. He claimed that although he had heard talk of the planned closing of the two installations, he had received no official information about any such plans. The relieved Rotarians spread the news to the community, but the celebration abruptly terminated when a startling statement issued from Mayor H. A. Coffield confirmed his office had been told by federal authorities on April 24 that the rumors about the closings were in fact true. The mayor had assumed that the airfield's commander was to break the dire news to the public, but a later inquiry proved that Colonel Baxter had not received word of the closing until he learned it from the mayor. At any rate, the message from Washington was now clear that both installations would cease operations by May 25. The last class of Marfa-trained pilots received their silver wings on May 23, 1945. Following the graduation of Class 45-C, all other trainees, including those from China, were reassigned to other airfields. For the first time since December 7, 1942, the skies over Marfa fell silent. The area's residents, shocked by both the silence and the impending economic disaster that the tandem closures were sure to bring, held informal meetings to seek some sort of recourse from the army that had departed almost as suddenly as it had arrived. Within less than a month, the town's future again looked bright.

On June 30, 1945, five weeks after the airfield closed, the War Department advised an astonished but overjoyed Mayor Coffield that it had changed its bureaucratic mind. Rather than being permanently deactivated, the airfield would soon be reopened with a new troop-carrying mission and a complement of 2,000 men. Almost immediately following that welcome news, the army announced that 4,000 men—nearly twice as many as originally stated, and only 1,000 troops fewer than were at the field at the peak of its operation—would soon be on their way to Marfa. The same message from Washington declared the deactivated Fort D. A. Russell would also reopen in support of some other undisclosed mission. The entire Marfa region instantly basked in a state of euphoria enhanced by an almost palpable sense of dreams coming true and prayers being answered. To celebrate all the good military news, a festive open

At its operational peak in late 1943, Marfa Army Airfield supported nearly 500 aircraft. There were five runways, each a mile and a half in length, on its 2,800-acre expanse as well as a complete military city. On average, over 3,100 personnel were serving on the base. US Army Air Forces Airport Directory, *vol. 3, 1944.*

house took place at the once again bustling airfield. A huge crowd inspected the fleet of recently landed aircraft, cheered as thousands of newly arrived troops paraded past the reviewing stand, and thoroughly enjoyed the food and beverages donated by grateful members of the Marfa and Alpine chambers of commerce. As one celebrant recalled years later, "The speeches were numerous and lengthy and it was terribly hot, but no one minded. Marfa Army Airfield had come back to life." Five days later, an atomic bomb fell on Hiroshima, Japan. That act led directly to the end of World War II as well as to the final closure of the Marfa military installations so recently resurrected. Within three months' time, both the field and the fort had become ghostly remnants of their wartime glory. Only two pilots remained at the airfield where 8,000 others had once flown. Ironically, not a single airplane remained at their disposal.

Regional historian Cecilia Thompson put the situation in perspective in her two-volume *History of Presidio County.* "The glory days of military activity were over," she wrote. "Marfa would never be the same." According to the blunt-speaking Fritz Kahl, "The town fell on its face. The economy of the entire region plummeted right along with the spirits of the people." The population shrank and over half the town's busi-

Only concrete footprints remained in 2004 to indicate the once impressive size of Marfa Army Airfield. The unusual 45-degree ramp/taxiway is clearly visible across the top of the photograph, as is the slab that once supported a 32,000-square-foot hangar (upper left). *Thomas E. Alexander Collection.*

nesses closed as the region's two former military installations, one long proud of its old army cavalry traditions and the other once resonant with the sounds of countless aircraft engines, began a rapid descent into destruction, desolation, and decay.

The buildings at old Fort D. A. Russell have at least marginally survived the test of time. Some have been restored for use as unique settings for modernistic sculptures owned by the Chinati Foundation. The Officers' Club, Building 98, has been refurbished to become Hacienda del Arcon, the International Women's Foundation headquarters. Down the hall from the officers' bar, where legend has it George S. Patton occasionally enjoyed good bourbon, is a large room still bearing colorful decorations by artistic prisoners of war during World War II. These fanciful paintings depict a stylized Wild West, as incarcerated German eyes beheld it in 1944. On the other edge of Marfa, very little remains to be easily seen of its old airfield. On the side of US Highway 90 that parallels the site of the field, however, two five-foot-tall whitewashed walls mark the location of the field's main gate. Anyone standing at the gate's opening to look south across the vast acreage in hopes of spotting some visible remains of the hundreds of structures that once stood there will only search in vain. From that vantage point, it would seem that all of Marfa's airfield has been swept away by time. The view from the air, however, is more rewarding. The large main runways are clearly visible, as are the ramps and taxiways. The imprints of roadbeds define the precise grid outlines that contain foundations and slabs of onetime warehouses, barracks, and a hospital. The path of the railway spur that connected the field with the main line of the Southern Pacific is indelibly etched on the otherwise barren landscape. Some of the buildings that once stood on the empty slabs eventually graced other locations. Workers moved one of the distinctively army-style chapels over the nearly mile-high Paisano Pass to accommodate a congregation in Alpine. A large gymnasium later took the same route to serve as a school gym.

Although the boom-to-bust story of Marfa and its military history is not unique, some of its elements are significantly different. The fact that the small village had two World War II installations is unusual. Such an example of fortunate economy of scale is rarely found in army records. Further, it is clear that the government's rationale for placing an airfield at Marfa was truly more pragmatic than political. The site was strategic, the land was vast and inexpensive, and the transportation facilities in the region were excellent. Few other World War II airfield sites offered such positive inducements. More than a few, in fact, came into being primarily because some powerful congressman saw the political rewards implicit in snaring a military installation for his constituents. Nearly every community in Texas, and elsewhere, was eager to have an airfield during the war. A combination of altruistic patriotism and powerful economic need drove that desire. Marfa's proven reputation as a hospitable and tolerant host to military personnel was clearly an additional element in the ultimate decision to place the airfield nearby. Although no significant vestige of that field remains, its contribution to the winning of World War II is undeniable.

Location: The site of Marfa Army Airfield is nine miles east of town on US Highway 90. A Texas Historical Commission marker indicates the site.

Access: No public access, but a roadside park affords a good panoramic view of the site.

SOURCES

Alexander, Thomas E. *The Stars Were Big and Bright: The United States Army Air Forces and Texas During World War II*, vols. 1 and 2. Austin: Eakin Press, 2000–2001.

The Avenger (Sweetwater, Texas), May 11, 1943; August 12, 1943; March 17, 1944; July 4, 1944.

Big Bend (Texas) Sentinel, May 1, 1942; May 22, 1942; May 29, 1942; October 10, 1942; December 1, 1942; December 28, 1942; February 8, 1943; August 20, 1943; June 8, 1943; September 17, 1943; May 6, 1945; May 13, 1945; August 3, 1945; August 10, 1945.

Blumenson, Martin. Patton: *The Man Behind the Legend.* New York: Quill-William Martin, 1985.

Bonine, Mindy L., and James W. Steely. *Transformation of the Culture and Physical Landscape: Historical Archaeology and Oral History at Camp Bowie, Brown County, Texas.* Austin: SWCA Environmental Consultants, 2006.

Brownwood, Texas, Public Library vertical files.

Choate, Mark. *Nazis in the Pineywoods.* Lufkin: Best of East Texas Publishers, 1989.

Cochran, Jacqueline. *The Stars at Noon.* Boston: Little, Brown, 1954.

Cole, Jean Hascall. *Women Pilots of World War II.* Salt Lake City: University of Utah Press, 1971.

Dailey, Janet. *Silver Wings/Santiago Blue.* New York: Poseidon Press, 1984.

Davenport, Bill. Interview with Thomas E. Alexander. Pecos, Texas. October 3, 1998.

Deaf Smith Historical Society. *The Land and Its People, 1876–1981: Deaf Smith County, Texas.* Hereford, TX: Deaf Smith Historical Society, 1982.

Dictionary of American Naval Fighting Ships Online. www.hazegray.org/danfs/destroy/dd569txt.hem. Accessed on September 24, 2010.

Fairchild, Louis. *They Called It the War Effort: Oral Histories from World War II, Orange, Texas.* Austin: Eakin Press, 1993.

Fickle, James E., and Donald W. Ellis. "POWs in the Piney Woods: German Prisoners of War in the Southern Lumber Industry, 1943–1945." *Journal of Southern History* 56 (November 1990): 695–724.

"400,000 Acre Timber Plan to be Started." *Lufkin Daily News,* February 20, 1944, 1.

Granger, Byrd Howell. *On Final Approach.* Scottsdale, AZ: Falconer Press Publishing Co., 1991.

Graves, Debe. Three-part article series in the *Hereford Brand* on the POW camp at Hereford, June–July 1981. Clippings in the Official Texas Historical Marker files, Deaf Smith County. Texas Historical Commission, Austin.

Grube, Susanne. "A Brief History of Camp Marfa and Fort D. A. Russell." Marfa, TX: Chinati Foundation, n.d.

Harrison, Addie. Interview with Thomas E. Alexander. Abilene, TX. June 8, 1998.

Henegar, Lucielle, "Hereford Military Reservation and Reception Center." In *The New Handbook of Texas,* 3:569–70, ed. Ron Tyler. Austin: Texas State Historical Association, 1996.

Hennigan, J. R. Interview with Thomas E. Alexander. Odessa, TX. August 12, 1998.

Kahl, C. M. (Fritz). Interview with Thomas E. Alexander. Marfa, TX. October 11, 1999.

Keefer, Louis E. *Italian Prisoners of War in America, 1942–1946: Captives or Allies?* New York: Praeger, 1992.

Keil, Sally Van Wagenen. *Those Wonderful Women in Their Flying Machines.* New York: Four Directions Press, 1990.

Krammer, Arnold P. "When the Afrika Korps Came to Texas," *Southwestern Historical Quarterly* 80, no. 3 (January 1977): 247–82.

Kuykendall, Lucy Roundtree. *P.S. to Pecos.* Houston: Anson Jones Press, 1945.

Maxwell, Robert S., and Robert D. Baker. *Sawdust Empire: The Texas Lumber Industry, 1830–1940.* College Station: Texas A&M University Press, 1983.

McHenry, Robert, ed. *Webster's American Military Biographies.* Springfield, MA: G&C Merriam Co., 1978.

Monde, Bennet B. *Wings over Sweetwater: The History of Avenger Field.* Privately published, 1983.

Nalty, Bernard C., ed. *Winged Shield, Winged Sword: A History of the United States Air Force,* vol 1. Washington, DC: United States Air Force, 1997.

"Nazi Prisoners Will Undertake Forestry Work," *Lufkin (Texas) Daily News,* December 1, 1943, 1.

Odessa (Texas) American, December 31, 1937.

Pecos Army Airfield: 1998 Reunion Booklet. Pecos, TX: Pecos Publishing Company, 1998.

Pecos (Texas) Enterprise, December 19, 1941; January 23, 1942; January 27, 1942; April 2, 1942.

Pirtle, Caleb III, and Michael Cusack. *Fort Clark: The Lonely Sentinel on Texas's Western Frontier.* Austin: Eakin Press, 1985.

Pitts, Bill. Interview with Thomas E. Alexander. Pecos, TX. October. 3, 1998.

San Antonio Express News, April 6, 2009.

Schultz, Duane. *Hero of Bataan: The Story of General Jonathan M. Wainwright.* New York: St. Martin's Press, 1981.

Sweetwater (Texas) Daily Reporter, June 28, 1942.

Tanner, Doris Brinker, comp. *Who Were the WASP?* Sweetwater, TX: *Sweetwater Daily Reporter,* 1989.

Texas Almanac and State Industrial Guide, 1939–1940. Dallas: A. H. Belo Corporation, 1939.

Texas Historical Commission. Official Texas Historical Marker files, Angelina County, Castro County, and Orange County. Austin, TX.

Thompson, Cecilia. *History of Marfa and Presidio County, Texas 1535–1946,* vol 2. Austin: Nortex Press, 1986.

Thurmond, Marie H. Interview with Thomas E. Alexander. Pecos, TX. October 4, 1998.

Tyler, Ron, ed. *The New Handbook of Texas,* 6 vols. Austin: Texas State Historical Association, 1996.

United States Army Air Forces Airport Directory, vol 3. Washington, DC: War Department, 1944.

Verges, Marianne. *On Silver Wings: The Women Airforce Service Pilot.* New York: Ballantine Books, 1991.

Walker, Richard P. *The Lone Star and the Swastika: Prisoners of War in Texas.* Austin: Eakin Press, 2001.

Warnock, Kirby F. "Wings West of the Pecos" *Big Bend Quarterly,* Summer 1999.

Williams, Donald Mace. *Interlude in Umbarger: Italian POWs and a Texas Church.* Lubbock: Texas Tech University Press, 1992.

Williams, Howard C. *Gateway to Texas: The History of Orange and Orange County.* Orange: Heritage Museum of Orange, 1986.

Yeats, E. L., and Hooper Shelton. *History of Nolan County, Texas.* Sweetwater, TX: Shelton Press, 1975.

Epilogue

A CALL FOR PRESERVATION

The stories of the military sites discussed in this book reflect the great diversity that is inherent in Texas military history. The sites vary in their physical nature and geography, as well as their period of historical significance and accessibility. Each was included, however, because at some point in the past someone cared enough to preserve some element of the story. How much was left behind influenced our decision on whether or not to explore some stories further. A few stories initially intended for this book had to be eliminated because the trails had gone cold. While there was some information available on all the sites we considered, some clearly had more to offer the current researcher than others. It became a matter of historic preservation in its broadest sense.

Historic preservation deals not only with the past but also with the future. Fundamentally, it is a cultural process of deciding what is worthy of restoring, interpreting, recording, and commemorating, and then determining the best means for passing those resources along to the next generation. In order to succeed, any preservation project must be transgenerational in nature, taking the best available information from the past and bequeathing it to those in the future who will in turn have to make new determinations based on their own values, interests, and resources. It is a complex process that is always ongoing and depends on myriad factors, from historical relevance and community planning to available funding and current technology.

No matter how important a site might be, and regardless of how it contributes to the continuum of history, there are questions of vulnerability and viability. Historic resources, by their very nature, are fragile and often subject to such limiting factors as time, degradation, neglect, inaccurate interpretation, inadequate funding, and even well-intentioned but misguided restoration efforts. In the end, the best one generation can do to preserve history is to ensure it passes along historical resources in the most comprehensive and relevant ways it can. To that end, for persons interested in preserving sites and stories similar to those in this book, the following measures are time-tested ways of promoting sound practices of historic preservation.

Cultural Resource Surveys   In historical terms, a survey is an inventory of existing cultural resources, which can include such tangible elements as archival collections, photographs, oral histories, architecture, memoirs, books, artifacts, and historic landscapes, as well as intangible elements like folklore, tradition, language, interpretive arts, and a sense of place. Surveys can be basic, as in a visual reconnaissance—a so-called windshield survey—of a site. They can also be a review of available sources about the site, from archives and publications to oral histories and artifact collections. Such basic surveys provide a standard foundation for further work that might include more intensive forms of research, such as archeological investigations. All surveys, though, should lead to some consideration of the missing elements. Such "gap analysis" not only drives preservation planning but also provides future generations with a resource snapshot in time.

While basic cultural resource surveys can be coordinated through local historical organizations, such as county historical commissions or heritage societies, there are also professional firms with staffs trained in history, archeology, architecture, and other disciplines that can provide in-depth field investigations, background research, historical analysis, and master planning. Some firms can also take a story and provide public interpretation suitable for museum exhibits, heritage tourism efforts, educational programming, and publications. While funding can be a key factor in considering such services, it is important to remember that granting entities and other potential sponsors often look favorably on outside professional assistance, and in the end the intensive analysis might lead to a higher level of protection for a site.

Regardless of the level of surveys conducted, they can prove invaluable in raising public awareness and promoting the need for preservation. Care should be taken, however, to ensure that detailed information on known archeological deposits be protected through limited access to ensure security of the resource. (See the next item, "Site Recording.")

Site Recording   Closely related to surveys is the process of recording a site. The standards for the process are maintained through the Texas Archeological Site Atlas, set up by the Texas Historical Commission (THC) and operated in conjunction with the Texas Archeological Research Laboratory at the University of Texas at Austin. The site forms require some basic knowledge of archeological terms and methods, so it is best to enlist the assistance of a trained professional, if possible, to help with the recording. Another viable option is to work through the Texas Archeological Steward Network, a program of the Archeology Division of the Texas Historical Commission. The archeological stewards are trained volunteers who work on a regional basis to promote good practices and to assist interested citizens in preserving and recording sites. For contact information on the steward in your area, check the website of the Texas Historical Commission.

Oral History   The guided process of recording and preserving firsthand reminiscences—a process known as oral history—is one of the best means of collecting detailed information on recent military activities. It is equally effective in recapturing a sense of the historic landscape of a related site, whether it is a training base, a USO canteen, an induction center, or a military hospital. While oral history is one of the best methodologies for understanding emotions, feelings, and intent associated with a historical event, it provides a researcher with enough flexibility to explore myriad topics, including weapons, tactics, structures, unit commands, operational procedures, training, battlefield action, esprit de corps, and even the horrors of war and the difficulties of maintaining peace.

Internet searches for oral history will provide a number of resources, including books and beginning primers. One of the best places to start learning the basics is through the Texas Oral History Association, headquartered at the Institute for Oral History at Baylor University in Waco. Online materials associated with both the association and the institute offer directions related to workshops (including online workshops), publications, and conferences where individuals can receive basic training and also network with others interested in preserving oral memoirs. Other good resources can be found online through the Military Sites Program of the Texas Historical Commission, which maintains basic preservation guides on oral history in general and on military oral histories specifically.

In order to maximize long-term effectiveness, preservation, and access, oral history projects should be associated with organizations or entities fully prepared to archive recordings and transcripts using accepted professional standards. Check with local museums, archival collections, libraries, and universities to determine if they are interested in accepting and curating oral history materials.

When planning an oral history project, it is important to understand the limits of the process. First and foremost is the diminishing pool of possible interviewees. While there are still World War II veterans out there, the numbers decrease dramatically each year. Additionally, those who remain are usually able to tell only part of the larger story. Most of the war's primary decision makers have passed on, as have most of those in the flag officer corps. Many that remain represent the rank and file story of the war, and some of those already experience fading memories. Within a generation, the best remaining stories may relate to the home front or to the memories of children who lived through the war years. With time, though, even those stories will disappear, so an understanding of time limitations is vital to planning any project.

There are a number of institutions currently conducting World War II oral histories, and the reader is directed to three in particular: the General Land Office of Texas; the Library of Congress in Washington, DC; and the Voces Oral History Project (formerly the US Latino and Latina World War II Oral History Project) at the University of Texas at Austin. Each institution provides access to its collections, and information on the various projects can be found through online sources.

Historical Marker One of the best means of promoting public awareness about a historic site is to sponsor the placement of an Official Texas Historical Marker. The marker program is administered through the Texas Historical Commission, but the process begins with application to the county historical commission (CHC) where the resource is located. The CHC is the division of the county government charged with public assistance related to local matters of history and preservation. For the name of the CHC chair, contact the county judge's office or check the THC website.

The most common type of Official Texas Historical Markers are called subject markers, and they are designed to convey general information about a site or topic. They are educational and interpretive in nature and do not carry any legal restrictions on the property. The THC also offers building markers for restored historical structures deemed worthy of state recognition for their historical significance and architectural integrity. Building markers automatically convey the Recorded Texas Historic Landmark designation on a property that provides some measure of protection through THC review for any proposed changes to the structure. The THC also administers the Historic Texas Cemetery designation and markers for burial grounds, and such markers can be an effective way of bringing attention to sites where large numbers of military veterans are interred.

National Register of Historic Places The National Historic Preservation Act of 1966 provided for a register of historic sites that meet accepted federal standards of significance and preservation. Such sites can be individual properties, districts, or thematic groupings. Each state has a designated State Historic Preservation Office (SHPO) charged with reviewing applications to the National Register of Historic Places and ensuring proposed sites successfully meet the general criteria of the program. In Texas, the Texas Historical Commission serves as the SHPO and appoints a State Board of Review to make recommendations on applications.

The National Register provides an honorary designation for a site; there are no private property restrictions associated with the process. For properties included within project areas administered, funded, or reviewed by federal agencies, however, there is a lengthy and detailed process for evaluating the effect of such undertakings on eligible cultural resources. As a result, highway construction, mining operations, reservoir development, airport construction, and other similar projects require intensive surveys of existing cultural resources, both prehistoric and historic. The surveys can also take into account the effects on historical landscapes. While the National Register program deals with federal undertakings, some states, including Texas, have similar programs for dealing with potential impacts on cultural resources. Both state and federal oversights provide for adequate planning relative to projects and ensure that due consideration is given to mitigating any adverse effects.

The National Register, like the Official Texas Historical Marker Program, is an effective means of heightening public awareness of historic sites. It brings not only state and national recognition of historical significance but also a public awareness of the need for protective measures, whether through local preservation ordinances or other means.

State Archeological Landmark   An additional protective measure for historic sites is the State Archeological Landmark designation (SAL), also administered by the THC. Designed to provide the strongest measure of protection by means of a permitting process, it is an invaluable tool in planning for both public and private projects. While archeological sites can be designated through a regular review process involving the Antiquities Advisory Board, structures proposed for the SAL designation must first be listed in the National Register of Historic Places.

Photography/Measured Drawings   One of the easiest, most effective, and least expensive means of documenting the current condition of historic military sites is through a systematic, regular plan for photographing the resources. Detailed photography is a basic element of any survey plan, but it can also provide a process for documenting change over time. Photography used in conjunction with museum exhibits, promotional materials, publications, public interest stories, and websites can help to inform the public about the need for preservation, while underscoring the need for additional documentation.

Archival Collections   Whether associated with museums, universities, regional research centers, or libraries, archival collections provide a viable means of preserving materials associated with a historic military site. Such materials can include personal and organizational papers, photographs, maps, books, newspapers, and artifacts that add significantly to a broad understanding of a site's historical relevance. In those cases, like some of the sites documented in this book, an archival collection may represent the only means of reconstructing the past in a meaningful way. In the age of the Internet, the availability of archival materials is greatly enhanced by means of online markets and auctions. While many archival collections have limited budgets for acquisition, they welcome citizen assistance for donations of materials or funding.

Local Designations   In addition to the state and federal designations mentioned earlier, some municipalities provide for protective measures through local designations that can be important planning measures relative to public or private development projects. For information on local designations, contact city officials or check with the Certified Local Government Program of the Texas Historical Commission.

Easements and Covenants   Private landowners interested in providing current and future protection for military sites on their land may be able to use such legal proceedings as conservation easements and protective covenants that run with title to the property. Check with an attorney for additional information on these and similar measures.

Museums   As already noted, museums can be instrumental in a wide range of programs regarding the preservation of military sites and related information. Some institutions have mission statements specifically related to military history and would therefore be interested in site preservation or interpretation, as well as the acquisition of artifacts and records, including survey data and photographs. Others might have mission statements that provide for military holdings that help interpret broader themes as social and cultural history. Check with local museums to determine their interest in preserving Texas military history information.

Field Schools   The Texas Archeological Society (TAS) conducts regular workshops and onsite field investigations (field schools) on a wide range of topics, some of which might include military sites. Those who participate in the field schools work side by side with recognized leaders in the field of archeology to learn accepted standards for surveys, recording, and excavations. Check the TAS website or contact local archeological societies for additional information.

Historical Associations   There are a number of associations and organizations committed to preserving Texas military history and documenting historic sites. Among the most readily accessible are the county historical commissions—each county in Texas has one—which can help with historical marker applications, heritage tourism, and public education efforts. There are also groups such as the Daughters of the Republic of Texas, the United Daughters of the Confederacy, the Sons of

Union Veterans, and the Texas Old Missions and Forts Restoration Association which have programmatic mission statements that promote military history and scholarly research, as well as site preservation and interpretation. Check the Internet for current information on these groups and others. In addition, some historic sites, whether administered by the Texas Historical Commission, the Texas Parks and Wildlife Department, or the National Park Service, have groups of friends, or volunteers, that work to provide public assistance related to site preservation.

Regardless of the measures one selects to help protect Texas military sites and ensure the future viability of related records, the key objectives should be to collect as much information as possible and then to make it readily accessible through a wide variety of means. Recorded oral histories that have not been transcribed are vulnerable to quick and permanent loss, as are unlabeled historic photographs that languish in attics or closets for years, only to be disposed of by future generations unaware of their significance. Development without proper planning, including consideration of potential impact on unique cultural resources, denies future access to history, just as neglect, vandalism, and looting do. In a vast but also rapidly developing state such as Texas, there are many roadblocks to preservation, but there are also many solutions that can be implemented either collectively or individually. And those efforts can be effective even where a site seemingly no longer exists.

In the course of their work on this book, the authors followed various research trails using landmarks that could have easily been lost over the generations. Thanks to the efforts of heritage-minded individuals, though, the landmarks survive even while countless others have disappeared, only to be forgotten by those who came later. What remains and what fades away is a pressing concern for those interested in preservation, but it seems there are always those who make the effort and consider whatever they do worthwhile.

One research story in particular illustrates the great difference one person can make. At the Texas Collection at Baylor University in Waco is a series of files on both Camp MacArthur and Rich Field, important World War II sites in Central Texas. Included therein is a stack of ruled yellow tablet pages that, in single spaced but clearly legible handwriting, list details of all the known local newspaper stories dealing with the two sites. There are literally hundreds of entries dating from the time of the Great War up to a few years ago. No one knows why the writer took it on himself to record such information, but his meticulous records survive, though the newspapers themselves may be gone. What is known for certain, however, is that the papers ended up in a wastebasket after the individual died, and only the keen eyes of a Baylor archivist, Geoff Hunt, helped save the information for future researchers.

Such stories—some equally compelling but others with tragic endings—point to the fragility of the past and the need for preservation action. It is hoped the wartime stories in this book also serve similar purposes. They are, after all, only a small portion of a much broader context, one that continues to erode with time. This, then, is a call for preservation in the hope that similar sites and stories will continue to mark research trails for generations and that those seeking to understand why people engage in war for the sake of peace will have opportunities to have their questions answered before the historical connections simply fade away.

INDEX